Regulating sexuality

MANCHESTER
1824

Manchester University Press

Regulating sexuality
Women in twentieth-century Northern Ireland

LEANNE McCORMICK

Manchester University Press
Manchester and New York

distributed in the United States exclusively
by Palgrave Macmillan

Published by Manchester University Press
Oxford Road, Manchester M13 9NR, UK
and Room 400, 175 Fifth Avenue, New York, NY 10010, USA
www.manchesteruniversitypress.co.uk

Distributed in the United States exclusively by
Palgrave Macmillan, 175 Fifth Avenue,
New York, NY 10010, USA

Distributed in Canada exclusively by
UBC Press, University of British Columbia, 2029 West Mall,
Vancouver, BC, Canada V6T 1Z2

British Library Cataloguing-in-Publication Data is available

Library of Congress Cataloging-in-Publication Data is available

ISBN 978 0 7190 8510 9 paperback

First published by Manchester University Press in hardback 2009

This paperback edition first published 2011

The publisher has no responsibility for the persistence or accuracy of URLs for any external or third-party internet websites referred to in this book, and does not guarantee that any content on such websites is, or will remain, accurate or appropriate.

Printed by Lightning Source

For Mum and Dad

Contents

List of tables and figures   viii
Acknowledgements   ix
Note on terminology   xi
List of abbreviations   xii

Introduction   1

1   'Dirty girls and bad houses': prostitutes and prostitution   13
2   'Angels who have lost their way': the work of rescue and
    reform homes   37
3   'Modesty is the sister of virtue': moral prevention work with
    girls   79
4   'People should keep a grip of themselves': treatment and
    prevention of VD   113
5   'One Yank and they're off': interaction between US troops
    and Northern Irish women, 1942–1945   148
6   'Confused with prejudice and muddled thinking': preventing
    pregnancy   180

Conclusion   207

Bibliography   213
Index   243

List of tables and figures

Tables

1.1 Percentage of Catholic women who entered Belfast Union
     recorded as prostitutes   18
1.2 Percentage of the population of Belfast recorded as Church
     of Ireland and Presbyterian   18
1.3 Percentage of women who entered Belfast Union recorded
     as Church of Ireland or Presbyterian   19

Figures

1.1 Number of prosecutions for prostitution in Northern
     Ireland, 1902–1946   25
2.1 Number of admissions to Salvation Army Home, Belfast,
     1905–1946   43
2.2 Number of admissions to the Edgar Home, Belfast,
     1900–1926   43

Acknowledgements

This book originated as a PhD thesis and I owe a debt of gratitude to all those who have given me support and friendship along the long road to publication.

My initial thanks must go to my PhD supervisor, Professor Greta Jones, who has been unfailingly supportive throughout the long process and has been a constant source of help and encouragement. Her advice and criticism have always been constructive and her generosity of time and knowledge has been much appreciated.

Through the course of this research a large number of archives and libraries were visited, and my thanks go especially to the staff of the University of Ulster Library at Jordanstown, the Presbyterian Historical Society, Church of Ireland House and the US National Archives, Maryland. The staff of the Public Record Office of Northern Ireland (PRONI) deserve a special mention as I tortured them for closed and obscure files. In particular I am indebted to Stephen Scarth and Graham Jackson who were unfailingly cheerful and generous with their help and expertise.

Particular thanks and acknowledgement are due to the Salvation Army in Belfast who permitted me access to their records and provided me with space and privacy to work, and to Mrs Lorna Goldstrom who generously gave me access to the Ulster Pregnancy Advisory Service archive. A number of ladies very kindly gave up their time to be interviewed for the book and my thanks go to them all for sharing their fascinating stories with me.

There are a number of people who have been very generous with their own research and who have advised at various stages of the process: in particular thanks go to Professor Roger Davidson, Dr Gayle Davis, Dr Paul Gray, Dr Louise Jackson, Professor Keith Jeffery, Professor Maria Luddy, Dr Sean O'Connell and Father P. O'Donnell.

I received financial assistance from a number of sources while completing both my PhD thesis and the book, including the TK Daniel Memorial Scholarship, UU Library Travel Fund, Academy of Irish Cultural Heritages, Economic History Society and Wellcome Trust, for which I am appreciative and grateful.

My thanks to the editors of *Journal of the History of Sexuality* and *Social History of Medicine* for permission to use some material which had previously appeared in journal form. I am also appreciative of the help and patience of the Manchester University Press staff in the publication process.

On a personal level there are many people who have been provided invaluable friendship and support throughout both the PhD and book process at different times and different places. I don't have space to adequately thank and mention everyone, but a big thank you to: Anna, Annalise, Amy, Carol, Colleen, Diana, Diane, Kathryn, Frances, Janet, Judith, Lynsey, Kerrie, Michelle, Ned, Sarah, Shirley, Stephen and Sue.

My family have been unfailingly supportive and generous. Philip, Debbie and Mark have always been interested and encouraging from around the globe, providing a welcome distraction with their visits. Sharon, Steve, Andy and Isa have always been extremely kind and generous with their hospitality and support.

My husband Andrew trod the publishing path before me and gave of his expertise and help unconditionally. For his love, support, constant encouragement and unflagging re-reading of drafts I am eternally grateful. 'Wee Andrew' arrived in the middle of the writing process making my work more efficient and giving me greater perspective and laughter. Lastly thanks must go to my mum and dad, for their love, support and encouragement. They have proof-read, baby-sat, cooked, hoovered and been towers of strength; I would have been lost without them. I cannot adequately express my appreciation, and this book is dedicated to them.

Note on terminology

Any discussion of Ireland in the twentieth century encounters problems with language and political associations. As Northern Ireland was not established as a state until 1921, in this book the terms 'the North' or 'Ulster' are, as far as possible, used in discussion of the period preceding this. In the context of this book they refer to the six counties which were to make up Northern Ireland – Antrim, Armagh, Down, Fermanagh, Londonderry and Tyrone – rather than the nine which officially make up Ulster. For convenience of explanation, on occasion the term Northern Ireland is used in reference to the whole period under discussion.

The Republic of Ireland was known as the Irish Free State from 1922 until 1937 when it became Éire and then a republic in 1948. The terms Southern Ireland or 'the South' are often used in the book and at all times refer to the twenty-six counties of the Irish Republic.

In the case of Londonderry/Derry, it is noted that both terms refer to the same place – both city and county. As far as possible contemporary usage is maintained. In other cases, Derry is used with reference to the city and Londonderry in reference to the county.

List of abbreviations

BGCU	Belfast Girls' Club Union
BSCH	British Social Hygiene Council
BWWC	Belfast Women's Welfare Clinic
CD Acts	Contagious Diseases Acts
CLA	Criminal Law Amendment
CMAC	Contemporary Medical Archives Centre at Wellcome Trust for History of Medicine
DORA	Defence of the Realm Act
ETO	European Theater of Operations
FPA	Family Planning Association
GA	Girls' Auxiliary
GFS	Girls' Friendly Society
GSC	Good Shepherd Convent
LGB	Local Government Board
MD NAB	National Archives Building, Maryland, USA
MSOH	Medical Superintendent Officer of Health
NAI	National Archives of Ireland
NCCVD	National Council for Combating Venereal Diseases
NIFPA	Northern Ireland Family Planning Association
NSPCC	National Society for the Prevention of Cruelty to Children
NUWW	National Union Women of Workers
NVA	National Vigilance Association
PHS	Presbyterian Historical Society
PP	Parliamentary Papers
PRONI	Public Record Office of Northern Ireland
PSNI	Police Service of Northern Ireland
RCB	Representative Church Body
RCVD	Royal Commission on Venereal Diseases

RG	Record Group
RIC	Royal Irish Constabulary
RUC	Royal Ulster Constabulary
RVH	Royal Victoria Hospital (Belfast)
SPVD	Society for Prevention of Venereal Diseases
TNA	The National Archives, London (Kew)
UPAS	Ulster Pregnancy Advisory Service
WL	Women's Library
WPS	Women's Police Service

Introduction

Recent decades have seen an important growth in research and publication concerning women and sexuality in Irish history.[1] While many of these studies purport to be all-Ireland studies, in the majority of cases the position of women in Ulster or Northern Ireland has been overlooked. This is particularly lamentable as women living in Ulster were doing so in a social and political situation that was very different to the rest of the island.[2] The politics and political violence of twentieth-century Northern Ireland have overshadowed social history in general and women's history in particular. There has, however, been a partial move to redress this disparity and there appears to be a growing recognition of the need to investigate the lives of Northern Irish women as a distinct entity.[3] This book aims to further develop this by considering some of the ways in which female sexuality was regulated in Northern Ireland in the twentieth century, including the experiences of women involved in prostitution, who lived in rescue homes, and were suspected of having VD, as well as those who interacted with US troops and accessed family planning. The role of the Catholic and Protestant Churches in the regulation of female sexuality is considered, and it is argued that there was considerable unity across the religious and political spectrum in relation to female sexuality.

Historical background

The turmoil in Northern Ireland and the unique political, social and religious circumstances of the period provide the backdrop to this discussion of the regulation of female sexuality. The issue of Home Rule dominated the political landscape in Ireland in the first decades of the twentieth century. However, while the advent of the First World War halted political demands, the Easter Rising of 1916 and its aftermath heralded the political turmoil and violence which led to the partitioning of the island. The Government of Ireland Act of 1920 partitioned Ireland with the setting up of two governments and two parliaments, one for the six counties that were to form Northern Ireland and another for the twenty-six southern counties which became the Irish Free State.

The new state of Northern Ireland was faced with a situation where one-third of the population, Catholic nationalists, were hostile to its existence and wanted a united Ireland. The Northern Irish Parliament was dominated by unionists who were intent on maintaining links with Britain and not relinquishing any power to nationalists. Nationalists elected to the Northern Ireland House of Commons refused to take their seats until 1927.[4]

Local government in Northern Ireland consisted of two county boroughs – Belfast and Londonderry – with corporations, which were all-purpose authorities. There were six county councils and a lower tier of urban and rural councils. Responsibility for health lay with the Ministry of Home Affairs until 1944 when the structure of government in Northern Ireland was reformed and a Ministry of Health and Local Government was formed.[5] Throughout the period, medical services languished behind the rest of the United Kingdom, which was due in part to the financial difficulty experienced by the Stormont government.[6] The Health Services Act (NI) 1946 swept away all piecemeal health care and a free National Health Service was established in July 1948. The Act resulted in the establishment of the Northern Ireland Hospitals Authority, Northern Ireland Tuberculosis Authority, General Health Services Board, two County Borough Health Committees and six County Health Committees.

The population of the six counties that were to become Northern Ireland, was, in the period in question, around 1,300,000 of which Catholics made up around 30–35 per cent. The Protestant population was divided between a number of denominations, the largest two being the Presbyterian Church and the Church of Ireland, representing 26 and 23 per cent respectively of the population in 1926.[7] Church attendance and affiliation was strong in Northern Ireland and the Churches acted as powerful pressure groups.[8] Although the Protestant Churches had more direct access to the government, the government can also be seen to have been sensitive to the opinions and demands of the Catholic Church.

While Ireland, as a whole, was largely agricultural, the north-eastern counties, and Belfast in particular, had a strong manufacturing and industrial base. This was largely centred around shipbuilding and textiles and the associated industries of engineering and rope-making. Whiskey distilling and tobacco production also employed large numbers. Derry, in the north-west, possessed a thriving shirt-making industry. The situation was to change in the 1920s with the end of the industrial boom experienced during the First World War. As unemployment grew in the 1920s and 1930s, the government found it increasingly difficult to finance social benefits. The failure to help those out of work resulted in disturbances in Belfast in the early 1930s. In particular, in October 1932, there was a brief uniting of the Protestant and Catholic working class to demand increased unemployment relief. Industrial output did increase and unemployment correspondingly fell during the latter years of the Second World War. However, from its inception, Northern Ireland experienced higher unemployment and lower average incomes than the rest of the UK.[9]

Northern Ireland was therefore in a complicated political situation: part of the United Kingdom yet physically separated from it; politically separate from the Irish Free State yet sharing a land mass. This peculiar situation was most starkly evident during the Second World War, where Northern Ireland was at war on the side of the Allies while Éire remained neutral, leaving one quarter of the island under blackout conditions while the other three-quarters was lit up. Opposition to the partitioning of the island continued at a relatively low level until the late 1960s with the outbreak of civil unrest which was to become thirty years of violence popularly known as 'the Troubles'.

These political, social, economic and cultural features of Northern Ireland are essential to any discussion of sexuality and its regulation, and demonstrate the need to consider Northern Ireland as a separate entity worthy of particular consideration which can enhance our understanding of these issues.

Historiographical background

Historical research on prostitution and the associated philanthropic work of rescue and refuge homes in Ireland in the nineteenth and early twentieth centuries has been pioneered by Maria Luddy.[10] Although there has been some discussion of Protestant philanthropy in Dublin,[11] the focus has been largely on Southern Irish Catholic-run rescue homes.[12] In recent years the majority of the work published, along with the media coverage of Catholic-run Magdalen homes, has been extremely negative and has created an image of repressive and cruel institutions.[13] These exposés and scandals have impacted on the Catholic Church and have made it very reluctant to allow historical researchers access to records concerning their institutions. The Protestant-run rescue and refuge homes that existed in Northern Ireland, and in particular in Belfast, have often been neglected and deserve consideration because of their unique political, religious and social context.[14]

When the focus is broadened to consider the more general historiographical background, it is evident that much of the research on prostitution has centred on the attempts to regulate and control prostitution and is largely focused on governmental legislation in the nineteenth century.[15] The attempts to reform prostitutes have also prompted a body of research that has considered the institutions established to try and effect this reform and this also largely focuses on the nineteenth century. Paula Bartley's work considers the attempts to reform prostitutes in England between 1860 and 1914 and how prevention replaced reform as time progressed.[16] This work on England augments the work previously carried out by Maria Luddy on Ireland and Linda Mahood on Scotland.[17] Linda Mahood's work is more theoretically based than the work of Bartley, Luddy and Frances Finnegan, and uses Foucauldian, feminist and social control theories to expound a view of the Magdalen institutions of Glasgow and Edinburgh as gendered institutions which attempted to impose middle-class ideals of sexuality and maintain class roles.

Paula Bartley has also drawn attention to the previously neglected area of prevention work among girls: the attempts to prevent girls turning to prostitution rather than reform prostitutes. She focuses primarily on the work of Ladies' Associations for the Care of Friendless Girls, who worked in a variety of ways to guide young working-class women on the path of sexual purity.[18] There has been very little historical research carried out on the relationship between girls' organisations and moral prevention work. Carol Dyhouse, Brian Harrison and Bartley have all referred to the role of the Girls' Friendly Society (GFS) in the campaign to maintain female moral standards but the organisation has not received close scrutiny.[19] Similarly, discussion of the Girl Guides has tended to focus on their relationship with the Scout movement and the role of the organisation in assisting with empire building.[20] Richard Voletz has, however, expounded the theory that the Guides provided a solution to 'khaki fever' during the First World War, offering an outlet for the energy and emotions provoked by wartime conditions.[21] The concern generated by the behaviour of young women during the First World War and the measures employed to try and police their behaviour has been documented, centred in the main on the experience in England.[22]

The attempt to regulate female sexuality within the context of trying to prevent the spread of venereal disease (VD) is an important theme within recent historical research. Women who did not conform to accepted standards of sexual behaviour were regarded as responsible for the spread of disease and this was reflected in legislation. The situation was similar in many European countries where, even when the language of legislation was gender-neutral, women were still largely the focus of the action taken.[23] However, it is clear that consideration of age and class were also important factors determining the focus of legislation. Discussion of the measures taken and attitudes towards the regulation of VD have become part of a wider discourse concerning attempts to regulate sexuality and to control those considered 'deviant' in society.[24]

The impact of war, particularly the First World War, in stimulating legislation and the desire to protect the military has prompted considerable debate.[25] The establishment of a voluntary and free system to treat VD in Britain has also been documented,[26] as has the debate concerning the implementation of the recommendations of the Royal Commission on Venereal Diseases in 1916, which reflected the variety of moral and medical concerns associated with attempts to prevent VD.[27] The response of central government to VD and the formal policies and strategies employed have generated much discussion, with Peter Baldwin providing a comparative view of the responses in a number of European countries.[28] However, it is apparent from studies of the impact of VD legislation, at a local and regional level, that central governmental strategy and proclamations were often very different from the situation on the ground.[29]

Fears about female behaviour were also expressed during the Second World War and increased with the arrival of large numbers of US servicemen from 1942 onwards. The basing of US troops in Britain and the positive and negative interaction with the public has generated much discussion.[30] The involvement of local women in both Britain and Australia with US troops has been located in a wider debate surrounding changing female sexual identity and its impact on citizenship and international relations.[31] The subject of US troops in Northern Ireland has been discussed in a rather uncritical way by official war histories, local historians or those writing their wartime memoirs, with no real discussion of the nature of the relationships or involvement with local women.[32] The particular and unique situation in Northern Ireland requires attention to discover whether it impacted on the interaction between troops and local women and the wider debate on attempts to regulate female sexuality.

The reluctance to discuss issues relating to sex and sexuality was still evident several decades after the end of the war. The development of family planning services in Northern Ireland was slower than the rest of the UK, due to the unique religious, social and political circumstances. Research on the history of birth control and family planning has focused largely on the social politics surrounding provision.[33] Recent work has been carried out to consider these issues at a micro-level[34] and oral history interviews have been used to open new areas of debate surrounding the role of men in the process of limiting family size and the choice of birth control methods employed.[35] However, a lacuna still exists in relation to the establishment of family planning clinics and the issues involved at a local and regional level, particularly in the post-Second World War period.[36] The historiography of birth control has focused little attention on the establishment of clinics in the UK at a local or regional level, concentrating rather on decisions and debates at national and governmental level.[37] As has been contended, there is a need to consider local situations before assumptions and conclusions can be made about the nation as a whole.[38] Local and regional studies allow national generalisations to be tested and examined and often reveal a very different reality to that imagined by legislators. As with VD legislation, examination of how the situation in Northern Ireland differed from elsewhere is crucial in building a picture of regional difference and similarity which informs our understanding of the national and international picture.

There is, therefore, a significant gap in the literature surrounding all aspects of the regulation of sexuality in Northern Ireland. While issues such as prostitution and rescue homes in Southern Ireland have received increased attention, the situation north of the border has been notably neglected. The recognition of the separate identity and experience of Northern Irish women needs to be addressed, as do the issues of sexuality in a contested state.

Any discussion concerning the history of sexual regulation is extremely difficult to research given the sensitivity of many of the archives and problems of closure. The archival research for this book involved a number of problems in locating, identifying, and accessing archive material. A wide variety of public and private repositories and libraries were used and it took a considerable amount of time to find and gain access to much of the material. Issues of closure arose around a number of records of a sensitive nature, and this has meant that any names mentioned have been changed to protect anonymity. Most difficulty arose over attempts to access records held by the Roman Catholic Church relating in particular to Magdalen homes, girls' organisations and work with unmarried mothers. As has been mentioned, these difficulties have arisen in the light of the scandals and exposés involving the Catholic Church in recent years, which have led to a reluctance to allow researchers access to archives. This has meant that the material used in the discussion of these areas is often from the Protestant Churches and organisations that have a more open access policy. However, even with Protestant organisations the extant archive material is often rather scant. This is a particular issue with girls' organisations where records were often held in private hands and only partial records have been deposited with repositories. For example, the YWCA were obviously involved in preventative work, and they had a holiday home in Newcastle Co. Down. However the records for the organisation are very good for the Republic of Ireland, but very little is available for Northern Ireland.

It must also be recognised at the outset that activities such as prostitution are by nature clandestine, and those involved have not left written testimonies or records. The material used to create a profile of women who were involved in prostitution comes largely from the authorities, in the form of entrance registers to the workhouse or statistics for those arrested or imprisoned. Similarly, the backgrounds and case histories of women who entered rescue homes, and the information about life inside the homes, was written and recorded by those who ran the institutions rather than the women themselves. However, while the limitations of these sources are recognised, nonetheless they provide a clear insight into the attitudes and beliefs of the authorities at the time.

Oral history interviews were also carried out with twelve women who had been involved in girls' organisations before 1945. While this, admittedly limited, sample provided a fascinating and useful insight into the workings of the organisations and associated issues of acceptable female behaviour, the drawbacks must also be recognised. The women who agreed to be interviewed did so voluntarily having answered an advertisement; their views and experiences were largely positive, which prompted their interest in being interviewed. The women were all in their late 60s or 70s when interviewed and were from similar middle- or upper-working-class backgrounds. Interviews were also carried out with a nun from the Good Shepherd Convent in Belfast who had been at the Convent since 1935 and with a woman who had been employed by the US military authorities in Belfast to interview and report on the suitability of women who wanted to marry US troops, both of which provided fascinating insights in to the operations of these organisations and their own personal experiences.

In contrast to the difficulties in locating and accessing some archival material, there were also a number of rich, easily accessible, and under-utilised sources of material. These included the records held in the United States National Archives relating to the US troops based in Northern Ireland. They open up a new area of discussion relating to the attempts to regulate the interaction between US troops and Northern Irish women during the Second World War and the concerns of the military authorities. Similarly, the material relating to family planning in Northern Ireland has been neglected and provides fascinating insights into the concerns of those involved in trying to establish family planning clinics in the 1950s and 1960s.

The archival research which underpins this book demonstrates the unity of religious and political groups within Northern Ireland over a number of issues concerning female sexuality. It reveals how notions of female purity were not simply associated with Catholic Ireland and a post-colonial legacy, but were also common in Northern Ireland in the Protestant community. This, it is argued, was part of a wider view shared by Catholics and Protestants in the North and South of a Christian Ireland with higher moral standards of behaviour than its more secular English neighbour.

Notes

1 For example, Maria Luddy and Cliona Murphy (eds), *Women Surviving: Studies in Irish Women's History in the Nineteenth and Twentieth Centuries* (Dublin, 1989); Maria Luddy, *Women and Philanthropy in Nineteenth Century Ireland* (Cambridge, 1995); Mary Cullen and Maria Luddy (eds), *Women, Power and Consciousness in Nineteenth Century Ireland* (Dublin, 1995); Alan Hayes and Diane Urquhart (eds), *The Irish Women's History Reader* (London and New York, 2001); Margaret Kelleher and James Murphy (eds), *Gender Perspectives in Nineteenth Century Ireland: Public and Private Spheres* (Dublin, 1997); Mary O'Dowd and Sabine Wichert (eds), *Chattel, Servant or Citizen: Women's Status in Church, State and Society* (Belfast, 1995); Louise Ryan, *Gender, Identity and the Irish Press, 1922–37: Embodying the Nation* (Lampeter, 2002).

2 For more on the general political and social background to the period, see for example Jonathan Bardon, *A History of Ulster* (Belfast, 1992); Paul Bew, *Ireland: the Politics of Enmity, 1789–2006* (Oxford, 2007); Diarmaid Ferriter, *The Transformation of Ireland, 1900–2000* (London, 2004); Alvin Jackson, *Ireland, 1798–1998* (Oxford, 1999).

3 For example, Andrea Ebel Brozyna, *Labour, Love and Prayer: Female Piety in Ulster Religious Literature, 1850–1914* (Belfast, 1999); Janice Holmes and

Diane Urquhart (eds), *Coming into the Light: The Work, Politics and Religion of Women in Ulster, 1840–1940* (Belfast, 1994); Diane Urquhart, *Women in Ulster Politics, 1890–1940: A Story Not Yet Told* (Dublin, 2000).

4 Mary Harris, *The Catholic Church and the Foundation of the Northern Irish State* (Cork, 1993), p. 175.

5 Derek Birrell and Alan Murue, *Policy and Government in Northern Ireland: Lessons of Devolution* (Dublin, 1980), p. 133; Alvin Jackson, 'Local Government in Northern Ireland, 1920–1973', in Mary Daly (ed.), *County and Town: One Hundred Years of Local Government in Ireland* (Dublin, 2001), pp. 56–66.

6 Mary Daly, *A Social and Economic History of Ireland Since 1800* (Dublin, 1981), pp. 206–208.

7 W.E. Vaughan and J.A. Fitzpatrick, *Irish Historical Statistics: Population, 1821–1971* (Dublin, 1978), pp. 69–73.

8 Birrell and Murue, *Policy and Government*, p. 110.

9 John Simpson, 'Economic Development: Cause or Effect in the Northern Ireland Conflict', in John Darby (ed.), *Northern Ireland: The Background to the Conflict* (Syracuse, 1983), p. 81.

10 See for example Maria Luddy, *Prostitution and Irish Society, 1800–1940* (Oxford, 2007); Luddy, *Women and Philanthropy*; Maria Luddy, 'Women and Charitable Organisations in Nineteenth Century Ireland', *Women's International Studies Forum*, 11 (1998), 301–305; Maria Luddy, '"Abandoned Women and Bad Characters": Prostitution in Nineteenth Century Ireland', *Women's History Review*, 6 (1997), 485–503.

11 For example, Luddy, *Women and Philanthropy*; Oonagh Walsh, *Anglican Women in Dublin: Philanthropy, Politics and Education in the Early Twentieth Century* (Dublin, 2005); Margaret Preston, *Charitable Words: Women, Philanthropy, And The Language Of Charity In Nineteenth-Century Dublin* (Connecticut, 2004).

12 For example, James M. Smith, *Ireland's Magdalen Laundries and the Nation's Architecture of Containment* (Notre Dame, 2007).

13 For example, Frances Finnegan, *Do Penance or Perish: A Study Of Magdalene Asylums in Ireland* (Kilkenny, 2000); *The Magdalene Sisters* (written and directed by Peter Mullan, 2002); *Sinners* (BBC, 2001).

14 Exceptions include, Luddy, *Prostitution*, which discusses some of the Protestant homes in Belfast within an all-Ireland context, and Alison Jordan, *Who Cared? Charity in Victorian and Edwardian Belfast* (Belfast, 1993), which discusses the rescue and refuge homes in Belfast in the context of Victorian and Edwardian charity in the city.

15 For example, Judith Walkowitz, *Prostitution and Victorian Society: Women, Class and the State* (Cambridge, 1980); Paul McHugh, *Prostitution and Victorian Social Reform* (London, 1980).

16 Paula Bartley, *Prostitution: Prevention and Reform in England, 1860–1914* (London, 2000).

17 Linda Mahood, *The Magdalenes: Prostitution in the Nineteenth Century* (London and New York, 1990).

18 See Bartley, *Prostitution*; Paula Bartley, 'Preventing Prostitution: The Ladies' Association for the Care and Protection of Young Girls in Birmingham, 1887–1914', *Women's History Review*, 7 (1998), 37–60.

19 Carol Dyhouse, *Girls Growing Up in Late Victorian and Edwardian England* (London, 1981); Brian Harrison, '"For Church, Queen and Family": The Girls' Friendly Society, 1874–1920', *Past and Present*, 61 (1973), 107–138.

20 See for example Allen Warren, '"Mothers for Empire"? The Girl Guide Association in Britain, 1909–1939', in J.A. Mangan (ed.), *Making Imperial Mentalities: Socialism and British Imperialism* (Manchester, 1990) pp.96–110. Exceptions include Tammy Proctor, *On My Honor: Guides and Scouts in Interwar Britain* (Philadelphia, 2002).

21 Richard Voeltz, '"The Antidote to Khaki Fever"? The Expansion of the British Girl Guides During the First World War', *Journal of Contemporary, History*, 27 (1992), 627–638.

22 Angela Woollacott, '"Khaki Fever" and its Control: Gender, Class, Age and Sexual Morality on the British Homefront in the First World War', *Journal of Contemporary History*, 29 (1994), 325–347; Penny Summerfield, 'Women and War in the Twentieth Century', in J. Purvis (ed.), *Women's History: Britain, 1850–1945* (London, 1995), pp. 307–333; Phillippa Levine, '"Walking the Streets in a Way No Decent Woman Should": Women Police in World War I', *Journal of Modern History*, 66 (1994), 34–78; Lucy Bland, 'In the Name of Protection: The Policing of Women in the First World War', in J. Brophy and C. Smart (eds), *Women in Law: Explorations in Law, Family and Sexuality* (London, 1985), pp. 23–49.

23 See for example Anna Lundberg, 'Passing on the "Black Judgement": Swedish Social Policy on Venereal Disease in the Early Twentieth Century', in R. Davidson and L.A. Hall (eds), *Sex, Sin and Suffering: Venereal Disease and European Society Since 1870* (London, 2001), p. 41; Lutz D.H. Sauerteig, '"The Fatherland is in Danger, Save the Fatherland!": Venereal Disease, Sexuality and Gender in Imperial and Weimar Germany', in Davidson and Hall (eds), *Sex, Sin and Suffering*, p. 83.

24 For example, see Pamela Cox. 'Compulsion, Voluntarism, and Venereal Disease: Governing Sexual Health in England after the Contagious Diseases Acts', *Journal of British Studies*, 46:1 (2007), 91–115; Roger Davidson, *Dangerous Liaisons: A Social History of Venereal Disease in Twentieth-Century Scotland* (Amsterdam and Atlanta, 2000); Annet Mooij, *Out of Otherness: Characters and Narrators in the Dutch Venereal Disease Debates, 1850–1990* (Amsterdam, 1998); Richard Davenport-Hines, *Sex, Death and Punishment: Attitudes to Sex and Sexuality in Britain Since the Renaissance* (Glasgow, 1991); Davidson and Hall (eds), *Sex, Sin and Suffering*; Lucy Bland, '"Cleansing the Portals of Life": The Venereal Disease Campaign in the Early Twentieth

Century', in M. Langan and B. Schwarz (eds), *Crises in the British State, 1880–1930* (London, 1985) pp. 192–208; Frank Mort, *Dangerous Sexualities: Medico-Moral Politics in England since 1830* (London and New York, 1987).

25 See for example Bland, 'In the Name of Protection'; Suzanne Buckley, 'The Failure to Resolve the Problem of Venereal Disease Among the Troops in Britain During WW1', in B. Bond and I. Roy (eds), *War and Society: A Yearbook of Military History* Vol. 2 (London, 1977), pp. 65–85; Lesley Hal '"War Always Brings It On": War, STDs, the Military and the Civilian Population in Britain, 1850–1950', in R. Cooter, M. Harrison and S. Sturdy (eds), *Medicine and Modern Warfare* (Amsterdam, 1999), pp. 205–223; Lesley Hall, 'Venereal Diseases and Society in Britain from the Contagious Diseases Acts to the National Health Service', in Davidson and Hall (eds), *Sex, Sin and Suffering*, pp. 120–137.

26 David Evans, 'Tackling the "Hideous Scourge": The Creation of the Venereal Disease Treatment Centres in Early Twentieth-Century Britain', *Social History of Medicine*, 5 (1992), 413–433.

27 S.M. Tomkins, 'Palmitate or Permanganate: The Venereal Prophylaxis Debate in Britain, 1916–1926', *Medical History*, 37 (1993), 382–398; Bridget Towers, 'Health Education Policy 1916–1926: Venereal Disease and the Prophylaxis Dilemma', *Medical History*, 24 (1980), 70–87.

28 Peter Baldwin, *Contagion and the State in Europe, 1830–1930* (Cambridge, 1999).

29 See for example Ida Blom, 'Fighting Venereal Diseases: Scandinavian Legislation c.1800 to c.1950', *Medical History*, 50 (2006), 209–234; Davidson, *Dangerous Liaisons*.

30 Juliet Gardiner, *'Over Here': The GIs in Wartime Britain* (London, 1992); Norman Longmate, *The G.I.'s: The Americans in Britain, 1942–1945* (London, 1976); David Reynolds, *'Rich Relations': The American Occupation of Britain, 1942–1945* (London, 1996).

31 Marilyn Lake, 'The Desire for a Yank: Sexual Relations Between Australian Women and American Servicemen During World War II', *Journal of the History of Sexuality*, 2 (1992), 621–633; Michael Sturma, 'Loving the Alien: The Underside of Relations Between American Servicemen and Australian Women in Queensland, 1942–1945', *Journal of Australian Studies*, 41 (1989), 3–17; Sonya O. Rose, 'Girls and GIs: Race, Sex and Diplomacy in Second World War Britain', *The International History Review*, 19 (1997), 142–160.

32 See for example John Blake, *Northern Ireland in the Second World War* (London, 1956); James Doherty, *Post 381: The Memoirs of a Belfast Air Raid Warden* (Belfast, 1992); Derrick Gibson-Harries, *Life-Line to Freedom: Ulster in the Second World War* (Lurgan, 1990); John Hughes, *Toome's Wartime Airfield* (Draperstown, 1995).

33 See for example Walter Seccombe, 'Starting to Stop: Working-Class Fertility Decline in Britain', *Past and Present* 126 (1990), 151–188; Angus McLaren,

A History of Contraception from Antiquity to the Present Day (Oxford, 1990); Hera Cook, *The Long Sexual Revolution: English Women, Sex, and Contraception* (Oxford, 2004); Marcus Collins, *Modern Love: An Intimate History of Men and Women in Twentieth-Century Britain* (London, 2003).

34 See for example Claire Davey, 'Birth Control in Britain During the Interwar Years: Evidence from the Stopes Correspondence', *Journal of Family History* 13 (1998), 329–345.

35 Kate Fisher, *Birth Control, Sex and Marriage in Britain 1918–1960* (Oxford, 2006); Lucinda McCray Brier, '"We Were Green as Grass": Learning about Sex and Reproduction in Three Working-Class Lancashire Communities, 1900–1970', *Social History of Medicine* 16 (2003), 461–480.

36 General works on the establishment of Family Planning Clinics include Audrey Leathard, *The Fight for Family Planning* (London, 1980); Peter Fryer, *The Birth Controllers* (London, 1965).

37 Exceptions are Kate Fisher, '"Clearing up the Misconceptions": The Campaign to Set Up Birth Control Clinics in South Wales Between the Wars', *Welsh History Review*, 19 (1998), 103–129; Julie Grier, 'Eugenics and Birth Control: Contraceptive Provision in North Wales, 1918–1939', *Social History of Medicine*, 11 (1998), 443–458; Greta Jones, 'Marie Stopes in Ireland: The Mother's Clinic in Belfast 1936–47', *Social History of Medicine*, 5 (1992), 255–277.

38 Fisher, '"Clearing up the Misconceptions"', 104–105.

1

'Dirty girls and bad houses': prostitutes and prostitution

Prostitution, the exchange of sexual favours for monetary return, has conventionally been identified as a female occupation.[1] Women who were engaged in prostitution were drawn from across class divides and thus their experiences could be very different. Great Britain has never made prostitution illegal, rather it is solicitation or brothel keeping – matters of public order and decency – which are the criminal offences. It is difficult to give a precise figure for the number of prostitutes in Northern Ireland for the period under consideration in this chapter, 1900 to 1945. Judicial statistics, which are available for part of this period, record those who were prosecuted for brothel keeping and prostitution and indicate that the vast majority of prosecutions were made in Belfast. This, and the greater availability of source material for Belfast, has determined the focus of this chapter. The chapter considers prostitution up to 1945, just before the creation of a National Health Service and the closure of the workhouses in 1948. It encompasses both world wars which threw issues such as prostitution into sharper focus and generated most discussion. The closure of the majority of rescue and reform homes specifically for prostitutes also reflected the changing attitudes towards prostitution which had occurred by 1945.

In addition it must be recognised that there was also an 'invisible' group of women involved in prostitution – those who were either more careful in their behaviour, whose appearance was not that of the stereotypical prostitute, or whose role was more like that of the 'kept woman' or mistress. If they did not pose a visible threat to public order, or possess a criminal record, they were able to avoid the gaze of the authorities. These women, having avoided such attention, have left little trace for the historical record. The investigation is therefore slanted towards those who failed to escape prosecution or public labelling. The focus will be largely on those women who entered the Belfast workhouse and had their occupation recorded as 'prostitute', women convicted of prostitution, and those who were registered in official documents.

As mentioned above, one of the main difficulties in any discussion of prostitution or any attempt to identify the numbers involved in prostitution is that it is, by nature, a clandestine activity. Therefore any number suggested is only, at best, an estimate. While it is possible to use judicial statistics to identify the numbers prosecuted for brothel keeping and prostitution, and while Board of Guardian records can identify the number of women entering the workhouse recorded as prostitutes, these records give only a limited picture of the situation. They can only provide evidence about women who were arrested by the police and convicted, or those who were destitute and entered the workhouse. Police prosecutions also largely reflect the policing policy and priorities at that time, or the amount of public outcry about prostitution, rather than actual numbers of active prostitutes. Nonetheless, they are useful in providing a rough guide to numbers involved and, moreover, in identifying changes in both policing priorities and public opinion.[2] These sources are all, however, created by the authorities, those who were attempting to regulate, reform or classify. The voice of the prostitute is unfortunately lost. While assumptions can be made about motives, situations and experiences, it is impossible to know how the women viewed themselves and what the reality of their lives was.

The question of the terminology associated with prostitution needs to be clarified at the outset. From an examination of the records of the Board of Guardians of the Belfast workhouse, and those of various rescue homes, it is clear that the word 'prostitute' was a protean term which was used in a variety of situations and with regard to a wide variety of women. Those involved in the work of reform homes rarely used the word 'prostitute', employing a variety of euphemisms, such as 'fallen women', to indicate illicit sexual activity. As will be discussed in chapter 2, by the beginning of the twentieth century many of the women and girls who entered rescue and refuge homes were not prostitutes, but were more often either women who had fallen pregnant outside of marriage, girls whose behaviour was of concern to their families, or who were keeping bad company. The women entering these homes who had been involved in some form of prostitution had usually only been so very recently. As most homes preferred to admit young women, who were perceived to be more amenable to reform, older women identified as 'hardened prostitutes' did not usually enter them.[3]

Women considered to be 'hardened prostitutes' appeared to have used the workhouse as a place of refuge and respite more often than the reform and rescue homes. However, as will be discussed below, given the age and health of many of these women, the use of the term 'prostitute' was, as Linda Mahood suggests, a 'censure applied to women whose dress, behaviour, physical appearance or vocation caused them to be labelled a "prostitute".[4]

Contemporary debates concerning prostitution, particularly those which have involved sex workers themselves, have sought to argue for the acknowledgement of prostitution as a legitimate form of work within the labour market.[5] While we have no such arguments from prostitutes themselves in the period under consideration, the role of prostitution as part of the female labour market, rather than a moral issue, must be considered. Moreover, for many, prostitution was a temporary or seasonal occupation, which they had entered into due to straitened circumstances, rather than a premeditated career choice.[6] This was not a view shared by many contemporary observers and reformers, who preferred to regard prostitutes as victims who, having been seduced or betrayed, had fallen into a life of sin. Historians have contended that the prostitute should be considered as having historical agency and should be regarded as more than simply a victim.[7] While, admittedly, their choices were limited and constrained by economic and social circumstances, nonetheless they did have, and did make, choices about their lives.[8] For example, women identified as prostitutes who entered the workhouse were very poor and often destitute, yet they entered and left with a measure of independent decision and control. They used the workhouse as a place of respite when times were hard, as a means to get free medical treatment, and left when it suited them. For some women, therefore, it was preferable to enter the workhouse, rather than, for example, entering a rescue home, where there was the need for compliance with the rules of the home and the requirement to participate in some form of work activity.

Prostitutes and the workhouse

Women who entered the Belfast Union workhouse who were identified as prostitutes were obviously struggling economically or were destitute. The dread of having to go 'up the Lisburn Road' (where the workhouse was located) hung over the poor, and the stigma of pauperism was something to be avoided.[9] The indoor registers for the Belfast Union workhouse between 1901 and 1917 identify a number of women, whose occupation was noted as prostitute, entering the workhouse on a regular basis.[10] For these women prostitution was obviously not a particularly profitable occupation.

It is evident that the term 'prostitute', was applied to many women who were probably not actively engaged in prostitution, rather they may have been involved in prostitution in the past or their appearance, demeanour, address or company kept led the workhouse official to assume they were prostitutes. This is most clearly illustrated by several women who entered the workhouse on a regular basis between 1901 and 1915. 'Bridget'[11] entered the workhouse in 1903 aged sixty-eight and again many times every year until 1915. 'Sophia' had a similar entrance pattern, and her age was recorded variously between sixty and seventy-two. It would seem very unlikely that either of these women were actively engaged in full-time prostitution in their sixties and seventies. It is commonly assumed that most women had given up prostitution as an occupation by the time they had reached their forties.[12] There were also women listed as prostitutes, who were recorded as being, in one instance, blind, and in another, paralysed, which would seem likely to have restricted their successful engagement in prostitution.[13]

The most likely explanation is that these women were once engaged in prostitution and that the label had remained with them into old age.[14] The assumption can also be made that lower-working-class women who had no obvious occupation, who had illegitimate children, or whose appearance or companions were deemed unsuitable, were classed as prostitutes by the workhouse authorities. The question therefore arises as to whether the women entering the workhouse volunteered their occupation as prostitute, or whether the person recording the entry made the decision. The difficulty is in knowing how the women perceived themselves. Did they regard themselves as prostitutes or was this a judgement placed upon them? What is clear is that it was a pejorative term which was not necessarily restricted to women who were engaged in full-time employment as prostitutes. For example, the registers record women on some occasions as prostitutes and on others as, for example, 'working in the mill', 'servant' or 'dealer'. This would tend to support the contention that it was the workhouse authorities, rather than the women themselves, who decided on the choice of occupation. It may also have depended on who was filling in the register, whether they knew the women and made decisions based on prior knowledge rather than the answers given. While use of the term 'prostitute' in workhouse registers must be viewed with caution, the information provided in the entries does allow for a profile to be created for these women. Although they may not all have been practising prostitutes they were perceived by the institution as such.

By 1915 the use of the word 'prostitute' in the workhouse registers had largely declined. There were only four women recorded as being prostitutes and these were women who had been regular entrants from 1903. The decline in numbers may reflect a change in attitude of those recording the women entering the workhouse, with a move away from using the term 'prostitute'. The clearly defined areas from which women identified as prostitutes came were also changing. Belfast Corporation was engaged in a Housing Improvement Plan from 1911 which demolished some of the worst housing in the city. The improvement of areas that had traditionally been associated with prostitution and immoral behaviour may have removed some of the stigma previously attached to women from these areas on entering the workhouse. The increased employment caused by the First World War, combined with increased opportunities for women in factories, reduced the numbers seeking refuge in rescue homes and also in the workhouse. Similarly, the introduction of an old age pension in 1909 relieved the distress of some older women, who were now able to survive economically without having to enter the workhouse.

The workhouse as a survival strategy

Between 1903 and 1913, three women, recorded as prostitutes, were responsible for one-third of all the entries for such women in the workhouse register. Two of the women were in their sixties, and the third in her forties. They would typically stay in the workhouse for a few days, leave and then re-enter the same day or a day later. The addresses given by one of these women alternated between the workhouse, prison, the police office, no fixed address and areas of Belfast such as Millfield which were associated with prostitution and poor housing.

While these three women maintained a fairly permanent residence in the workhouse, for other women it was a more temporary solution, a survival strategy when things were difficult.[15] They were often women who had children, who were old, or who needed medical treatment. This casual use of the workhouse, Michael Boyle argues, 'consciously and deliberately exploited the Union'.[16] These women were not stereotypical vulnerable victims, for while their options were limited and their finances precarious, they nonetheless used the system for their own benefit. As will be seen in the following chapter, a number of women used rescue homes in a similar way, entering for short periods and moving between different homes.

Religious breakdown

The majority of women who entered the workhouse classed as prostitutes were Catholic:

Table 1.1 Percentage of Catholic women who entered Belfast Union recorded as prostitutes

Year	% Catholic
1903	60
1905	63
1907	54
1909	51
1911	63
1913	53

Source: Belfast Board of Guardians, *Indoor Relief Registers, 1903–1913*

While this was, in some years, a relatively small majority, it must be noted that the percentage of the total population in Belfast who were Catholic was less than twenty-five between 1901 and 1926.[17] Therefore, the number of Catholic women who entered the workhouse and were identified as prostitutes was more than double the total proportion of Catholics in the population of Belfast.

For the two main Protestant denominations, Presbyterian and Church of Ireland, the proportion of the population of Belfast claiming membership of these churches was as shown in the Table 1.2.[18]

Table 1.2 Percentage of the population of Belfast recorded as Church of Ireland and Presbyterian

Year	% of population Church of Ireland	% of population Presbyterian
1901	29.50	34.44
1911	30.54	33.74
1926	32.10	33.10

Source: Vaughan and Fitzpatrick, *Irish Historical Statistics,* pp. 64, 67, 70

Table 1.3 Percentage of women who entered Belfast Union recorded as Church of Ireland or Presbyterian

Year	% Church of Ireland	% Presbyterian
1903	29	12
1905	25	12
1907	37	9
1909	30	19
1911	32	5
1913	27	20

Source: Belfast Board of Guardians, *Indoor Relief Registers: 1903–1913*

The percentage of women from both denominations entering the workhouse, classed as prostitutes was as shown in Table 1.3.

The proportion of women claiming membership of the Church of Ireland was therefore relatively similar to the proportion of members of the Church of Ireland in Belfast as a whole. However, the Presbyterian proportion was much lower in comparison to its percentage of the total population. In addition to being the largest religious denomination, Presbyterians were also generally in a better position economically.[19] Presbyterian women were heavily over-represented in better-paid occupations such as clerks, dressmakers and seamstresses, in comparison with Church of Ireland women, who were over-represented in lower-paid occupations such as washing, linen work and factory labourers/machinists.[20]

In Belfast during this period, Catholics made up a higher proportion of those employed in lower-paid occupations, although as the city was three-quarters Protestant, there was still a higher actual number of Protestants employed in lower-paid and less-skilled occupations.[21] Catholic women were also over-represented in lower-paid work such as domestic service and in the less remunerative jobs in the linen trade.[22] In the early decades of the twentieth century the areas that many of the women who entered the workhouse identified as prostitutes came from, in particular the Smithfield area, were predominantly Catholic. These were areas that were placed under greater surveillance by the authorities and were economically marginal. Consequently, they were more likely to produce a greater number of women whose situation necessitated use of the workhouse and who were identified as prostitutes.

Living in bad areas

Considering the addresses given by women recorded as prostitutes in the workhouse registers, there were two areas which dominated in popularity. These were, first, the areas centred around Millfield/Smithfield and the surrounding streets such as Brown Street, Abbey Street and Winetavern Street and secondly, the Docks/Shortstrand area, incorporating Nelson Street and Lower Patrick Street. In addition, 1903, 1905 and 1907 saw a number of women giving addresses from an area south of the city centre, close to Queen's University and known as the Holy Lands.

The areas of Millfield/Smithfield and the Docks were located near the city centre and were areas of both overcrowding and urban decay. In 1900, there were 697 one-roomed tenements in Belfast of which two hundred were occupied by at least three people. The majority of this housing was found in what Emrys Jones describes as the 'zone of decay round the newly built centre of the city in St Anne's and Smithfield'.[23] Many of the houses in the Millfield area were built, as the name suggests, to provide housing for mill workers in the nineteenth century. However, by the 1880s they were already turning into slums.[24] It was not until 1910 that the Belfast Corporation agreed to adopt an Improvement Order to clear 700 of the worst slums in Millfield. However, it took until 1917 before any real work was carried out.[25]

These areas were more mixed, religiously speaking, than other parts of the city, which were becoming increasingly segregated. This was simply due to the fact that the housing here was cheap and the people who lived in these areas were not in a position to choose to live amongst those of a similar religious persuasion. It was to these areas that people moving from rural areas to Belfast in search of work went to first. Regardless of religion, they moved to better housing when they could afford to, which was generally in religiously segregated areas. Amongst the women identified as prostitutes who entered the workhouse, there appears to have been little religious segregation. It seems that they had more in common with each other than with members of the same religion who were wealthier; poverty was an important unifying factor.

The areas around Millfield and the Docks have been described by Hepburn and Collins as being, to some extent, a 'transient zone', characterised by a large number of lodging houses and a population which was constantly changing.[26] Many families rented out rooms in their houses, often to single women. Furthermore, it was not uncommon for several unrelated females to live with a family.[27]

It was particularly common for female-headed households to operate as unofficial lodging houses. In Belfast, just over a quarter of households were headed by women in 1901.[28] Of the official lodging houses that were registered after 1906, nearly 60 per cent were run by women. They were mostly situated in the area around Millfield, Smithfield and the Docks. Twenty-four official lodging houses were located in Upper Library Street, thirteen in Millfield and twelve in Winetavern Street. There were also six lodging houses all run by women in Amelia Street, a street which was particularly associated with prostitution.[29] There was a recognisable association between some female-run lodging houses and prostitution. These houses were not necessarily brothels per se, but the occupants were sympathetic to the engagement of women in prostitution as a means of paying rent and supporting the woman and family who ran the lodging house.[30]

Official lodging houses were inspected by the authorities on a random basis, often at night, to check that regulations were not being contravened. For example, they were not allowed to be used by nightly lodgers and, as one landlord found during a midnight inspection in 1926, their presence could lead to a court summons.[31] A further contravention of the regulations involved having both sexes occupying the same room. This offence led to Mrs Mary Corry in Upper Library Street being severely cautioned when inspectors visited her lodging house in 1924.[32]

For women who were engaged in prostitution, these areas not only provided cheap accommodation but also a space to earn money amongst a population that tolerated their lifestyle. These were areas where there were few 'respectable' families who were going to complain to the police. If they could, most people moved out of the areas into better housing and better neighbourhoods. Furthermore, if, as Luddy has suggested, the police restricted the activities of those engaged in prostitution to particular areas, then women involved in prostitution who kept to these areas increased their chances of escaping prosecution.[33]

The area of Millfield and the surrounding streets and the Docks area were, in the early decades of the twentieth century, synonymous with immoral behaviour and poor living conditions. The case notes of women entering the Salvation Army Home in Belfast illustrate this fact. The 'bad houses', which women had lived in prior to entering the Home or went to when they left, were predominately recorded as being in these areas. One twenty-year-old woman had lived in 'bad houses' in Abbey Street and Mitchell Street (close to Millfield) since she was thirteen.[34] The previous year, a sixteen-year-old was admitted to the Home, having been 'lodging

with Miss Cranston in Edward Street – a wicked place'.[35] Others were
described as having lived in 'bad houses' in Millfield, Abbey Street and
Mitchell Street.[36] The notorious Amelia Street was the destination for
'Florrie', who took lodgings there after leaving the Home. She was subsequently charged with soliciting and became ill because of a 'bad life'.[37]
A similar fate befell 'Maggie', who entered the Home when she was seventeen, having been living a 'bad life in the Docks', where she contracted
VD and was then admitted to the Lock Ward at the Union Infirmary.[38] In
case notes, 'Millfield' is used as a pejorative term to indicate an area of ill-
repute. It was an unsuitable location like the Lock Ward at the workhouse.
'Annie', who entered the Home in 1914, had her destinations upon leaving
the Home recorded as, 'Lock Ward, Millfield, Union'.[39]

These areas were so synonymous with immorality that any women
who were seen in these localities were believed to be 'doing wrong' and
risked gaining a bad reputation.[40] In particular, lodging houses in these
localities were regarded as unsuitable for young women.[41] They were
considered to be not only sources of moral danger but also unhygienic.
As the Salvation Army Home case notes for 'Sarah' recorded, 'she looked
dirty, as if living in a common lodging house'.[42] On leaving the Home,
'Sarah' went to live in Millfield before being sent to prison for stabbing a
police constable with a hatpin.[43]

Prostitute networks

As discussed above, women who entered the workhouse and were identified as prostitutes were clearly living close to each other in a small number
of areas. A number of these women returned to the same address or area
when they left the workhouse. Some historians have suggested that there
was a measure of community support amongst prostitutes who lived in
geographical proximity.[44] However, it has also been argued that this geographical proximity simply illustrates habitation of particular localities,
rather than proof that there existed any 'cohesive social community', in
addition to simply a geographical one.[45] Boyle has argued that the most
common factor of these areas was the availability of cheap accommodation, and that the prostitutes appeared to be a mobile group, often having
several changes of address, and that this transience would have worked
against the development of stable relationships. He also contends that
the fact that they entered the workhouse at all illustrates both a lack of
permanent residence and also a lack of adequate support from others.[46]

Although some of the women who entered the workhouse who were recorded as prostitutes, did offer a variety of addresses, and in a number of cases did not remain in the same location for very long, this does not necessarily imply a lack of support networks or a lack of social community. In short, transience does not necessarily imply rootlessness. It is also evident from the indoor relief registers that many of the women returned to the same address on leaving the workhouse, which does suggest some degree of permanence. Moreover, between 1903 and 1915 there were at least thirty houses which were given as the address for more than one woman. A number of these were recorded as lodging houses in the *Belfast Directory*.[47] This suggests not only some form of communication regarding accommodation, but also a physical proximity, which encouraged the establishment of relationships.

It is of course impossible to know the degree of association, community and friendship which existed amongst these women. However, while arguing against the existence of any social community, Boyle details the prosecutions of women for larceny associated with prostitution, and describes how women 'banded together' to carry out crimes.[48] This would seem to suggest some form of support network, even if it was only for criminal purposes.

These arguments must however, be qualified. As Walkowitz has suggested, any support system between women identified as prostitutes was unstable because many of the women were 'in an elementary struggle for survival'.[49] As contended above, prostitution was, for the majority of these women, not a lucrative occupation, but one which helped them survive on a daily basis. Engagement in prostitution was a choice, but a choice from limited possibilities. It was in many cases due to circumstances, such as an illegitimate child, problems with alcohol, lack of family support, or adequate employment, and often a combination of a number of these.

Prosecuting prostitution

Soliciting or brothel keeping were public order offences, and prosecutions were often made at the discretion of the policemen involved. Prostitutes in Belfast were prosecuted under the 1845 Belfast Improvement Act which provided that:

> Every common prostitute or night walker loitering or being in any public place or thoroughfare for the purpose of prostitution or solicitation, to the annoyance of the inhabitants or passengers shall be liable to a penalty of 40/- or in default of payment to one month's imprisonment.[50]

This was similar to the provision in the Towns Improvement Act (Ireland) 1854, which applied to many of the smaller towns in Northern Ireland.[51] The Criminal Law Amendment Act of 1885 provided for the summary conviction of brothel keepers with a fine of up to £20 or three months' imprisonment for a first offence and £40 or four months' imprisonment for subsequent convictions. In 1912, a new Act increased fines for brothel keeping and required landlords to evict tenants who were convicted of using their homes for prostitution. This was further developed in Northern Ireland with the 1923 Criminal Law Amendment Act which set a fine of £100 for a first offence and £250 for a second prosecution for brothel keeping and raised the prison sentence to six months for repeat offenders.[52]

In 1926, the strategies employed for the policing of prostitution in Northern Ireland were explained in two government memoranda: one on the measures used to combat venereal diseases in Northern Ireland; and the other on the measures available for combating prostitution in Northern Ireland. They suggested that the application of the Acts to prosecute prostitutes did not present much difficulty. The danger which the authorities felt needed to be avoided was the arrest of a 'frivolous girl, who, though her conduct may not be all that is desirable, is not, in fact, a prostitute'.[53] It was explained that identifying the common prostitute posed no difficulty for experienced constables, as she usually associated with other known and convicted prostitutes and spoke to men who were obviously strangers to her.[54]

In cases where it was suspected that premises were being used as a brothel, policemen with local knowledge kept watch on the premises and made a note of the number of 'women of loose character' who entered in the company of men, and how long they stayed. The Ministry of Home Affairs was confident that these measures had been found to be 'sufficient to keep prostitution in check in Northern Ireland'.[55]

Section 14 of the Licensing Act of 1872 also stated that publicans who allowed their premises to be the 'habitual resort or meeting place of reputed prostitutes', who stayed longer than was necessary to obtain 'reasonable refreshment', were liable for a penalty and endorsement of their licence. Similarly, under Section 15 of the same Act, if they allowed their premises to be used as a brothel they could be deprived of their licence to sell alcohol indefinitely.

The general impression from official sources between 1900 and 1945 is that prostitution was never viewed as a great problem in Northern Ireland, and that numbers were always felt to be small. In 1942, the City

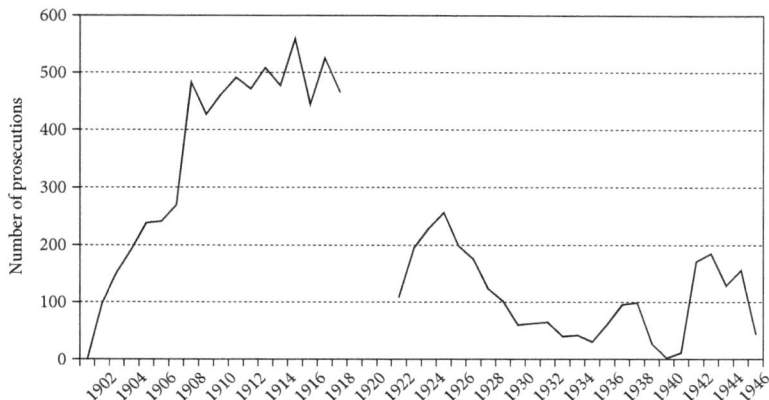

Note: Statistics for the number of prosecutions for prostitution are not available for 1919–1921

Sources: *Judicial Statistics (Ireland) 1902–1918*; Government of Northern Ireland, *Home Office Services, 1927–46*

Figure 1.1. Number of prosecutions for prostitution in Northern Ireland, 1902–1946

of Belfast Royal Ulster Constabulary (RUC) Commissioner's Office explained that there were 'not many prostitutes in the city who actually solicit on the street and they all operate in the centre of the city'.[56] In 1941 it was estimated that there were about forty-five prostitutes operating in the city, with only twelve women prosecuted.[57] Similar arguments were put forward, in April 1942, by the Ministry of Home Affairs at a meeting with the Belfast Council of Social Welfare and the Church of Ireland Moral Welfare Association, both of whom were concerned about the moral state of the city.[58]

Figure 1.1 shows the prosecutions for prostitution for the whole of Northern Ireland. Over 90 per cent of the prosecutions made were in Belfast. For the whole of Ireland, both North and South, between 1906 and 1918, the number of convictions for Belfast made up, on average, 42 per cent of the total number of prosecutions. In 1918, prosecutions in Belfast accounted for nearly three-quarters of all prosecutions for prostitution in Ireland. However, the political situation and the level of unrest experienced throughout Ireland, and Dublin in particular, were likely to have had an important effect: police attention was focused on more pressing issues of law and order than on the activities of prostitutes.

As Figure 1.1 indicates, the number of prosecutions rose rapidly between 1907 and 1908, from 269 to 483, followed by consistently high numbers of prosecutions between 1908 and 1918, peaking at 559 in 1915. The high number of prosecutions between 1908 and 1914 reflected the increased concern with female morality in the years leading up to the First World War, particularly surrounding the White Slave Trade.[59] Similarly, during the First World War, concerns arose over 'Khaki Fever' which was believed to be a dangerous social and psychological affliction, which affected girls and young women of Britain, causing them to act in 'unrestrained, even bold and brazen ways, thus threatening the very moral order of the country'.[60] Women's Patrols were organised to try and prevent prostitution and 'protect' girls on the streets. Military fears concerning the spread of VD to the armed forces, and the belief that women were responsible for its spread, led to increased police vigilance and regulation of women on the streets at night or in the company of soldiers.[61] During the First World War, the numbers of women prosecuted for prostitution in Derry City also increased, from four prosecutions in 1913 to thirty-eight in 1916.[62]

While prosecutions were considerably lower in the 1920s, Figure 1.1 illustrates the peak in the number of prosecutions between 1924 and 1926. This may be largely explained by the concern about prostitution generated by the new Criminal Law Amendment (CLA) Act introduced in Northern Ireland in 1923. The Act brought Northern Ireland into line with the rest of the United Kingdom, where a new CLA Act had been passed in 1922. However, it was felt that the Northern Irish Parliament needed to debate the issues for themselves rather than simply include the Act in the Uniformity of Laws (Northern Ireland) Act.[63]

In keeping with the CLA Act passed in the Imperial Parliament, the Northern Ireland CLA Act maintained the age of sexual consent as sixteen.[64] However, the legislation removed two defences which were used in cases of indecent assault: the argument that consent had been given and 'reasonable cause to believe' that a girl was over sixteen. The latter defence had previously allowed those under twenty-three to be acquitted if it was their first offence. The time limit of bringing a charge of indecent assault was also extended to nine months, which was to allow pregnancies to come to full term, and the fines for brothel keeping were also increased.[65]

In the months leading up to the debate on the Criminal Law Amendment in the Northern Ireland Parliament, the government received a number of letters and a deputation representing a number of organisations including: the Girls' Friendly Society; Edgar Home; Presbyterian Deaconesses Hostel; Church of Ireland Workers' Settlement; the Social Wing of Salvation Army and the NSPCC. These organisations urged the adoption of the Act and the raising of the age of consent.[66] A number of these organisations, including the Ballymacarrett Women's Adult School (BWAS) and the Society of Friends, argued that the age of consent should be increased further to eighteen.[67]

Such sentiments were echoed in debates in the Northern Ireland House of Commons over the Act, with a number of MPs also keen to raise the age of consent.[68] Mr Coote, Member for Fermanagh and Tyrone, suggested raising the age of consent to eighteen, as he felt that it was impossible to discriminate between the mind of a girl of fourteen, fifteen, sixteen or seventeen years of age. He felt that the law was needed to protect girls when they left home and the care and protection of their mother.[69]

During the debate, most anger was reserved for those engaged in brothel keeping. Mr Lynn, Member for Belfast West, suggested flogging as a suitable punishment. When asked by the Minister of Home Affairs, Sir Dawson Bates, whether this punishment would be carried out on women who were convicted of brothel keeping, Mr Lynn explained that:

> when a woman behaves in that way there is no reason why she should not get the same punishment as a man. We have reached a stage where we have equality with regard to responsibility and there must be equality when an offence has been committed.[70]

It was, however, decided that judges would be reluctant to pass this sentence and it was not included in the provisions of the Act.[71]

Dr Morrison, the MP for Queen's University, used the debate to express his fears that there were those who were naive about what was really happening in Belfast. He contended that 'if you get beneath the surface of Belfast you will find a very dark picture'.[72] He supported stiff penalties for brothel keeping, as he believed that brothels were 'hot-beds in which VD is developed and from which it is spread to innocent people'.[73] It was hoped that:

> experiences such as this Bill is intended to prevent might prove the turning point in the career of a young girl that might lead her into the path of absolute immorality.[74]

Mr McGuffin, who represented Belfast North, also believed that this 'evil is certainly more common that is supposed'.[75]

The intensification of attention towards prostitution and associated moral concerns in the North in the 1920s was likely to have been assisted

by Catholic moral purity movements in Dublin in the 1920s. These movements focused attention on a variety of issues in addition to prostitution
such as: 'obscene' publications; unmarried mothers; female behaviour
and sexual laxity.[76] Prominent in these movements were figures such as
the Jesuit Father R.S. Devane, and Frank Duff who founded the Legion of
Mary.[77] They focused their attention on the red-light districts of Dublin
and, between 1923 and 1925, worked with the Dublin police to close down
brothels in the infamous 'Monto' district. Following a police raid in March
1925 the campaign ended with 120 arrests and the closure of brothels.[78]
No such action was taken in Belfast, and while Amelia Street was notorious for prostitution, there was no red-light district, equivalent to Monto,
in Belfast. However, it is arguable that the discussions and debates which
took place in the Irish Free State influenced policing and public awareness
of the issues in Northern Ireland, with all-Ireland organisations, such as
the Legion of Mary, and the Protestant and Catholic Churches, involved.

Prostitution and war

As in the First World War, prosecutions for prostitution saw a large
increase in the Second World War, particularly from 1942 with the
arrival of US servicemen in Northern Ireland.[79] Numbers of prosecutions increased rapidly to 171 in 1942, peaking at 185 in 1943, and then
remained high during 1944 and 1945 before decreasing to 45 in 1946.
The increase in numbers does not necessarily indicate an increase in
prostitutes; rather it may reflect increased vigilance by the police under
governmental and military pressure concerning the spread of VD and the
subsequent need to protect troops from infected women.[80] Nonetheless,
it is probable that, with such an increased market, the actual numbers of
women involved in prostitution rose accordingly. In Armagh Prison in
May 1944, there were twenty-three women charged with brothel keeping
or solicitation, just under a quarter of all the female inmates.[81]

Often simply associating with servicemen was enough to prompt an
arrest and prosecution for prostitution. This was an issue which trou-
bled the Church of Ireland Chaplain at Armagh Women's Prison, Revd
Bloomer. His concern was that women were being wrongly arrested for
solicitation, and gave an example of one girl who had been sentenced to
three months' imprisonment for solicitation but was not even aware of
the meaning of the word until she went to jail. He contended that it was
'very easy to lift a girl seen speaking to a man on a charge of solicitation,
whereas she might be engaged in innocent conversation'.[82]

The RUC in Belfast were, however, convinced that there had been a considerable increase in the numbers of prostitutes who frequented hotels in the city centre in 1942, whose detection was made difficult by the blackout conditions.[83] These concerns prompted a similar reaction to that during the First World War, with an appeal for female police or patrols to try and prevent soliciting and supervise girls on the streets of the city centre.[84] These appeals resulted in the authorisation by the Minister of Home Affairs and the police commissioner of a Women's Volunteer Patrol in Belfast in September 1943.[85] It was to function until a women's police force was established and up to four members patrolled the city centre from 7.30pm until 10.30pm and provided 'friendly supervision'.[86]

Prostitution and poverty

In the early part of the twentieth century, women who were prosecuted for prostitution were often involved with associated crimes of larceny and theft. For many women, a conviction for soliciting made up only a small proportion of their total convictions, and they were more frequently prosecuted for other crimes.[87] For example, between 1900 and 1907, twice as many prostitutes were received into Belfast Prison as the number actually prosecuted for prostitution.[88] As with the workhouse authorities it is evident that a number of women were identified as prostitutes on the basis of something other than their criminal offence, whether this was their appearance, associates, address, past history or previous convictions.

The association of many women identified as prostitutes with criminal offences such as larceny or theft suggests that, for these women, prostitution alone did not provide an adequate income. While there may have been some higher-class prostitutes who provided for a wealthy clientele, this was not the experience of the majority of women who were prosecuted. Women who came under the gaze of the authorities labelled as prostitutes were generally living in relative poverty. Economic difficulties are regarded as a major factor in the move into prostitution. Luddy has suggested that, in Ireland in the late nineteenth century, it was a lack of employment opportunities other than domestic service which led to women turning to prostitution.[89] However, the situation in Belfast in the latter decades of the nineteenth century and the early decades of the twentieth century was very different. Belfast's workforce was notable for its high proportion of women. Between 1900 and 1926, approximately 40 per cent of the Belfast workforce was female, which was much higher

than the rest of Britain and Ireland.[90] The textile industry, and in particular linen production, employed three-quarters of these women.[91]
This high proportion of women employed in manufacturing resulted
in only a small proportion of women employed in domestic service,
less than 10 per cent in 1911.[92] Female migrants were drawn from rural
areas in search of work in manufacturing industries as an alternative to
agricultural work or domestic service. Belfast was different to other cities
in the rest of Ireland, in that it was not necessarily a lack of employment
that was a 'push' factor in some women entering prostitution, but more
specifically poor wages, and the fluctuations of a market that involved
seasonal work.

Brenda Collins has suggested that women chose employment in the
mills as they offered superior wages and more freedom than domestic
service.[93] While it is true that working in the mills offered more independence than living-in as a domestic servant, it is evident that the wages
for female mill workers were not extremely high and were less than half
those of equivalent male workers.[94] Female wages in Belfast in 1911
were around 9 to 12 shillings a week, as opposed to 20 to 40 shillings
for men.[95] For single women, and in particular, single women with children, having a job did not guarantee a high standard of living. Particular
occupations, including the spinners in the mills,[96] were also often associated with immorality, though it is argued that these were unfounded
insinuations.[97]

It was not only women employed in mills and factories who suffered
from poor wages and who may have used prostitution as a means to sup-
plement their income: at the beginning of the twentieth century, women
who worked in shops were paid on average 4 shillings a week for an
eleven-hour day. They were expected to be better dressed than women
who worked in the mill, which led in some cases to women turning to
prostitution to earn some extra money.[98] The case notes for the Salvation
Army Rescue Home in Belfast record the story of 'Lena', who entered
the Home in 1910. She worked in the lace department of Robinson and
Cleaver (a large department store in the centre of Belfast) and was so
badly paid that, along with another girl, she went onto the streets at
night to earn more money.[99] For some young women, then, prostitution
simply offered a way to improve their economic prospects. They did
not necessarily live in absolute poverty, but had ambitions or desires for
material goods which were beyond their earnings. Prostitution potentially offered better hours and working conditions than could the linen
mills.

In addition to poor wages, there were other reasons that prevented some women from keeping regular employment and led them to turn to prostitution. For some women this was a dependency on alcohol. A belief in the connections between alcohol and prostitution was firmly held by contemporary observers and reformers.[100] It was believed that alcoholism had caused women to turn to prostitution in order to support their addiction, while for others the habit was developed as a consequence of their occupation, as public houses were important locations for finding clients.[101] Alcohol prevented some women from keeping regular hours and coping with the physical demands of factory work. Furthermore, having a reputation for drinking often prevented a women from being offered a job. 'Sophia', a woman who was in and out of the Belfast workhouse between 1903 and 1917, and was recorded as being a prostitute, exemplifies the close association of prostitution and alcohol. She was sentenced to a month in prison when she appeared in court in 1913, charged with being drunk for the two hundred and fiftieth time.[102]

For other women, family commitments prevented them from taking regular work. There were limited alternatives in the first half of the twentieth century for unmarried mothers, living outside their family support network, who wanted to keep their children with them. For those who were willing to give up their children for adoption, entrance to a rescue home, such as the Good Shepherd Convent, Edgar Home or Magdalen Asylum, offered a residence while they were pregnant and assistance in having the baby adopted.[103] However, having more than one illegitimate child made entrance to a rescue home more difficult, as such women were considered to be harder to reform. Dr Darling from Co. Armagh, giving evidence to the Poor Law Reform Committee in 1903, explained that women with more than one child were not sent to reform homes: 'we do not put the obnoxious class there at all . . . I always make a distinction between a girl who has made her first slip and a woman who has come in for the third or fourth time'.[104] For some, prostitution offered an opportunity to make money and support their children, as it offered more flexible working hours than formal employment. It has been argued that having an illegitimate child was not an important factor on the path to becoming a prostitute;[105] however, the entrance registers for the Belfast workhouse indicate that a majority of those who entered, identified as prostitutes, did have illegitimate children with them.[106] Clearly then, for some women, having an illegitimate child was an additional precipitating factor in their entrance into prostitution or at least in their identification as prostitutes by the authorities.

Conclusion

The reasons for women entering prostitution were complex. For many, relative poverty encouraged the move into prostitution, whether it was the need to earn money to provide for the basic necessities or to provide for their children, or for others ambitions which stretched beyond poor wages and limited opportunities. Walkowitz moots that in many cases it was not simply 'sheer want' that led women to prostitution, but a combination of different circumstances.[107] Family disruption or the removal of family or other support networks, more particularly the death of a parent or parents, were also important factors. Similarly, disruption of 'normal work' through either alcohol or illness may have made prostitution a more attractive option. The need to support illegitimate children and the desire to keep the children rather than have them adopted appears to have been a determining factor for a number of women in Belfast in the first decades of the twentieth century.

The area of residence clearly played a very important part in both the move into prostitution and continued identification as a prostitute. When residing in an area where prostitution was tolerated, or in a lodging house where it was encouraged as a means to pay the rent, prostitution may have appeared an acceptable and legitimate means to obtain an income. Areas such as Millfield and the Docks in Belfast were far removed from respectable society and unsurprisingly, people living in those areas were often effectively excluded from such society.

It is evident from the numbers who entered the workhouse that prostitution was for many women not a lucrative occupation, but one which they entered when all other avenues were closed to them. It was, nonetheless, a necessary means of gaining money rather than simply evidence of moral depravity, as many contemporary observers believed. Similarly, contrary to contemporary views, the use of the workhouse indicates a level of agency and choice, These women were not simply victims: while their options were clearly limited, they did choose to enter and leave at will, using the system to suit their needs.

The examination of women entering the workhouse throws into stark reality the lack of real understanding of the lives and experiences of these women. The limited picture obtained is one based on the voices of the authorities, those prosecuting, classifying or attempting to reform. It is impossible to know how the women viewed themselves and whether their classification as prostitutes was an accurate reflection of their occupation, or rather a judgement based on their appearance, family circumstances, company or address.

Notes

1 For the purposes of this book prostitution is considered as a female occupation as contemporary discussion of prostitution saw it as exclusively female.
2 Michael Boyle, 'Women and Crime in Belfast 1900–1913' (unpublished doctoral thesis, Queen's University, Belfast, 1997), p. 190.
3 Walkowitz, *Prostitution and Victorian Society*, p.18.
4 Mahood, *The Magdalenes*, p. 13.
5 For example in 2000 the International Union of Sex Workers was formed in London: it is now a branch of the GMB Union and recognised by the Trade Union Council.
6 Walkowitz, *Prostitution and Victorian Society*, p. 14.
7 Luddy, *Prostitution*, p.49; Walkowitz, *Prostitution and Victorian Society*, pp. 26–28.
8 Maria Luddy, 'Prostitution and Rescue Work in Nineteenth Century Ireland', in, Luddy and Murphy (eds), *Women Surviving*, p. 51; Walkowitz, *Prostitution and Victorian Society*, p. 9.
9 Dr Florence Stewart, 'Reminiscences of a GP in Northern Ireland, 1914–1970', D/3612, Public Record Office of Northern Ireland (PRONI).
10 For logistical purposes, the alternate years between 1901 and 1917 were selected. The registers for the years not selected were randomly sampled to ensure the selected years were representative of the period.
11 All names have been changed to preserve anonymity.
12 Luddy, 'Prostitution and Rescue Work', p. 57.
13 Belfast Board of Guardians, Indoor Relief Registers, 1901–1917, BG/7/50–117, PRONI.
14 Judith Walkowitz has illustrated that in Plymouth and Southampton, after the repeal of the Contagious Diseases (CD) Acts, the average age of women engaged in prostitution increased. Various reasons for this trend are suggested, including the stigma that was attached to women registered under the Acts. Although the CD Acts were never imposed in Belfast, the same situation, with the label of prostitute remaining over time, is seen.
15 See chapter 2.
16 Boyle, 'Women and Crime', p. 249.
17 A.C. Hepburn, *A Past Apart: Studies in the History of Catholic Belfast, 1850–1950* (Belfast, 1996), p. 4.
18 There were five women recorded as Methodists and two as members of the Salvation Army.
19 A.C. Hepburn, 'Work, Class and Religion in Belfast, 1871–1911', *Irish Economic and Social History*, 10 (1983), 44, 49.
20 Hepburn, *A Past Apart*, p. 77.
21 Ibid., p. 110.
22 Boyle, 'Women and Crime', p. 70.

23 Emrys Jones, *A Social Geography of Belfast* (London, 1960), p. 62.
24 Jonathan Bardon, *Belfast: An Illustrated History* (Belfast, 1982), p. 125.
25 W.A. Maguire, *Belfast,* (Keele, 1998) p. 124.
26 A.C. Hepburn and B. Collins, 'Industrial Society: The Structure of Belfast, 1901', in P. Roebuck (ed.), *Plantation to Partition: Essays in Honour of J.L. McCracken* (Belfast, 1981), p. 215.
27 Boyle, 'Women and Crime', p. 57.
28 Hepburn, *A Past Apart*, p. 55.
29 Register of Lodging Houses in Belfast, Records of Belfast Corporation, LA/7/9C/1, PRONI.
30 Walkowitz, *Prostitution and Victorian Society*, p. 28.
31 Register of Lodging Houses in Belfast, LA/7/9C/1, PRONI.
32 Ibid.
33 Luddy, 'Prostitution and Rescue Work', p. 78.
34 Entrance Register, Salvation Army Home, Belfast, 11 January 1906.
35 Ibid., 27 May 1905.
36 Entrance Registers, Salvation Army Home, Belfast, 1905–1915.
37 Entrance Register Salvation Army Home, Belfast, 11 February 1909.
38 Ibid., 7 June 1905.
39 Ibid., 11 May 1914.
40 Entrance Registers, Salvation Army Home, Belfast, 1905–1945.
41 The concern over suitable lodgings for young women in Belfast prompted the establishment of a variety of hostels, which are discussed in chapter 3.
42 Entrance Register, Salvation Army Home, Belfast, 20 May 1912.
43 Ibid.
44 Luddy, 'Prostitution and Rescue Work', p. 78; Walkowitz, *Prostitution and Victorian Society*, pp. 26–27.
45 Boyle, 'Women and Crime', p. 213.
46 Ibid.
47 *Belfast and Province of Ulster Directory* (Belfast), 1903, 1905, 1907, 1911, 1913, 1915.
48 Boyle, 'Women and Crime', p. 202.
49 Luddy, 'Prostitution and Rescue Work', p. 78; Walkowitz, *Prostitution and Victorian Society*, pp. 26–27.
50 Belfast Improvement Act, 1845, 8 & 9 Vic., c.142, s.167.
51 Towns Improvement Act (Ireland) 1854, 17 & 18 Vic., c.103, s.72.
52 Criminal Law Amendment Act (Northern Ireland) 1923, c.8, s.3.
53 Memorandum on the Measures Available in Northern Ireland for Combating Venereal Diseases, February 1926, CAB/9B/23/1, PRONI; Memorandum on Measures Available in Northern Ireland for Combating Prostitution 1926, General 'H' Files, Ministry of Home Affairs, HA/5/1378, PRONI.
54 Memorandum on Measures Available in Northern Ireland for Combating

Prostitution 1926, General 'H' Files, Ministry of Home Affairs, HA/5/1378, PRONI.
55 Ibid.
56 Letter from City of Belfast RUC Commissioner's Office to the Inspector General, 31 March 1942, Police Service of Northern Ireland (PSNI) Museum.
57 Ibid.
58 Minutes of Meeting of Belfast Council of Social Welfare and Church of Ireland Moral Welfare Association with Minister of Home Affairs, Belfast, 1 April /1942, PSNI Museum.
59 See chapter 2.
60 Voeltz, '"The Antidote to Khaki Fever"?', 627. For more on Khaki Fever see chapter 3.
61 For more on the attempts to control female behaviour during the First World War see chapter 3, and for the Second World War see chapter 5.
62 Judicial Statistics (Ireland), 1916–1918.
63 Memorandum Regarding Legislation for Coming Session Emanating From the Ministry of Home Affairs, 30 November 1922, Criminal Law Amendment Act, 'B' Files, Ministry of Home Affairs, CAB/9B/157/1, PRONI.
64 The age of sexual consent in Northern Ireland was raised to 17 in 1950.
65 Criminal Law Amendment Act (Northern Ireland) 1923, c.8, s.3.
66 Criminal Law Amendment Act, CAB/9B/157/1, PRONI.
67 Miss W.J. Sayers to Sir James Craig, 17 December 1922, Criminal Law Amendment Act, CAB/9B/157/1, PRONI; W.A. Green, Chairman Society of Friends to Sir James Craig, 14 December 1922, Criminal Law Amendment Act, CAB/9B/157/1, PRONI.
68 Northern Ireland House of Commons Debates, 13 March 1923.
69 Second Reading of the Criminal Law Amendment Act, Northern Ireland House of Commons, 13 March 1923.
70 Ibid.
71 Ibid.
72 Ibid.
73 Ibid.
74 Ibid.
75 Ibid.
76 Luddy, *Prostitution*, pp. 209–227.
77 Sandra L. McAvoy, 'The Regulation of Sexuality in the Irish Free State, 1929–1935', in G. Jones and E. Malcolm (eds), *Medicine, Disease and the State in Ireland, 1650–1940* (Cork, 1999), p. 254.
78 McAvoy, 'The Regulation of Sexuality', pp. 262–263; 'Suppression of Prostitutes', 1946–48, File Relating to Prostitution, Department of Justice, 72/94A, National Archives of Ireland (NAI).
79 See chapter 5.

80 See chapters 4 and 5.

81 Twenty-four women were convicted of vagrancy.

82 Revd Cannon J. Bloomer, Church of Ireland Chaplain to Armagh Prison, Discharged Prisoners Aid Society, 20 February 1943, Armagh Prison Records, Prisons/Prisoner 'PI' Files, HA/9/2/491, PRONI.

83 Letter from City of Belfast RUC Commissioner's Office to Inspector General, 27 April 1942, PSNI Museum.

84 *Belfast Newsletter*, 8 January 1943, p. 3; 10 April 1943, p. 2.

85 *Northern Whig*, 27 September 1943, p. 3.

86 Ibid.

87 Boyle, 'Women and Crime', pp. 210–211.

88 Judicial Statistics (Ireland), 1900–1907.

89 Luddy, 'Prostitution and Rescue Work', p. 78.

90 Maguire, *Belfast*, p. 70; Alison Morrow, 'Women and Work in Northern Ireland, 1920–1950' (unpublished doctoral thesis, University of Ulster, 1995), p. 46.

91 Boyle, 'Women and Crime', p. 61.

92 Margaret Neil, 'Women at Work in Ulster, 1845–1911' (unpublished doctoral thesis, Queen's University, Belfast, 1996), p. 33.

93 Brenda Collins, 'The Edwardian City', in J.C. Beckett (ed.), Belfast: The Making of the City, 1300–1914. (Belfast, 1983) p. 178.

94 Neil, 'Women at Work', p. 42; Hepburn, *A Past Apart*, p. 76.

95 Hepburn, *A Past Apart*, p. 76; Emily Boyle, '"Linenopolis": The Rise of the Textile Industry', in Beckett (ed.), *Belfast*, p. 54.

96 Luddy, *Prostitution*, p. 43.

97 Betty Messenger, *Picking up the Linen Threads: A Study in Industrial Folklore* (Austin and London, 1978), p. 173.

98 Boyle, 'Women and Crime', p. 218.

99 Entrance Register, Salvation Army Home, Belfast, 1910.

100 See chapter 3.

101 Boyle, 'Women and Crime', p. 198.

102 *Northern Whig*, 4 April 1913, p. 2.

103 See chapter 3.

104 Evidence of Dr Darling, Co. Armagh, to Vice-Regal Commission on Poor Law Reform in Ireland, *Minutes of Evidence*, PP 1906, Cd 3204, vol. LII, 1 December 1903.

105 Walkowitz, *Prostitution and Victorian Society*, p. 18.

106 Belfast Board of Guardians, Indoor Relief Registers, 1901–1917, BG/7/50–117, PRONI.

107 Walkowitz, Protitution and Victorian Society, p. 19.

2

'Angels who have lost their way': the work of rescue and refuge homes

The previous chapter discussed the difficulty in accurately determining the numbers of prostitutes operating in Belfast from 1900. The problems of terminology were also discussed and it was argued that the term 'prostitute' was applied to women whose behaviour or appearance was outside that of acceptable social norms, most often poor lower-working-class women. Regardless of the actual numbers involved, concern about prostitution and female sexual behaviour clearly existed and was expressed through the establishment of a variety of penitentiaries and rescue homes for women during the nineteenth and early twentieth centuries.

Penitentiaries and rescue homes were founded initially for the rescue and reformation of prostitutes. In Belfast there were a number of homes affiliated to all the major denominations. There are references to the existence of an Ulster Female Penitentiary from around 1816, which subsequently became the Edgar Home, and was run by the Presbyterian Church.[1] The Ulster Magdalen Asylum was opened in 1849, ten years after building work had originally begun, and was attached to the Church of Ireland Magdalen Chapel on Donegall Pass. The Catholic Church was represented by the Good Shepherd Sisters, who came to Belfast in 1867. They established a 'Home for Destitute Penitents' in the centre of the city before moving to premises on the Ormeau Road.[2] The Belfast Midnight Mission, a non-denominational organisation, was established in the 1860s, and sent a missionary out onto the streets at night to find women and bring them back to the rescue home.[3] The Salvation Army opened its rescue home in Wellington Park in 1905 before moving to larger premises on the Antrim Road. It had a wider remit than the other homes, and a more flexible entrance and exit policy, accepting women of all ages on a short-term basis if required. Elsewhere the Londonderry and North West of Ulster Women's Home had been established in 1829 and appears to have closed in 1911; it was also non-denominational, admitting 'fallen women and girls' who after two years' probation were encouraged to emigrate.[4] In Lisburn the Rosevale Home, a rescue home and laundry, had been founded by a Miss Moore in 1862. It was still operating as a rescue home in 1914 as a notice appeared in the *Lisburn Standard* in which the Lady Superintendent of the home thanked 'all those kind friends who so kindly gave the girls at Rosevale House a pleasant evening at Hallowe'en. Although Rosevale House is often forgotten, it does quiet and unobtrusive work amongst the unfortunate ones. Will kind-hearted people please remember the nights are cold.'[5]

By the beginning of the twentieth century, however, the women who were admitted to all of the above institutions were generally not prostitutes. They were more likely to be: unmarried mothers; girls whose parents were concerned about their moral well-being, the company they were keeping and their behaviour; girls who had been in trouble with the police; or girls who appeared to be sexually precocious. The word 'prostitute' was rarely used in reference to the work of rescue homes in Belfast after 1900. The women were most commonly referred to in terms such as 'fallen women', 'unfortunates' or those who had lived a life of 'degradation and shame'.[6] While the rhetoric employed in describing the work of the institutions gave the impression that all those who entered had been on the streets, living sin-filled lives of moral depravity, this was not the reality in the majority of cases. Those who may have been involved in some form of prostitution, had been arrested for soliciting or had been 'living a bad life', had usually only been on the streets for a short time and were in the minority. However, for the purposes of fund raising the image of a degraded fallen woman saved from destitution on the streets was much more emotive than the reality.

What the majority of those admitted had in common was that they had engaged in sexual activity outside marriage, and in doing so were, in the eyes of respectable society and reformers, in need of rescuing and reformation. As Marian Morton argues, successful prostitutes were unlikely to need or want reformation. She goes on to contend that it was not those who had been paid for sexual favours who needed refuge and rescue, 'but those who had given them freely'.[7] Women who had chosen a career in prostitution, as the previous chapter has shown, often decided not to enter rescue homes. If they were in desperate financial straits or in poor health, they were more likely to use the workhouse as a refuge. As will be discussed more fully below, even if they had desired admittance, women who were believed to have been engaged in prostitution were considered a bad influence on younger women and refused entry to rescue homes.

Religion and rescue

Religious beliefs directed the work of rescue and refuge homes and the names of the institutions reflect the variety of religious thinking. Paula Bartley describes the use of the term, 'penitentiary' as evoking images of 'a triple fusion of sin, punishment and penitence'.[8] Similarly, the name 'Magdalen Asylum' combined that of the most famous female sinner, Mary Magdalen, with the offer of protection and sanctuary.[9] However, there was clearly an awareness from the end of the nineteenth century of the importance of the choice of name for the institutions. Fearing negative associations with the term 'penitentiary' the Ulster Female Penitentiary changed its name to the Edgar Home in 1892.[10] It was felt that the term 'penitentiary' conjured up the wrong image for the establishment, that of a prison rather than of a 'loving home'.[11] While the name may have changed it was unlikely that life within the institution changed markedly. There is no doubt that for many of the women in charge of reform institutions their actions were directed by Christian love and the desire to rescue and protect the women who came into their care. However, this is not to deny the fact that life in the institutions was one of strictness and structure, with evidence of repentance required and the belief that hard work was necessary for reform.

The main purpose of rescue homes was based on the Christian principle of seeking and saving the lost. As the Revd John Waddell, the Honorary Secretary of the Edgar Home, declared at the Home's Annual Meeting on 11 December 1901:

> the primary objective of the institution is to rescue the unhappy inmates from a life of sin and to bring them to a saving knowledge of Him who came to seek and save the lost.[12]

The fact that the Order of The Good Shepherd ran a number of Catholic penitentiaries in Ireland, including Belfast, is of particular significance, reflecting the image of Christ the good shepherd who protected his flock, who laid down his life for them, and who brought other sheep into the fold.[13] The parable of the 'lost sheep' was used to illustrate the importance of rescue work, the saving of those who had wandered from the fold. The work of saving girls who had gone astray, or were in danger of going astray, was seen as directly reflecting the work of Christ. It was thus one of the highest forms of Christian work that could be carried out. As Bartley asserts, the 'reclamation of a single soul from eternal damnation was considered an important offering to God, as his Son had died on the cross in order to save humanity'.[14]

The emphasis was upon forgiveness and on how even the worst sinners who repented and came to God in faith would be completely forgiven and made whole. This forgiveness was available to all, and even those 'fallen and defiled sisters who [had] lost all beauty of holiness' could 'by God's grace, yet show themselves partakers of the Divine nature and become the crown jewels of Immanuel'.[15] This redemption required repentance. The women needed to be made aware of their sin, shown God's love and encouraged to turn from their past wrongs and start anew. In short, the desire was to bring these women back from the 'paths of sin and make them into useful and godly people'.[16]

Entering the homes

Admission to rescue homes was, in theory, voluntary. However, while some girls did volunteer themselves, many were placed in the homes by parents or relatives. The only entrance registers of rescue homes in Belfast that it has been possible to gain access to are those of the Salvation Army Home. These provide detailed background information about those admitted.[17]

Of the 1,329 women who entered the Salvation Army Home between 1905 and 1946, 579 women were admitted on personal request, 416 were recorded as having been 'brought' to the home and 337 as having been 'sent'. When the totals of those who were 'sent' or 'brought' are added together, it is apparent that 753, fifty-seven per cent of women, entered the home at the request or demand of others. This was most often either parents or relatives, or members of the clergy. Young women who were in domestic service and became pregnant were often brought by their mistress when their situation became physically obvious.[18]

Increasingly as the twentieth century progressed a number of women were admitted to the homes via the police courts. Women could be sent to a rescue home, as an alternative to prison, for offences which were considered to be relatively minor. The Edgar Home employed the services of a Miss McClean, who attended the police courts and, with the consent of the magistrate, brought girls to the home in an attempt to effect some form of rehabilitation.[19] The Salvation Army Home also received admissions from the police courts and, from the late 1930s, from social workers, probation officers and slum officers, reflecting a growing professionalism of services. It acted as a 'safe house' for several women who were witnesses to a murder, and also as a remand home for women who were accused of serious crimes. One woman entered the home on remand for murder, after the bodies of four babies were found in a suitcase.[20] The Good Shepherd Convent (GSC) acted in a similar way for Catholic girls who had committed crimes.[21] In a description of the work of the Good Shepherd Sisters in Belfast in 1944, it was explained that they were, 'ready and eager to receive and be responsible for the care and custody of Catholic girls who may be committed by the courts'. The hope was that the government would grant 'reasonable aid' to assist them in their work.[22]

The Protestant homes adopted a pro-active approach in encouraging admissions. In addition to visiting courts, they employed missioners to visit women in their own homes or on the streets at night. Their mission was to try and show the women concerned the error of their ways and persuade them to enter the home. From 1901, the Edgar Home employed a Miss Collins as a visitor to women 'out-of-doors' (those seeking outdoor relief) and in hospital.[23] The committee of the Home recognised the difficult job she had, 'going about street to street trying to lead the poor captives of Satan to that Home of rest'.[24] The visitors also engaged in preventative work, holding classes for 'respectable young women' who were in danger of going astray.[25]

Miss Clarke was employed in 1909 as a missioner for the Edgar Home, and like Miss Collins, she visited 'all the parts of the city where our dishonoured sisters congregate'. She was, apparently, almost invariably well received.[26] As Jesus was the Good Shepherd, seeking and saving the lost sheep, Miss Clarke's work was described as akin to leading sheep out of the miry clay in to which they had sunk. By trying every technique, she had 'the satisfaction of leading many of them, through the Home to a better life'.[27] The job of visiting was strictly a female one, as it was felt that the motives of men doing this work could be misconstrued. Revd Dr O'Loughlin, in a sermon in aid of the Magdalen Asylum, explained that this work was not suitable for all, but rather 'this is women's work, a woman whose heart is made gentle and patient by the constraining power of love'.[28] While the Belfast Midnight Mission had a male missioner, Thomas Clokey, in the 1860s and 1870s, this situation had changed by 1900, as it was felt that women could more effectively reach their fellow sisters.

For the Salvation Army, their role on the streets formed the heart of their work, as officers patrolled the streets at night and directed those they felt were in need to their home. This is reflected in the wide variety of women who entered the Salvation Army Home, often only for a few nights. Some had missed trains, argued with their husbands, lost their job, or were drunk, but all needed refuge for the night.[29]

The entrance registers for the Salvation Army Home also highlight a degree of co-operation between refuge homes, particularly the Protestant or non-denominational ones. If women had requested admission to a particular home and it was full, they were directed to another home. Similarly, women who were pregnant were often sent to Malone Place Maternity and Rescue Home (formerly Belfast Midnight Mission) to give birth.[30] It has been argued that there was a degree of rivalry amongst reform institutions,[31] but this was not evident amongst the Protestant homes in Belfast where there appears to have been a shared concern and awareness of a unity of purpose. This unity also encompassed financial concerns. For example, the funds from the Magdalen Asylum, when it closed in 1916, and the Edgar Home, when it closed in 1926, were given to other organisations engaged in rescue work.[32] However, this spirit of co-operation and support does not appear to have extended between Protestant and Catholic homes. It would appear that the fears that existed were to do with the belief that homes, on either side of the religious divide, were engaged in proselytisation. The Salvation Army records state that one woman left the Home because, 'the Roman Catholics got to know that this girl was with us and we believe that they influenced her mother to make other arrangements for her'.[33] Similarly, the case history for another inmate records that the Salvation Army would have, 'befriended her until she was ready for service but she was taken away by a Roman Catholic woman the day after she entered the Home'.[34] However, as will be discussed below, the concerns about proselytising and the need for religious segregation were more pressing for those running the homes rather than the women who entered them,

Women who entered the homes

It is possible to gain an impression of the background of women who entered the various homes in Belfast by examining their age and religion. As previously mentioned, the only available entrance registers are for the Salvation Army Home. However, numbers who entered the Edgar Home are available from their annual reports. Furthermore, the Census records for 1901 and 1911 provide a snapshot of the inmates of the various homes on these dates.

Figure 2.1 shows the number of admissions to the Salvation Army Home each year between 1905 and 1946.[35] As can be seen, the numbers entering follow an erratic pattern, with a general decline from 1913 and a marked, permanent decline from 1924 onwards. This pattern was

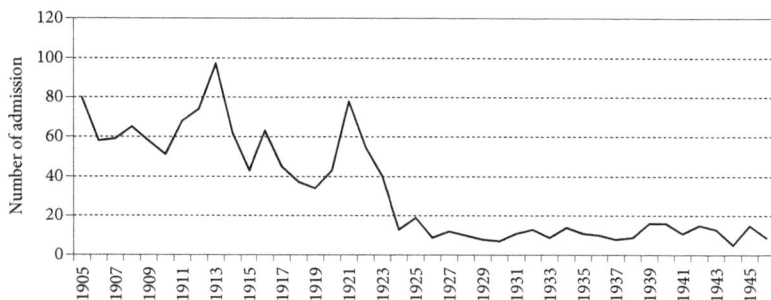

Source: Entrance Registers, Salvation Army Home, Belfast

Figure 2.1 Number of admissions to Salvation Army Home, Belfast, 1905–1946

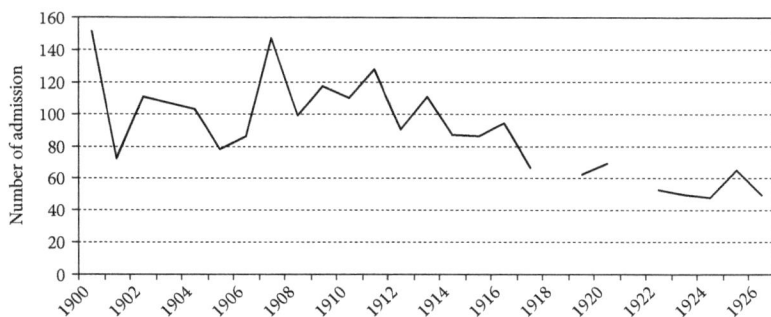

Note: Numbers of admissions are not recorded for 1919 and 1922

Source: *Annual Reports of Edgar Home, Belfast*

Figure 2.2 Number of admissions to the Edgar Home, Belfast, 1900–1926

experienced in other homes, as the graph for the admissions to the Edgar Home, Figure 2.2, also indicates.

Both homes had relatively high numbers of admissions from 1908–1915. The years preceding the First World War also saw a high number of arrests for prostitution. This reflects concerns about issues such as the White Slave Trade, which were growing throughout the British Isles.[36] In 1912, the Irish Women's Suffrage Society held a meeting in the Ulster Hall in Belfast, appealing for support for the Criminal Law Amendment Bill to be passed to help stop the White Slave Trade.[37] These fears, the discussions surrounding the Criminal Law Amendment Bill, and growing expressions of eugenic concerns about the feeble-minded, combined to create a moral panic centred on young women. Rescue homes were therefore used as an important means of attempting to reform those whose behaviour was causing concern.

It is also evident that in the first two decades of the twentieth century rescue homes were increasingly regarded as the most suitable place for unmarried mothers. Viscount Corry, giving evidence to the Poor Law Reform Commission (Ireland), explained that such 'unfortunate women', instead of going to the workhouse, should 'go to a religious institution for reform'.[38] Revd R.H. Smythe, the Presbyterian Chaplain of Monaghan Workhouse, was also in favour, and described sending pregnant, single, young women to a reformatory as 'one of the greatest acts of mercy that could be performed'.[39] However, it is also apparent that as the century progressed it was felt that specific homes for unmarried mothers were more suitable than rescue homes.

The decline in admissions, which began during the First World War and continued more rapidly in the 1920s, may also reflect a change in social and cultural attitudes. By the end of the First World War, women had experienced greater emancipation, and young women who had lived independently from their families were not as willing to submit to the discipline of a rescue home. Similarly, as will be seen in the next chapter, prevention was seen as a better alternative than the 'cure' that rescue homes offered. It was believed that by putting in place organisations that offered positive alternatives to young women, they would be protected from the dangers of city life and the numbers entering rescue homes would decline.

The committee members of the Edgar Home felt that the 'great unrest' following the war was a major contributing factor in the decline of admissions, combined with the ready availability of jobs in factories during the First World War.[40] The growth of industry in Belfast during the First World War had ensured that there were increasing employment opportunities for women. The high demand for workers meant that jobs could now be obtained without having a reference of good character. Girls, who the Committee felt would previously have been deemed unemployable unless they had spent the required period of reformation in an institution, could now gain employment without entering such homes. They considered these girls very poor employees who tended to flit from job to job until they were forced by poverty or disease to enter 'the shelter of a Home and listen to friendly advice'.[41] However, as the number of admissions illustrates, those forced to seek shelter were declining.

Size of homes

The Census records for 1901 and 1911 reveal the differences in size between the GSC, the Edgar Home, Magdalen Asylum and the Salvation Army Home.[42] In 1901 the GSC had 127 inmates[43] compared with thirty-four in the Edgar Home and twenty-one in the Magdalen Asylum. These figures are very similar to 1911 with 135 recorded in the GSC, forty-seven in the Edgar Home and twenty in the Magdalen Asylum. In addition in 1911 there were twenty-four women in the Salvation Army Home.[44]

The difference in size reflected, amongst other things, different attitudes to reformation. The Good Shepherd Sisters felt a large institution was most suitable, whereas the smaller size of the other institutions reflects the view, popular in Protestant Evangelical circles, that a smaller, more home-like situation was most effective.[45] It may also indicate a stricter entrance policy for the smaller homes, with convent institutions being more willing to receive any applicant 'regardless of character, age or physical condition'.[46]

For most homes, age was an important factor determining entrance.[47] The Ulster Magdalen Asylum was specific about their ideal applicants who should be under twenty, in good health, and able to give satisfactory evidence of a sincere disposition to reform their lives. Those above twenty and under twenty-five were only admitted under 'peculiar and encouraging circumstances'.[48] However, both the 1901 and 1911 Census indicate that the asylum clearly did not stick rigidly to this policy. In 1901 there were only three women under twenty in the asylum, five who were between twenty and twenty-five, eight women between twenty-five and forty and four who were in their forties and fifties. In 1911 the average age had increased even further with no women in the asylum under thirty and the average age of the inmates was forty-six.[49] Interestingly in 1901 all the inmates of the asylum are recorded as laundresses, whereas in 1911 only six of the women are recorded as laundresses, ten as servants, one linen mill weaver, one dressmaker, one cook and one post office worker. Although these occupations may have been those of the women prior to their entry to the home, it is evident that laundry work in the home was clearly on the decline. Through most of its existence the asylum was in financial difficulties, and closed due to lack of funds in 1916, unable to generate enough income from running a laundry.

The average age of inmates in the Edgar Home was slightly lower at twenty-one in 1911 compared with twenty-five in 1901. The Salvation Army Home in 1911 had a similar average age of twenty-two whereas the

GSC average age in both 1901 and 1911 was thirty-one, reinforcing the suggestion that it possessed a more flexible entrance policy. Between 1905 and 1946, the average age of those entering the Salvation Army Home was twenty-five and from 1928, the yearly average was always below twenty-five. The policy of admitting young women was influenced by the belief that older women, who had perhaps been involved in prostitution for a considerable amount of time, would be a bad influence on those who had only recently 'fallen'. It was also felt that older women were less amenable to reform than younger women.[50] The preferred candidates were young women who showed willingness to reform and who, if they had been involved in prostitution, had only been so for a short time.[51] It was argued that as younger women, who had recently 'fallen', were much more compliant and offered greater possibilities for redemption, they offered a much higher success rate for institutions. Those lay institutions, such as the Edgar Home and Magdalen Asylum, which depended on fund raising and donations to operate, needed to justify their existence by demonstrating they were able to reform and rehabilitate. Habitual offenders and so-called 'hardened women' were avoided as relapse rates were high.[52]

Similarly, women who had had more than one child out of wedlock were also discouraged from entering rescue homes. An initial 'fall' could be excused, but more than one illegitimate child was clearly a sign of moral failure and, as the twentieth century progressed, mental instability. By entering a rescue home those who had only 'fallen' once were kept away from the workhouse and, the 'obnoxious class', those 'lusty, vicious women', who had 'fallen' three or four times.[53] In the maternity ward of the workhouse, girls would, 'acquire a deeper knowledge of evil and come out later, hopeless, helpless, reckless and without a friend to help her and her child'.[54]

Religious affiliation

Examination of the 1901 and 1911 Census Returns illustrates how the Edgar Home, Salvation Army Home and the Magdalen Asylum were used by both Protestant and Catholic women. While all of these homes had a majority of Protestant inmates, in 1901 there were seven Catholic women in the Edgar Home and in 1911, thirteen; there were five Catholics in the Magdalen Asylum in 1901 and four in 1911. There were only two Catholic women in the Salvation Army Home in 1911, However over the period 1905–1908, when the religious persuasion of those entering the home was recorded, thirty-three Catholics had entered the home.

Grainne Blair has argued that in the late nineteenth century, to the majority of Roman Catholics in Ireland the Salvation Army symbolised the 'oppressor and the British proselytising overlord'.[55] In Belfast, however by the early twentieth century, this view does not seem to have prevented Catholic women from entering the Salvation Army Home. The records also indicate that a number of these Catholic inmates had spent time in other Protestant homes, such as the Edgar Home, Malone Place and Magdalen Asylum, in addition to Catholic convents. One Catholic woman, for example, had spent time in the Edgar Home, a convent in Dublin and the GSC in Belfast before entering the Salvation Army Home.[56]

The Protestant denominations recorded for the women resident in the homes were dominated by the two largest churches, Church of Ireland and Presbyterian. In the Magdalen Asylum there were ten members of the Church of Ireland in 1901 and fifteen in 1911 compared with six Presbyterians in 1901 and one Presbyterian in 1911. The Edgar Home had a similar Church of Ireland majority with eighteen members in 1901 and twenty-two in 1911 compared with eight Presbyterians in 1901 and nine in 1911, along with two Methodists and one Salvation Army member. In the Salvation Army Home the Church of Ireland also predominated with fourteen members compared with eight Presbyterians. The records for 1905–1908, however, show an increase in the number of Presbyterians with thirty-seven recorded, compared with twenty-three members of the Church of Ireland, ten members of the Church of Scotland, seven from the Church of England, three Methodists and one Congregationalist.[57]

The higher proportion of Church of Ireland women in comparison with Presbyterian women entering rescue homes has also been identified in the previous chapter for women entering the Belfast workhouse identified as prostitutes. This is most probably a result of the stronger economic position enjoyed by Presbyterian women ensuring they were less likely to resort to prostitution or become destitute and need to enter either type of establishment.

This religious mix did not operate in the opposite direction and the records do not show any Protestant women who had been in a convent before entering the Salvation Army. Similarly, the 1901 Census does not record any Protestant women in the GSC and the 1911 Census records only one Church of Ireland and one Church of Scotland member.[58] The reason was perhaps the identification of convents as strictly Catholic, as opposed to the other homes which had a more open religious policy and profile. As the GSC was obviously run by nuns, who were clearly identifiable and associated with the Catholic Church, this may have dissuaded Protestants from entering. Also, within Belfast, there were more Protestant/non-denominational homes to choose from. Nonetheless, it does appear that while concerns existed, for many women who were in desperate straits and who were pregnant outside marriage or whose families had disowned them, the religious affiliation of a particular home was not necessarily the most important consideration.

Survival strategies

As discussed in chapter 1, a number of women used the workhouse when their situation was desperate and entered and left as it suited them, thus involving it in their survival strategy. For another group of women, rescue homes played a similar role: they entered and left when they pleased and as their situation necessitated. One third of the women who entered the Salvation Army Home between 1905 and 1946 were recorded as having been in another home previously, with over half of those having been admitted to two or more homes.[59] The example of a twenty-two-year-old woman, who entered the Salvation Army Home in 1907, illustrates the point. She had been in the Victoria Children's Home, Edgar Home, Magdalen Asylum (several times) and the Rosevale Home in Lisburn, before entering the Salvation Army Home. She stayed there for six months before going back to the Magdalen Asylum, returning to the Salvation Army, going back again to the Magdalen Asylum and finally going to Canada to live with her sister.[60] As Peggy Pascoe has contended, for some women rescue homes offered the possibility of getting back on their feet, of getting a job or an education. Their entrance to the home however, did not necessarily imply they accepted the moral authority of the rescue home or its identification of them as in need of moral reform.[61] The fact that so many women moved between homes and clearly entered and left as they pleased indicates a measure of choice and the freedom to make decisions about their future. It is evident that, like women entering the workhouse, these women were not simply victims, and although their choices were limited they were able to make some decisions.

One of the popular beliefs about Magdalen homes was that women were unable to leave the homes and were, as Frances Finnegan has described, 'victims, hopelessly submitting to their situation'.[62] However, the statistics which Finnegan herself uses demonstrate that the overwhelming majority of women left of their own accord.[63] Maria Luddy has argued that between 1890 and 1899 eighty-five per cent of the women who entered the GSC in Belfast left the asylum rather than being incarcerated for life.[64] Similarly, a comparison of the Census Records for 1901 and 1911 for the GSC in Belfast indicates that there were only twelve women in the home in 1911 who had also been in the home in 1901.[65] While the Good Shepherd Sisters may have encouraged women to stay for longer periods of time than many other institutions, it is evident that many women left of their own accord when they wished. Nevertheless, in the grounds of the former GSC in Belfast, a number of women still live in sheltered housing, having never left the institution. The fact that they have remained is perhaps more to do with becoming institutionalised and unable to survive in the outside world with no family support, rather than being prevented from leaving.

The Protestant-run homes and in particular the Salvation Army Home, had a more relaxed entrance and exit policy, and while two years was seen as the ideal period to effect rehabilitation, women were not prevented from leaving if they were determined to do so. In the Edgar Home the overwhelming majority, 1009 (thirty-nine per cent) are recorded as having left of their own accord[66]

Societal perceptions

The view that was presented to society by those running the homes was that the women who entered them were corrupted innocents. The terms used to describe women in the homes, such as, 'unfortunate creatures, unhappy sisters, fallen women, defiled, wrecks', all convey a picture of victims who were in this position due to their ignorance and trustfulness, often having been betrayed by wicked men.[67] They were portrayed as pathetic, aimless women, who wandered the streets like 'withered leaves driven in the wind',[68] or drifted about like 'derelict vessels'.[69] They had lost their sexual purity, and with it their sense of direction and purpose. The Annual Reports of the Edgar Home and descriptions of the work of the other homes and the Midnight Mission, present a picture of the 'fallen woman' who was 'suspected or guilty of sexual delinquency', and who had started, or already was, on the path to becoming a prostitute.[70] In reality, as discussed above, those who entered the homes were not generally prostitutes. However, the image of the young betrayed and seduced woman, who had 'fallen' and needed to be rescued and saved from a life of wickedness was not only more appealing to the public but would hopefully encourage donations.[71]

Living a bad life?

A more detailed consideration of the wealth of information available in the entrance registers of the Salvation Army Home in Belfast provides a vivid illustration of how the case histories of the women who entered were constructed, and the situations which generated most sympathy and most concern from the staff. The registers reinforce the point that the majority of women entering such homes were not prostitutes. From over one thousand admissions to the Salvation Army Home between 1905 and 1946, less than 70 entries or case histories refer to women who had been prosecuted for soliciting or were living a 'bad or wicked life'.[72] There were twenty references to either the Lock Ward (Ward 26) at the Union Infirmary, which was where those with venereal disease were treated, or of a woman entering a home with VD.[73] Prostitution was never mentioned explicitly, and a variety of euphemisms were employed to describe the lives that some of the girls were leading before entry. These descriptions included, 'living wickedly', 'living a careless life', living in 'bad houses' or 'being on the streets'. Others had been charged with soliciting and several are recorded as being 'fond of sailors'.[74] One girl in particular apparently had the nickname 'the dry-land sailor', implying an involvement in prostitution in the docks area.[75]

The majority of the case histories made reference to the women entering the home as either being pregnant, a 'maternity case', or having previously had a baby.[76] The number of maternity cases or unmarried mothers increased appreciably from the late 1920s onwards. This increase reflected the changing role of the home: as with the majority of homes, as the twentieth century progressed their work moved away from rescue work to focus on unmarried mothers.[77] The Salvation Army was one of the few organisations that permitted women to keep their babies with them once they had given birth. However, the folklore associated with the Salvation Army Home in Belfast suggested that women who gave birth there were given no pain relief, in order to teach them a lesson and to make sure they did not end up in the same situation at a future date.[78] Even in the 1940s and 1950s the Salvation Army Home was seen as a place that no respectable girl would ever want to enter and those women who ended up there were used as salient reminders of the need for good behaviour.[79]

Babies born to mothers in the GSC went to the Nazareth Home, an orphanage conveniently situated across the road from the convent. Unmarried mothers posed a particular difficulty for homes as they represented both the highest pinnacle of achievement for women, which was motherhood, and were also visible statements of immorality and inappropriate sexual behaviour.[80] Unmarried mothers were acceptable cases for entry into rescue homes as the objective was to prevent them continuing down the slippery slope that could lead them to prostitution. It was felt that the fact that they had fallen once, and the difficulty of having to support a child alone, could easily lead them into prostitution.[81] As discussed above, women who had more than one child outside marriage were generally refused entry to rescue homes and were often considered to be both sexually and mentally dissolute.[82]

This belief was influenced in the early decades of the twentieth century by eugenics. Unmarried mothers with more than one child were believed to be mentally deficient, being described as 'imbeciles [and] hopeless cases'.[83] Concerns surrounding 'feebleminded' women having children were part of wider concerns in the early decades of the twentieth century about national degeneration.[84]

Innocent victims

The impression given from annual reports and entrance registers is that, in the majority of cases, the women who entered homes were viewed as the innocent parties. They had been taken advantage of by male aggressors and left to face the consequences alone or had been introduced to alcohol or drugs by 'bad company'. The story emerges of innocent and naive girls who had been unaware of the consequences of their actions and had been 'led astray'.[85] From 1913 onwards, the phrase, 'seduced under the promise of marriage', appears frequently in the Salvation Army case histories. Women had acquiesced to sexual intercourse, after receiving assurances and promises that marriage would follow. Unfortunately for many, marriage did not inevitably follow and they were left pregnant and alone.

The First World War added a new dimension to 'seduction under the promise of marriage'. In many cases, after the seduction came the enlisting of the young man in the army, and frequently his subsequent disappearance. For example a twenty-year-old woman from Ballygawley, Co. Tyrone, whose parents were 'very respectable small farmers', was engaged and expected to marry soon. Her fiancé had enlisted and apparently 'seduced her under the promise of marriage' on his first leave. Since then she had not heard from him, and her parents were 'in a terrible state about her'.[86] For others in the same situation who had become pregnant, the father of their child may have joined up but still kept in touch, writing regularly. However, this was of no immediate help and the woman was often forced to enter a home until such time as he returned and could fulfil his promise of marriage.

Betrayal was an important feature of many of the stories of how women became pregnant outside of marriage. As Regina Kunzel suggests, the idea of seduction and abandonment created sympathy, with the woman at the centre of the story being lured by the promise of a happy life and becoming ensnared and deceived. This reinforced the idea of female sexuality as dormant and passive and male sexuality as animalistic, brutalistic and predatory.[87] Terms such as 'seduction', 'betrayed', 'wronged', and 'taken advantage of' were all associated with melodrama; the idea of an innocent girl being seduced by a predator male. The use of such terms may also have enabled women to speak about sex in an acceptable way, and no doubt tells more about the attitudes of those writing the records than gives accurate information about those entering the home.[88] Reformers preferred to see women as unwilling or innocent partners who needed rescuing and protection. For the women seeking admittance, portrayal as an innocent victim may have been necessary for their admission to the home. As General William Booth, the founder of the Salvation Army, declared, many of the women who entered the homes would have:

> escaped their evil fate had they been less innocent. They are where they are because they loved too utterly to calculate the consequences and trusted too absolutely . . . to suspsect evil.[89]

For the majority of those who entered rescue homes under the shadow of sexual sin, the blame was largely redirected. For those who had been living a 'bad life' or living in 'wicked houses' their fall into such a life was often perceived as being due to 'nameless aggressors'. These men had taken advantage of friendless girls from the country, who were often unaware of the perils of city life.[90] It was an unthinkable premise that the women would be active participants or that prostitution would be an active career choice. Rescuers were unwilling to accept that women could chose prostitution as a viable means of earning or supplementing their income. In their view, it was obviously something that was forced upon them.[91] Defining the fallen woman as a victim may have been a way of negotiating fears and disarming the threat and power of the prostitute. As Lynn Nead suggests, by feeling sympathy towards prostitutes, their threat was displaced and their power redistributed in terms of a 'conventional paternal relationship organised around social conscience, compulsion and philanthropy'.[92]

Alcohol

Alcohol also played a prominent role in leading to the admission of many women to rescue homes. The Salvation Army entrance registers had a specific category for whether the woman was a 'drink case' or not, which illustrates both the frequency of alcohol problems and also the association with vice. The Revd J. Waddell, at the Annual Meeting of the Edgar Home in 1906, commented how 'truly sad to find so many of those admitted who are victims of strong drink'. He explained that on the streets of Belfast there were 'wallowing in intemperance and impurity, degraded beings in whom there are infinite possibilities'.[93] These 'twin evils' of intemperance and impurity were considered responsible for the downfall of many women. It was reported that the inmates themselves testified that 'a close connection exists between intemperance and incontinence' and that it led to 'the downfall of hundreds of young girls a year as well as their continued degradation'.[94]

The Church of Ireland Rescue League and the Edgar Home were among the organisations that saw alcohol as the chief cause of immorality and proposed the prohibition of the alcohol trade.[95] The Annual Meeting of the Edgar Home in 1921 heard the Revd Dr MacMillan express the hope that 'this province and the land would soon be swept clear of that [drink] traffic, which caused so much demoralisation and destroyed so many souls and bodies of women'.[96] Alcohol was considered to be responsible for leading many women into prostitution and preventing them from leaving such a life. It was believed that alcohol was necessary to dull the senses and its addiction meant that women would do anything to satisfy their need.[97] Mrs Clarke, a missionary employed by the Edgar Home, described how she was often told how unhappy the girls were, how they 'couldn't lead a life without drink' and therefore 'must drown the voice of conscience or be converted'.[98]

Of the admissions to Salvation Army Home between 1905 and 1946, one quarter were described as 'drink cases' or their case notes referred to alcohol as a reason for their entry.[99] As the image of women who entered rescue homes as victims of circumstances and events was important for reformers, alcohol was portrayed as another factor on the slippery slope that led to a sexual 'fall' and then ultimately could lead to a life of prostitution. The case histories of those who entered the Salvation Army

Home in Belfast provide vivid illustrations of the part alcohol played in the lives of those who entered the home. For example, one girl who was a 'half-timer'[100] in the mills got into bad company when she was eleven and was subsequently introduced to alcohol. She ran away from home and soon ended up in bad houses.[101] The tragic consequences of alcohol were further illustrated in the case notes of 'Mary'. She had been a 'delicate' child and was given spirits as medicine, with the result that she was 'nearly a drunkard at thirteen'. Her life then degenerated; she mixed with bad company and had several children. Failure to stop drinking led to Mary's children being taken away by a priest and placed in children's homes. She then entered the Magdalen Asylum in Belfast but fell into bad company again and had another baby. Soon after the baby's birth 'Mary' was found in a field in a drunken stupor with her baby dead beside her. She was subsequently found guilty of infanticide and sentenced to twelve months in prison.[102]

Alcohol or drugs formed an important part of the image of the innocent being seduced. This is seen in the case of 'Margaret'. She went to a dance, had some port wine and woke up the next morning in bed with other girls. She was so ashamed that she did not go home and, after having been led astray, subsequently contracted syphilis. From that point on her life was on a downward spiral: she mixed with prostitutes and lived in a 'bad house' for three years, had a baby but gave it away, and finally went on the streets again. Following the birth of another baby who subsequently died, she again turned to drink.[103] Alcohol was seen as instrumental in having led her into a life of sin and in having caused her further degeneration. 'Rose' entered the home in 1910, her notes recording that she had been drugged and 'ruined'. Following her 'fall' she had ended up on the streets working as a prostitute. She remained in the home for five months, but no reformation was clearly effected as she was recorded as being in and out of prison and still drinking.[104]

Lack of support networks

The lack, or removal, of support networks has been suggested as the fundamental reason why women came to rescue homes.[105] The family support network was perhaps the most important, and for many women the consequences of this being withdrawn necessitated entrance to a rescue home. As discussed above, a number of those who entered homes had been or were pregnant outside marriage. This eventuality in many cases ensured the removal of parental or family support until either the baby was born or it was felt a reformation of behaviour had taken place. Across the class divide, pregnancy outside marriage carried a great stigma. Girls who became pregnant were often rapidly removed from the family home to avoid anyone noticing their condition.[106] For many parents, therefore, rescue homes provided an important service in removing a problem child from the family domicile.

The disgrace and shame which parents felt about daughters who became pregnant is clearly apparent from the case histories of the Salvation Army Home. A number of women were recorded as fearing their parents' reaction to the news of their pregnancy. In many cases they had simply left home to avoid them finding out and having no other means of support, ended up in the home. One young woman became pregnant after apparently being 'seduced'. She was afraid her father would find out and so went to Belfast. She was assisted in leaving by her mother who was also afraid of her husband's reaction.[107]

For some parents, it was preferable for daughters to be placed in a home until they gave birth. The baby could then be adopted and the woman would be able to return home. Illegitimacy also created issues concerning land inheritance and legitimate heirs. This was of particular importance in rural areas where the removal of the woman from the locality took on greater urgency.[108] One father was so anxious to keep his daughter's condition from being known in the village that he sent her to her sister in Belfast. The baby was born in the workhouse and after its birth the girl entered the Salvation Army Home.[109] The pregnancy of unmarried daughters was seen as bringing disgrace on a whole family. In one extreme case, the fact that his daughter had become pregnant outside of marriage distressed a father so much that he had to be taken to the asylum the day that his daughter's baby was born.[110]

The attitudes and sympathies of those recording the case histories are clearly seen when referring to the backgrounds of women entering the home. Greatest sympathy was given to girls from 'respectable' families who became pregnant. The impact of an out-of-wedlock pregnancy on these families was recorded in greater detail than for other girls. The language used in the cases of 'respectable' families suggests that the parents were present when the case history was recorded and it is their views, rather than their daughter's, that are recorded. This is illustrated in the case of one young woman whose family was deemed very respectable, her father being a Sunday School superintendent and a local preacher. She had apparently been 'drawn away' and subsequently 'wronged' by a local farmer, who was a 'low common man'. Her parents were described as being 'heartbroken as she was their joy and their right hand in the house and a Sunday School Teacher'.[111]

The disintegration of parental support networks by death or abandonment were important factors. It is apparent from the case histories that many of the girls and women were orphans. Out of 486 entries between 1905 and 1917, 176 (thirty-six per cent) were recorded as having no parents, and this lack of parental influence was seen as an important factor in the 'falling into sin' of many of the girls who lacked discipline and had been allowed to run 'wild'.

However, while not having parents was seen as damaging, bad parents were equally problematic. One young woman who entered the Salvation Army Home was described as having had a mother who was 'a gypsy, a godless woman who would not let her mix with anyone who would lead her to the right'.[112] For another girl, having a 'very bad drunken' mother meant she received very little schooling and went into service at a young age. Her mother took her wages from her, before turning her out onto the street. Another case involved a drunken father who sent his children out to sell matches, and then on to the spinning room to earn money. It was here that his daughter got in with bad company.[113] The epitomes of bad parenting were mothers who encouraged their daughters to enter prostitution. In one case a stepmother who was said to have 'mixed with soldiers', supposedly led her stepdaughter astray by putting her on the streets. In another case, a mother who was believed to be keeping a house full of young girls for 'immoral purposes' had her daughter removed from her care by the police. Similarly, another mother was reported to have been trying to make her daughter 'sin with men'.[114]

The problem of bad parents contributed to the image of the young woman as victim, betrayed by both 'negligent parents or faithless seducers'.[115] Again, outside influences and circumstances had led to these women 'falling'. They were thus to be pitied, not blamed. Pascoe, discussing rescue homes in the American West, described how the typical unmarried mother was seen as 'motherless, weak and untaught – not wicked', and that most 'impure' women were regarded as the innocent victims of male aggression.[116] Rescue homes hoped to replace a lack of parental guidance and protection and to provide structure and paternal influence.

Feebleminded

Another group of women who were perceived to be in need of rescue and reform were those classed as 'feebleminded'. Women suffering from a wide spectrum of mental health problems were often placed in rescue homes by parents, relatives or the authorities. They ranged from those classed as 'dull', 'backward' or 'simple' to women suffering from hysteria, fits or delusions as well as those believed to be 'morally deficient' or 'degenerate'.[117] There was a growing connection through the nineteenth and into the twentieth century, between 'feeblemindedness' and female sexual activity.[118] Women who were defined as being 'feebleminded', it was felt, were 'more sexually precocious than the rest of the population since their limited intellect made their powers of inhibition and moral constraint correspondingly low'.[119]

The Poor Law Commission for Ireland (1906) was also concerned about the problem of 'simple-minded' girls, who believed 'everything that is said to them and they will do everything that is told to them – good or bad' and didn't 'understand the difference between good and evil'.[120] Miss Hamilton of Portrush Board of Guardians giving evidence to the Commission went on to explain that such girls could be identified by their language and conduct. She further believed that the fact that they were not married, and that their mother and grandmother were not married either was a clear sign of mental weakness. When these girls 'became a danger and an expense to the country', Miss Hamilton argued that the authorities should 'have the power to lock them up and be kind to them'.[121]

It is difficult to know whether women who had learning difficulties or who were suffering from mental illness were more likely to spend longer in institutions such as the Good Shepherd Convent than other women. It may have been the case that their mental state led to longer and perhaps permanent stays. However, it is evident from Salvation Army Home records that women who were classed as 'mental', were generally sent to the asylum or the workhouse, as it was felt that adequate care could not be provided in the home.[122] As the case notes for one woman explain:

> [she] proved to be more mental than we were given to suppose and she would have needed more watching than is possible to give her here. Miss Bane thought she could be trained, but she is not capable of being taught.[123]

Another woman, it was explained, 'could not stay, is mental case, went to Union'.[124] It is clear that the term 'mental' was used to cover a wide range of disorders and proved to be a useful label for any type of behaviour considered 'strange'. Women who were 'hysterical', in a 'low state' or had a 'mania for suicides', were all sent to the asylum,[125] where they would most likely be classified as suffering from 'mania' or 'melancholia', vague terms with little scientific basis.[126] Moreover, the term 'mental', was used to refer to those whose behaviour was in any way antisocial, such as one woman who was 'always laughing' or another who was described as being 'very sour, [and] sits in [her] bedroom all day'.[127] Others who were 'out of control' or were accused of stealing were given the same diagnosis.[128] As Matthew Thomson argues, mental deficiency provided a convincing biological explanation for the plight of women in Magdalen and refuge homes. Their 'mental deficiency left them with no restraint over their sexual instincts and unprotected against abuse from men'. It was also a powerful justification for placing them under the care and control of refuges and homes.[129] Similarly, Rosen suggests the idea of 'feeblemind-edness' had little to do with mental capacity, but was a useful way of clas-sifying female aggressive sexuality and explaining their behaviour.[130]

Preventative cases

Those who were classed as 'feebleminded' or 'mental' were seen as needing protection, both from themselves and from others who would take advantage of them. Rescue homes provided a similar service for girls who were felt to be at risk from others due to their naivety or innocence, those who were keeping bad company, or whose behaviour was felt to be beyond parental control. These were often classed as 'preventative cases'. Several examples, again from the Salvation Army case histories, illustrate this fact. One sixteen-year-old girl's mother had died, and her father's concern that she was mixing with bad company led him to place her in the Salvation Army Home.[131] A similar case recorded in 1912 con-cerned a fourteen-year-old girl who was in service. She was mixing with what were considered to be bad girls and her father was worried that she would get into trouble. His solution was to admit her to the 'good influ-ence' of the home.[132] A mother's fear that her daughter was developing 'bad habits', having previously been in trouble for stealing and running away, resulted in her admission to the home in 1915.[133] There was a clear belief that time in a home, such as the Salvation Army Home, would help ensure that girls remained on the straight and narrow path, surrounded by good influences.

For other parents, rescue homes were the last resort if they couldn't control their daughter. One father was very worried about his daughter who apparently had a 'hasty temper', and had been spoiled.[134] Another young woman was recorded as being disobedient, wayward and had a habit of staying away from work in the afternoon to go to music halls, picture palaces and dancing classes. Her parents were concerned that she was fraternising with girls who 'were not particular what they did if they needed money'.[135] The most common behavioural concerns included staying out all night, drinking alcohol, running away, and generally uncontrollable behaviour. Such behaviour clashed with the standards and acceptable morals of many parents, who used the homes as a solution to their problems.

The homes were therefore an important disciplinary tool for working-class families, not simply a middle-class construction to impose middle-class values. Working-class parents could remove troublesome daughters who generated concern or who had the potential to bring disgrace to their family. The homes could not have continued to function without the support of working-class families who placed their daughters in them. While middle-class reformers may have created and operated institutions which aimed to control female sexuality, working-class parents 'actively used them for their own needs and purposes'.[136] Mary Odem, in her discussion of adolescent female sexuality in the United States, contends that the behaviour of sexually active young women clashed not only with middle-class morality, but with the moral codes of many working-class parents, who used rescue homes and reformatories to deal with their problem daughters.

Daily life

On entrance to a rescue home, a change of clothing was provided, often in the form of a uniform. This, it has been suggested, removed any physical attachment to the entrants' past life and clearly identified them as penitents.[137] A photograph of the Edgar Home Laundry, taken around 1901, shows the inmates in a uniform of white hat and long white apron.[138] To further remove any attachment or connection with their past life, women who were admitted to the GSC had their names changed on entry, often to a saint's name to reflect their reforming intentions. It has been suggested by a nun involved in running the home that this was also to keep the woman's identity a secret, even from the nuns, who only knew her by her new name.[139]

Life in rescue homes was based on the principles of religious instruction and hard work. These were considered as essential requirements to the inmates' reform.[140] Religion informed all that took place: if the women were not praying, they were working.[141] Daily life in the homes was carefully structured in the belief that this was necessary for reformation.[142] A series of rules and regulations governed the inmates' activities, and contact with the outside world was carefully controlled.[143]

Attendance at religious services and worship formed a crucial part of life in the homes. Some form of religious observance took place both in the morning and evening. Furthermore, a weekly Sunday service or Mass was taken by a member of the clergy. Some former inmates of the Edgar Home returned for Sunday evening services: one of them wrote to the matron apologising for being unable to attend the service, relating how 'sometimes I feel lonely when I think you are having worship . . . I hope you still remember me in your prayers'.[144]

As the twentieth century progressed, there were growing attempts to make many of the homes more pleasurable places to live. For the Edgar Home, the concern that it was perceived as a prison led to the changing of its name from the Ulster Female Penitentiary. Letters from past residents were read at the Annual Meetings, to demonstrate that the women enjoyed a measure of freedom in the home. It was hoped to make life in the home like that of a normal home, with as much variety as possible.[145]

This variety took the form of entertainment provided for the women, aimed at 'brightening their lives'. Various people came and provided musical entertainment, with the intention of 'relieving the monotony of the Home life'. Groups such as the 'Cripple hand-bell ringers' provided the entertainment at New Year and on other occasions Sunday School children came and presented the girls with bouquets of flowers. For occasional treats there were magic lantern shows and a cinematograph.[146] By the 1940s, the GSC had its own 16mm projector, which one of the Sisters operated, on which to play hired films. In addition, there were also netball and tennis courts in the large grounds of the convent.[147] The matron of the Edgar Home requested a piano to make the inmates' life 'bright and cheery' and, in the GSC, plays and operas were performed. It has been contended that games and other activities acted as 'mechanisms of control', as they directed energy into positive sources while relieving boredom and perhaps 'compensating for the loss of liberty'.[148] However, it must also be recognised that many of those running the homes were sincere in their attempts to try and improve the lives of the women under their care.

Groups and organisations often took an interest in the homes, donating gifts and money. In the Edgar Home, a Christmas tree and Christmas dinner were provided, as were presents for the girls. Throughout the year various gifts and contributions of fruit, food, magazines, books, clothes and sweets were donated to the home.[149] The involvement of women visitors played an important function, particularly in the Protestant homes. The purpose of these visits from 'friends' was to introduce the inmates to what were considered ideal role models. In 1904, the committee of the Edgar Home appealed for Christian mothers and daughters to 'take an interest in friendless girls, ignorant of the traps set for them in the city'. The aim was that, by example and teaching, they would prevent the girls getting the idea that 'true happiness consisted in being well dressed and living in idleness and pleasure'.[150]

Inmates also engaged in sewing and knitting and other suitable feminine activities in their spare time. Women in the Salvation Army Home embroidered tablemats, which were sold at bazaars to raise funds for the home. Residents of the Edgar Home were encouraged to knit for the foreign missions and, during 1915, spent most of their spare time knitting for the soldiers. The aim was to try and create an awareness of the needs of the world and their ability to be useful, and carry out 'worthwhile' activities for those less well off than themselves.[151]

Importance of work

Combined with their leisure activities, the women were required to work. This was seen as a crucial part of their rehabilitation, giving discipline and teaching them new skills. As Mr Justice White contended in 1923, his encounters with people whose virtue was questionable had taught him that 'the great thing required in the Home was to give the people work, work, work'.[152] One of the most popular forms of work within rescue homes was laundry work, and in Belfast the GSC, Edgar Home and Magdalen Asylum all possessed laundries. The laundry at the GSC was operational until 1977.[153]

Linda Mahood has argued that laundry work was central to the operation of reform homes because it generated essential income.[154] However, it is apparent that in the Edgar Home, conflict existed for some of the Committee between the idea of Christian charity, the considered necessity of keeping the women occupied productively, and the provision of essential funds. While expressing satisfaction that the laundry at the Edgar Home was making money, and that the earning power of the inmates was considerable, the Revd Park, speaking at the Annual Meeting for the Home in 1900, made it clear that,

> the place was not kept up as a public laundry or for the express purpose of earning money. The object was to bring erring girls and women away

from evil influences and put them on the path of virtue, honesty and usefulness.[155]

The work of the laundry was considered secondary to the greater task of 'saving souls to shine as jewels in Emmanuel's crown forever'.[156] Nonetheless, while saving souls was the major priority, it was also essential that the institutions had some means of support other than public donations which often fell short of running costs.[157] The Ulster Magdalen Asylum was forced to close in 1916 when it became economically unviable, due to lack of public support, and a laundry that failed to make money.

Laundry work was seen as the most suitable work for penitent women to be involved in. It was believed to be therapeutic and had undertones of religious sanctification, where the unclean was made clean again.[158] One of the nuns involved in the work at the GSC in Belfast, described what she felt were the therapeutic effects of the work, with washing having a cleansing effect by removing dirt and making clean again, and ironing smoothing crumbled garments; a similar process to that occurring in the lives of the women in the convent. This process, it was suggested, gave a sense of satisfaction and fulfilment.[159]

Peter Hughes has argued that there was a symbolic function of laundry work in Good Shepherd Convents based on the link between 'the fallen woman and the dirty linen'.[160] He has identified particular significance between the washing process, where linen is neither clean nor dirty, and the condition of short-stay penitents, where, 'as dirt is an affirmative pre-condition of cleanliness, so is sin of virtue'.[161] The close connections between the transformation of soiled linen to its former clean pristine form, and the transformation of penitents from their former sinful ways to become cleansed and renewed through the power of salvation, was summed up in the hope of the Committee of the Edgar Home that 'many of our past and present laundresses will be found amongst those who have washed their robes and made them white in the blood of the lamb'.[162]

Laundry also gave the homes a greater justifiable sense of purpose. It was crucial in gaining further support that the inmates were seen to work for their keep. The homes did not want to be perceived as 'homes of rest', but as places where those who entered were 'kept fully employed in helping towards their own support'.[163] The women would gain not only essential skills, but also discipline, and have structure put back into their lives. As the Edgar Home Annual Report of 1911 explained, the laundry enabled the women to 'earn their bread by working with their hands' and while 'occupied in making soiled linen clean and white they have been taught higher things as well'.[164] It has been further suggested that laundry work was favoured, as 'hard physical labour acted as a penance'.[165] It is clear that the work was physically demanding, so much so that in the Edgar Home there was a growing realisation that this tough physical regime was counter-productive. Steam power was introduced in 1909/10, and it was felt this would ensure that 'suitable girls would no longer be deterred from entering the Home through fear of drudgery'.[166] There was a fine line between ensuring that the women worked for their keep, and that the prospect of too much work did not lead to falling numbers of entrants.

Leaving the home

Domestic service was seen as the most suitable destination for women on leaving rescue homes as 'they would be under good influence, given the option of honest work'.[167] Ideally they would be placed in houses where they would be set a Christian example and their activities would be closely supervised, with contact with men and unsuitable companions being severely curtailed.[168] They would be kept away from the temptations of city life and provided with protection and guidance and respectability.[169] Domestic service in a suitable home maintained a support network, the loss of which was believed to have precipitated many admissions to rescue homes. It was a much more 'honourable' form of work than the more lucrative but morally dubious employment that was to be had elsewhere.[170] This more lucrative employment that was frowned upon was generally to be had in factories or mills. It was actively discouraged because these environments were blamed for the downfall of many women. In workplaces such as these, it was believed that impressionable young women were likely to come into contact with bad company and were able to mix freely with men. It is evident that in Belfast in particular, the availability of jobs for women in manufacturing, with better hours, higher wages and more independence, was a preferable alternative to domestic service. The 1911 Census recorded fifty servants per thousand of the population in Dublin, and only twenty-two per thousand in Belfast.[171]

It has been argued that one of the benefits of laundry work was that it prepared women for work in domestic service.[172] However, as Paula Bartley has argued, the reality was that very few women who left institutions actually entered domestic service.[173] This pattern is clear when the available evidence from the Edgar Home is examined. Between 1900 and

1926, there were 2,786 recorded admissions to the Edgar Home. Of the destinations of women leaving the home which were recorded, only 437 women, sixteen per cent, were placed in service, with another 140, five per cent, recorded as going to situations. Of the remainder, 189, seven per cent were restored to family and friends, with the overwhelming majority, 1,009, thirty-nine per cent, leaving of their own accord.[174]

The Salvation Army records indicate a similar pattern, with 278 women, twenty per cent, recorded as leaving the home to enter domestic service situations. However, one hundred of these women did not remain in their situations, and ended up back on the streets, pregnant, drunk or unemployed. 307 women went to parents or friends; 201 left wilfully to seek work; 147 were hospitalised, and thirty placed in the asylum. Forty-four went to other homes, while fifty-one were known to be living 'bad lives'. Finally, seventy-two of the women were dismissed or ran away. Clearly the aim of training inmates in the homes to be domestic servants was not entirely successful.

It was felt by many reformers that eighteen months to two years spent in a rescue home was adequate to effect reformation and reha-bilitation.[175] It removed inmates from bad influences and immersed them in an atmosphere of Christian example. In the Edgar Home, and the North-West Ulster Home those inmates who were most convincing in their signs of reform had the possibility of being assisted to emigrate. It was essential that they had spent their required two years in the home, and 'only those who give real proof of reclamation sent out'.[176] This was considered to be a new beginning, away from the bad influences of a past life and a chance to create a new identity. The Edgar Home authorities considered that 'amidst strange surroundings and entirely separate from old associations and companionships, the path to a good and pure life is not so difficult'.[177]

The Salvation Army Home did not implement a two-year policy and women stayed for anything from a few days to more than a year. Conversely, inmates in Good Shepherd Convents often remained there for life.[178] As mentioned, at the GSC in Belfast there are elderly women living in sheltered accommodation in the grounds of the convent who have been there since their admission as young women.[179]

Discipline and bad behaviour

Issues of discipline and bad behaviour were features of life in rescue homes. While not generally openly discussed there were often oblique references to unrest. In 1909 the matron of the Edgar Home explained that there had been fewer requests from the girls to leave the home, and that the general conduct of those who had remained was good. She went on to record that, many 'settled down to work heartily with no desire for a change until ready to go to service'.[180] Also in 1909 the Committee of the Edgar Home passed a resolution to cover the top of the back wall with broken glass, as inmates were talking to young men outside. The windows in the lavatories were also to be replaced with ribbed glass to prevent the women from seeing over the wall.[181]

The description of the behaviour of some of the inmates as 'self-willed' and 'lacking in restraint' implies that there was a certain level of unrest and resistance to rules and regulations in the home.[182] As a letter to the matron of the Edgar Home, from a former inmate attests:

> I and many others could tell the story of ignorance, wilfulness and sin you and Miss Williams have to contend with and this is not now and again, but year in and out. I know I was a very troublesome naughty girl when I first went to you, but I was young and did it ignorantly not knowing the sorrow I caused.[183]

Similarly, a number of women in the Salvation Army Home were identified as 'bad influences',[184] or as 'deceitful and quarrelsome',[185] causing trouble within the Home and amongst the other girls. Several incidences of stealing were also recorded, along with broken windows in the home. Furthermore, a number of inmates were dismissed, as their behaviour was deemed unacceptable.[186]

A number of those who left the homes may have run away. It has been suggested that the term 'left of their own accord' indicates absconding.[187] It is also apparent that a number returned to their previous 'bad lives'. The Annual Reports of the Edgar Home record the disappointment felt concerning the number who returned to their old way of life: 'some girls go back and back again until their case becomes hopeless'. These 'backsliders' who lapsed back into sin were not condemned and rejected, rather they were 'tenderly dealt with and their feet once more guided onto straight paths'.[188]

The Salvation Army entrance registers also record the women who returned to the home. One woman arrived back in a terrible condition with 'not enough clothes to cover her' and pregnant.[189] However, not all women were taken back. Those considered to be a bad influence, or who had lied about their situations, were refused entry. For some of those who wanted to return to the Salvation Army Home, but who had left wilfully, or who had been badly behaved while in the home previously, the punishment was often a month in the Union Workhouse. The threat of spending time in the workhouse was obviously used to make the women aware of how fortunate they were to be living in the Salvation Army Home and where bad behaviour would lead.

However, more attention was understandably drawn to the success stories of women who had been rehabilitated and reformed. Annual Reports often contained extracts of letters from girls who were doing well, and had written back to thank the matron. Mention was made of those women who had achieved more than was really expected. For example the Edgar Home highly praised those women who had overcome the odds and trained as nurses.[190] Also deemed deserving of praise were those who had married and were doing well running their own homes.[191]

Declining numbers

As identified above, there were fewer women entering the homes from the beginning of the 1920s. Furthermore, the role of the homes was changing. In 1923 the Edgar Home visitor found that it was 'exceedingly difficult to induce young girls, who would most need a Home such as this kind to enter its walls'.[192] She was of the opinion that smaller establishments with a less rigid system of control stood a better chance of success.[193] Unwillingness to enter homes may have been due to a number of factors, including the ready availability of jobs without references, dislike of the length of time expected to stay, the type of work engaged in within the homes, and the discipline and strict conditions.[194] While the Edgar Home and the Magdalen Asylum, both of which had operated a traditional laundry reform home, had closed by 1926, the Salvation Army Home remained in existence. This was because it operated a more flexible system, allowing women to enter and leave much more easily, and did not demand participation in laundry work. The Salvation Army work also began to focus more closely on unmarried mothers, as did the Belfast Midnight Mission, which changed its name in 1944 to Malone Place. There had been no Midnight rescue work carried out since the beginning of the century and very few real rescue cases were received at this point. Most of those who entered as rescue cases were prostitutes who would arrive at 4am – using the home as simply a place to stay after a night's work.[195]

Another factor which led to the closing of the Edgar Home and

Magdalen Asylum was a lack of funds. The Committee of the Edgar Home appealed every year for donations, but interest in the work of such institutions was waning and patrons who had supported the work in the past grew older and died. As suggested above, interest was increasingly being directed towards preventative work.[196] As the Salvation Army Home was part of a wider organisation with a large membership, its financial position was much more secure. The GSC was in a similar position, as part of an international Order and a wider international Church, both of which provided sources of funding.

While many of the Protestant homes were finding it difficult to attract entrants, and parents and relatives were not bringing daughters for admission in the same numbers, the GSC remained open. The Sisters had under their care a 'penitentiary and laundry' into the 1940s, before it became known as the 'Home for Friendless and Wayward Girls' in 1948. The name of the home changed again in the 1960s, becoming a home for the re-education of problem girls with a separate home for unmarried mothers. Added to these homes in the 1970s was a hostel for broken families which continued operating until the late 1990s. Both the centre for problem girls and the unmarried mother's home had closed by 1990.[197] Throughout Ireland, a number of convents continued to operate as penitential institutions and laundries, some up until the 1990s.[198]

Magdalen Homes in popular culture

Since the early 1990s there has been a growing interest and representation of Magdalen laundries in the media.[199] This has included several documentaries such as, *Washing Away the Stain* (1993) and *Sex in a Cold Climate* (1998) as well as plays, songs and works of art. Much of the media interest followed the 1993 reporting of the exhumation and reburial of over one hundred women who had been buried in the grounds of the High Park Magdalen Asylum in Drumcondra and the closing of the last laundry in Dublin in 1996. However, gaining the greatest audience and media attention has been Peter Mullan's 2002 film *The Magdalene Sisters*.[200] Set in the Republic of Ireland in the 1960s, it tells the story of four young women who for different reasons are placed in a Catholic-run Magdalen Asylum: Margaret was raped by her cousin at a family wedding and taken to the asylum by a priest at the request of her parents; Bernadette was an orphan whose attractiveness and flirtatious behaviour caused her teachers to be concerned that she was in danger of falling into sin; Rose became pregnant outside marriage and had her baby adopted while she was placed in the Magdalen Asylum; Crispina had learning difficulties and was also an unmarried mother. The film follows the life of these girls in the asylum until Margaret is taken away by her brother, Bernadette and Rose escape, and Crispina is admitted to the mental asylum after a public outburst at the priest who has been sexually abusing her.

The characters associated with the Catholic Church are portrayed as uniformly unsympathetic. The nuns are presented as evil, money-grabbing, malicious, sexually frustrated and abusive. James Smith has argued that The *Magdalene Sisters* 'contributes to a broader understanding of Ireland's female religious in their specific cultural context' and he also challenges 'interpretations of the film that exclusively indict Ireland's Catholic Church for the scandal depicted on screen'.[201] However, while a detailed academic analysis of the film may support these arguments, it is clear that the public perception and response to the film did not recognise these more complex representations. As Smith himself suggests, the film 'reduces most of the nuns on-screen to mere stereotype'[202] and both the film and the responses to it 'present the nuns as the primary agents of abuse and . . . singularly responsible for the historic abuse of women in the laundries'.[203] This is the main difficulty with a film such as The *Magdalene Sisters*: the stereotypes and the stories presented in the film have come to represent the true picture of life inside Magdalen laundries. To offer any alternative position has come to be seen as condoning the brutalities of the institutions and, moreover, supporting the abuse of power by the Catholic Church. Consequently, the fiction of a motion picture has become the accepted historical reality. This is not to suggest that Magdalen asylums and laundries were pleasant places, and undoubtedly many women were treated badly in these institutions. The testimonies of those who spent time in these institutions are not being questioned. However, the story of these institutions is wider than image and narrative generated by The *Magdalene Sisters* and it may be argued that films such as this have a damaging effect on the research of academic historians of the subject. Religious orders will not permit access to records covering the period after 1900, and any attempt to view any archive material connected with the Good Shepherd Convent in Belfast in recent years has been met with polite refusal and the claim that there are no existing records. Ironically, the restriction of access to archives contributes and encourages the perpetuation of the representation of Magdalen asylums as the bleak, hopeless, cruel institution of the *Magdalene Sisters*. The image of the Magdalen asylum therefore exists in the public arena as a 'story' rather than 'history'. However, as Smith also suggests, while it is important to tell this story, cultural representations can 'sensationalise and exploit . . . appropriate survivor testimony for its shock value. . .eroticize traumatic memories of abuse . . . scapegoat easily identifiable targets as culpable while ignoring the collusion and complicity of other social and political agents'.[204] This failure to consider any of the wider societal or cultural conditions that allowed these institutions to continue to operate is perhaps one of the most important omissions of the film. They were kept open by the support of the general public, who placed their daughters in them, sent their laundry to them and donated funds when required. The parents of the girls in the film are simply shown as turning their heads and handing their daughters over to the representatives of the Church or, in the case of the father played by Mullan himself, returning his daughter to the asylum, beating her and calling the girls 'whores'. While the power exerted by the Catholic Church in the Republic of Ireland over social and moral behaviour is undeniable, if women did not enter homes voluntarily, in many cases it was parents who made the decision to have their daughters placed in them. The asylums offered an alternative for families who felt ashamed by their daughters' behaviour. However, as many parents in the same position made the decision not to place their daughters in homes, the Catholic Church cannot be held entirely accountable or held responsible for forcing parents to utilise the institutions. The continued existence of Magdalen laundries run by the Catholic Church in Ireland in the second half of the twentieth century was a reflection of a failure of the states on both sides of the border to provide for and protect vulnerable young women in society.

For many women who became pregnant outside marriage, Magdalen asylums or homes for unmarried mothers were some of the few options available to them other than the workhouse or the streets. Even in the second half of the twentieth century, pregnancy outside of marriage in Ireland, both North and South, carried huge social stigma and parents of all religious denominations were keen to remove pregnant daughters from the eyes of society. For some this involved being sent to relatives, often in England, until the baby was born and subsequently adopted, or perhaps the child being passed off as belonging to a married family member.[205] In Belfast, some of the Protestant-run rescue homes became homes for unmarried mothers where women could go to have their babies and stay for a period after the birth. Catholic-run homes for unmarried mothers were also established, such as the Regina Coeli Home and the Mater Dei Hostel in Belfast, both of which were run by the Legion of Mary. In the

Irish Free State there were a variety of institutions established by the 1930s to cater for unmarried mothers, including county homes, homes run by nuns, privately run maternity homes and a Regina Coeli Home in Dublin.[206]

It is undeniable that the existence of Magdalen asylums was a story that needed to be told. Life in such establishments was undoubtedly strict, disciplined and hard. However, it is arguable that not all those running such establishments were entirely without compassion, and many felt they were providing an important religious and practical charitable function, offering an opportunity for rehabilitation and rescue to those whom society had shunned. The danger lies in the presentation of films such as *The Magdalene Sisters* as historical documents. At the end of the film a coda appears telling what became of the four girls, as if they actually existed, when in reality they are fictitious characters and a conglomeration of stories from women who had been in asylums. The synopsis of the film also claims that young girls, as a consequence of their sinful behaviour 'worked 365 days a year unpaid, they were half starved, beaten, humiliated, raped and had their children forcibly removed from them. Their sentence was infinite.' It concludes with the statement, 'this is a fictional film that unfortunately, happens to be true'.[207] This synopsis has become the accepted 'truth' concerning Magdalen asylums.

Conclusion

The power and influence which the Catholic Church had on both society and the state in the Irish Free State explains in part the continued existence of Magdalen laundries.[208] As the Church dictated the moral standards and religious orders were responsible for the majority of the reformatory institutions, people were more willing to accept their continued existence. In Northern Ireland, while the Protestant run rescue homes either closed or largely focused their attention on unmarried mothers and vulnerable women on remand, the GSC continued to operate as a home for 'friendless and wayward girls' and as a laundry, the laundry only closing in 1977. It is difficult to explain why this occurred. The arguments of a 'nation-state containment culture', presented for the continued operation of Magdalen laundries in the Republic of Ireland, cannot be applied to Northern Ireland, and within such discussions the GSC in Belfast has been conveniently excluded.[209] It does perhaps reflect the reluctance of the Stormont Government to interfere in the work and operation of Catholic institutions, for fear of causing further alienation of the Catholic community. This concern is also evident over other potentially contentious issues such as birth control and venereal disease.[210] The continued operation of the laundry clearly depended on a public using the service and may have reflected a desire from the Catholic community to maintain control over their own institutions, and a fear that state-run institutions were fundamentally Protestant and posed a threat of proselytisation.[211]

As suggested above, social mores and the advancement of female emancipation are likely to have assisted the closure of rescue homes. In the interwar period, while female behaviour was still criticised and policed, there was greater acceptance of female independence. The cinemas and newspapers were projecting images of women in new roles, and institutions such as the Edgar Home did not have a place in this altered vision. This is not to ignore the fact the homes such as the Salvation Army Home, which catered mainly for unmarried mothers, were still utilised by large numbers of women. The stigma attached to illegitimacy remained largely unchanged in Ireland, in both North and South until the 1960s and 1970s and society still demanded that unmarried mothers be hidden away.[212]

It is clear that the function which the founders of the homes envisioned, and which may have existed during the nineteenth century, had changed in the early decades of the twentieth century. Those who entered were no longer mainly penitential prostitutes who were rescued and reformed. Many who entered did so due to lack of family support networks and needed help to get on their feet and become established in the workplace. For others, the homes provided a place to stay while pregnant, when they had no other options. The police and the courts placed others in the homes as an alternative to prison in the hope that their good influence would effect an improvement in their behaviour.

Notes

1 Luddy, *Women and Philanthropy*, p. 109.
2 *Irish Catholic Directory and Almanac* (Dublin, annually). Good Shepherd Homes for 'friendless and wayward girls' were opened in Derry and Newry in the late 1940s; both continued to operate homes until the late 1980s.
3 Jordan, *Who Cared*, p. 67.
4 *Ulster Directory*, 1910.
5 Quoted in E.J. Best, 'Health and Wealth in the Borough of Lisburn', *Lisburn Historical Journal*, 2 (1972).
6 *Edgar Home Annual Reports*, 1900–1926; *Minutes and Annual Reports of*

the Church of Ireland Rescue League, 1912–1937; *Annual Report of the Ulster Magdalen Asylum*, 1905; Entrance Registers, Salvation Army Home, Belfast, 1905–1946; *Minutes of Belfast Midnight Mission*, 1936–1944; *Irish Catholic Directory*, 1900–1945.

7 Marian Morton, 'Seduced and Abandoned in an American City: Cleveland and its Fallen Women, 1869–1936', *Journal of Urban History*, 11 (1985), 447.

8 Bartley, *Prostitution*, p. 31.

9 Ibid.

10 This was in honour of the Revd John Edgar, who had been a prolific fund raiser for the home in the nineteenth century and greatly enhanced the home's public profile.

11 Jordan, *Who Cared*, p. 173.

12 *Edgar Home Annual Report, 1902*, Presbyterian Historical Society (PHS).

13 St John, Chapter 10 verses 1–18.

14 Bartley, *Prostitution,* p.35.

15 *Edgar Home Annual Report, 1913.*

16 Sermon by Revd William Park at the opening of new premises of Edgar Home, 29 May 1902, Records of Edgar Home, PHS.

17 The entrance registers date from 1905. There are two types of register, one running from 1905–1917, which records the details of women who appeared to stay in the home for a longer period of time. The second register runs from 1905–1946 and the women recorded in many cases stayed for shorter periods of time, some only a few days. The home had a number of separate functions: as shelter, industrial and rescue home and home for unmarried mothers. Both books have similar headings for entering information. They record: name; age; where born; where they entered the home from; manner of application; date of entry; cause of 'fall'; had they been in prison before; were they a 'drink case'; had they been in other homes; religion; next of kin; conduct in home; date left; help given and destination on leaving.

18 Entrance Registers, Salvation Army Home, Belfast, 1905–1945.

19 *Edgar Home Annual Report, 1903.*

20 Entrance Registers, Salvation Army Home, Belfast, 1921, 1932.

21 Jordan, *Who Cared?*, p. 178.

22 Letter from GSC Belfast to NI Minister of Home Affairs, 25 June 1944, Religious, Box 9, 'B' – relating to Convents, Cardinal Macrory Archive, Cardinal O'Fiaich Library and Archives, Armagh.

23 *Edgar Home Annual Report, 1901.*

24 *Edgar Home Annual Report, 1907.*

25 Annual Meeting of the Edgar Home, 1907.

26 *Edgar Home Annual Report, 1909.*

27 *Edgar Home Annual Report, 1911.*

28 Revd Dr O'Loughlin, *Sermon in Aid of the Magdalen Asylum*, 27 March 1900, Exhibition Hall Belfast, Linenhall Library.
29 Entrance Registers, Salvation Army Home, Belfast, 1905–1946.
30 Ibid.
31 Bartley, *Prostitution*, p. 28.
32 *Edgar Home Annual Report, 1926.*
33 Entrance Register, Salvation Army Home, Belfast, 1936.
34 Ibid., 1934.
35 Between 1905 and 1917 the numbers of admissions are taken from both long-and short-stay homes.
36 See chapter 3.
37 *Northern Whig*, 11 March 1912, p. 5.
38 Evidence of Viscount Corry to Vice-Regal Commission on Poor Law Reform in Ireland, *Minutes of Evidence*, PP 1906, Cd 3204, vol. LII, 11 November 1903.
39 Ibid., evidence of Revd R.H. Smythe, Presbyterian Chaplain, Monaghan Workhouse.
40 *Edgar Home Annual Report, 1921.*
41 *Edgar Home Annual Report, 1923.*
42 The Salvation Army Home opened in 1905, so Census Records for 1911 only are available.
43 'Inmates' is the term used in the Census.
44 Census of Ireland, 1901 and 1911.
45 Bartley, *Prostitution*, pp. 29–30.
46 Finnegan, *Do Penance or Perish*, p. 41.
47 Bartley, *Prostitution*, p.36.
48 *Annual Report of the Ulster Magdalen Asylum, 1887*, Linenhall Library.
49 Census of Ireland, 1911.
50 Bartley, *Prostitution*, p. 36.
51 Frances Finnegan, *Poverty and Prostitution: A Study of Victorian Prostitutes in York* (Cambridge, 1979), p. 167; Walkowitz, *Prostitution and Victorian Society*, p. 18.
52 Oonagh Walsh, 'Protestant Female Philanthropy in Dublin in the Early Twentieth Century', *History Ireland*, 5 (1997) 27.
53 Evidence of Dr Darling, Co. Armagh to Vice-Regal Commission on Poor Law Reform in Ireland, *Minutes of Evidence*, PP 1906, Cd 3204 vol. LII.
54 Ibid, evidence of Dr Elizabeth Bell.
55 Grainne Blair, '"Equal sinners": Irish Women Utilising the Salvation Army Rescue Network', in M. Kelleher and J. Murphy (eds), *Gender Perspectives in Nineteenth Century Ireland: Public and Private Spheres* (Dublin, 1997), p. 188.
56 Entrance Register, Salvation Army Home, Belfast, 1907.
57 Entrance Registers, Salvation Army Home, Belfast, 1905–1908.

74 *Regulating sexuality*

58 Census of Ireland, 1911.
59 Entrance Registers, Salvation Army Home, Belfast, 1905–1946.
60 Entrance Register, Salvation Army Home, Belfast, 1907.
61 Peggy Pascoe, *Relations of Rescue: The Search for Female Moral Authority in the American West, 1874–1939* (Oxford, 1990), p. 87.
62 Finnegan, *Do Penance or Perish*, pp. 4, 64, 74, 108, 154, 237, 244.
63 Ibid., pp. 46, 74, 108, 154, 237, 242.
64 Luddy, *Prostitution*, p. 101.
65 Census of Ireland, 1901 and 1911.
66 Edgar Home Annual Reports.
67 Revd Dr O'Loughlin, *Sermon in Aid of Ulster Magdalen Asylum*.
68 Moderator of Presbyterian Church, Annual Meeting of the Edgar Home, 1902.
69 Revd Dr O'Loughlin, *Sermon in Aid of Ulster Magdalen Asylum*.
70 Morton, 'Seduced and Abandoned', p. 44.
71 Luddy, *Prostitution*, p. 84.
72 Entrance Registers, Salvation Army Home, Belfast, 1905–1946.
73 Ibid.
74 Ibid.
75 Entrance Register, Salvation Army Home, Belfast, 1905.
76 Around one quarter of all entrants were recorded as such.
77 Luddy, '"Abandoned Women and Bad Characters"', 90; Luddy, *Prostitution*, p. 111.
78 Interview with Mrs D., 11 April 2002.
79 Ibid.
80 Bartley, 'Preventing Prostitution', 45.
81 Mahood, *The Magdalenes*, p. 70.
82 Maria Luddy, 'Moral Rescue and Unmarried Mothers in Ireland in the 1920s', *Women's Studies*, 30 (2001), 801.
83 Evidence of Dr Darling, Co. Armagh to Vice-Regal Commission on Poor Law Reform in Ireland, *Minutes of Evidence*, PP 1906, Cd 3204, vol. LII; Luddy, 'Moral Rescue', 801.
84 For further discussion of these ideas see Greta Jones, *Social Hygiene in Twentieth Century Britain* (London, 1986).
85 Entrance Register, Salvation Army Home, Belfast, 1912.
86 Ibid., 1915.
87 Regina G. Kunzel, *Fallen Woman, Problem Girls: Unmarried Mothers and the Professionalization of Social Work, 1890–1945* (New Haven and London, 1993), pp. 20–22.
88 Ibid., p. 24.
89 General William Booth, *In Darkest England and the Way Out* (London, 1890).
90 Annual Meeting of the Edgar Home, 1909.

91 Luddy, *Women and Philanthropy*, p. 103.
92 Lynn Nead, 'The Magdalen in Modern Times: The Mythology of the Fallen Woman in Pre-Raphaelite Painting', in R. Betterton (ed.), *Looking at Images of Femininity in the Visual Arts and Media* (London, 1987), p. 83.
93 Annual Meeting of the Edgar Home, 1913.
94 *Edgar Home Annual Report, 1916.*
95 *Church of Ireland Rescue League Annual Report 1916*, Church of Ireland House, Belfast.
96 Annual Meeting of the Edgar Home, 1921.
97 Bartley, *Prostitution*, p. 6.
98 Annual Meeting of the Edgar Home, 1909.
99 Entrance Registers, Salvation Army Home, Belfast, 1905–1946.
100 'Half-timers' went to school half time and worked in the mill half time.
101 Entrance Register, Salvation Army Home, Belfast, 1907.
102 Ibid., 1914.
103 Ibid., 1909.
104 Ibid., 1910.
105 Gillian Tyler Ball, 'Practical Religion: A Study of the Salvation Army's Social Services for Women, 1884–1914' (unpublished doctoral thesis, University of Leicester, 1987), p. 240.
106 Luddy, 'Moral Rescue', 804–807; Lindsey Earner-Byrne, *Mother and Child: Maternity and Child Welfare in Dublin, 1922–60* (Manchester, 2007), p. 186.
107 Entrance Register, Salvation Army Home, Belfast, 1914.
108 Mary Odem, *Delinquent Daughters: Protecting and Policing Adolescent Female Sexuality in the United States, 1885–1920* (Chapel Hill and London, 1995), p. 44; for a discussion of illegitimacy in Northern Ireland, see William Paul Gray, 'A Social History of Illegitimacy in Ireland from the late Eighteenth Century to the Early Twentieth Century' (unpublished doctoral thesis, Queen's University, Belfast, 2001).
109 Entrance Register, Salvation Army Home, Belfast, 1916.
110 Ibid., 1911.
111 Ibid., 1913.
112 Ibid., 1912.
113 Entrance Registers, Salvation Army Home, Belfast, 1912, 1915.
114 Ibid., 1907, 1910, 1911.
115 Pascoe, *Relations of Rescue*, p. 60.
116 Ibid., p. 50.
117 Entrance Registers, Salvation Army Home, Belfast, 1905–1946.
118 Bartley, *Prostitution*, pp. 119–152. A similar situation existed in the United States: see Marian Morton, *And Sin No More: Social Policy and Unwed Mothers in Cleveland, 1855–1990* (Columbus, 1993), p. 82.
119 Bartley, *Prostitution*, p. 127.

120 Evidence of Miss Hamilton, Portrush Board of Guardians to Vice-Regal Commission on Poor Law Reform in Ireland, *Minutes of Evidence*, PP 1906, Cd 3204 vol. LII.

121 Ibid.

122 It is likely that a similar situation existed in other Protestant-run homes, with women being removed to the asylum or the workhouse.

123 Entrance Register, Salvation Army Home, Belfast, 1935.

124 Ibid., 1923.

125 Entrance Registers, Salvation Army Home, Belfast, 1914, 1915.

126 Aine McCarthy, 'Hearths, Bodies and Minds: Gender Ideology and Women's Committal to Eniscorthy Lunatic Asylum, 1916–1925', in Hayes and Urquhart (eds), *Irish Women's History*, p. 121.

127 Entrance Registers, Salvation Army Home, Belfast, 1922, 1945.

128 Ibid., 1929, 1940.

129 Matthew Thomson, *The Problem of Mental Deficiency: - Eugenics, Democracy and Social Policy in Britain c.1870–1959* (Oxford, 1998), p. 22.

130 Ruth Rosen, *The Lost Sisterhood: Prostitution in America 1900–1918* (Baltimore and London, 1982), pp. 22–23.

131 Entrance Registers, Salvation Army Home, Belfast, 1908.

132 Ibid., 1912.

133 Ibid., 1915.

134 Ibid., 1917.

135 Ibid., 1916.

136 Odem, *Delinquent Daughters*, p. 4.

137 Bartley, *Prostitution*, pp. 38–39.

138 Maguire, *Belfast*, p. 84.

139 Interview, Sister O., 4 April 2001.

140 Luddy, *Women and Philanthropy*, p. 114.

141 Kunzel, *Fallen Women*, p. 26.

142 Mahood, *The Magdalenes*, p. 78.

143 Minutes of Edgar Home Committee.

144 Annual Meeting of the Edgar Home 1903.

145 *Edgar Home Annual Reports, 1900–1926.*

146 *Annual Reports* and Meetings of the Edgar Home, 1900–1926.

147 Interview, Sister O., 4 April 2001.

148 Bartley, *Prostitution*, p. 57.

149 *Edgar Home Annual Reports, 1900–1924.*

150 Annual Meeting of the Edgar Home, 1904.

151 *Edgar Home Annual Report 1915.*

152 Annual Meeting of the Edgar Home, 1923.

153 Women in the Good Shepherd Convent also made vestments, altar linen and other kinds of needlework to order. In the Salvation Army Home, embroidery done by the women was sold to raise funds for the home.

154　Mahood, *The Magdalenes*, p. 87.
155　Annual Meeting of the Edgar Home, 1900.
156　Ibid., 1904.
157　Mahood, *The Magdalenes*, p. 87.
158　Bartley, *Prostitution*, pp. 52–53; Mahood, *The Magdalenes*, p. 91; Walkowitz, *Prostitution and Victorian Society*, p. 71.
159　Interview, Sister O., 4 April 2001.
160　Peter Hughes, 'Cleanliness and Godliness: A Sociological Study of the Good Shepherd Refuges for the Social Reformation and Christian Conversion of Prostitutes and Convicted Women in Nineteenth Century Britain' (unpublished doctoral thesis, Brunel University, 1985), p. 376.
161　Ibid., p. 378.
162　*Edgar Home Annual Report, 1916.*
163　Revd Dr O'Loughlin, *Sermon in Aid of Ulster Magdalen Asylum.*
164　*Edgar Home Annual Report, 1911.*
165　Bartley, *Prostitution*, p. 53.
166　*Edgar Home Annual Report, 1910.*
167　Annual Meeting of the Edgar Home, 1908.
168　Linda Mahood, *Policing Gender, Class and Family: Britain 1880–1940* (London, 1995), p. 127.
169　Kunzel, *Fallen Women*, p. 52.
170　Pascoe, *Relations of Rescue*, p. 167.
171　Morrow, 'Women and Work in Northern Ireland', p. 27.
172　Mahood, *The Magdalenes*, p. 163; Frank Prochaska, *Women and Philanthropy in Nineteenth Century England* (Oxford, 1980), p. 148.
173　Bartley, *Prostitution*, p. 52.
174　This figure obviously includes re-admissions, so the real figure will be less.
175　Bartley, *Prostitution*, p. 39; James M. Smith, *Ireland's Magdalen Laundries: and the Nation's Architecture of Containment* (Notre Dame, 2007), p. 26.
176　*Edgar Home Annual Report, 1901.*
177　*Edgar Home Annual Report 1902.*
178　Bartley, *Prostitution*, p. 40; Finnegan, *Do Penance or Perish*, p. 36.
179　Interview, Sister O., 4 April 2001.
180　Annual Meeting of the Edgar Home, 1909.
181　Edgar Home Committee Meeting, 30 July 1909.
182　*Edgar Home Annual Report, 1924.*
183　*Edgar Home Annual Report, 1904.*
184　Entrance Registers, Salvation Army Home, Belfast, 1912, 1913, 1924.
185　Ibid., 1921, 1936.
186　Ibid., 1905–1946.
187　Bartley, *Prostitution*, p. 61.
188　*Edgar Home Annual Report, 1904.*
189　Entrance Register, Salvation Army Home, Belfast, 1909.

190 *Edgar Home Annual Report, 1902.*
191 *Edgar Home Annual Report, 1910.*
192 Annual Meeting of the Edgar Home, 1923.
193 Ibid.
194 Bartley, *Prostitution*, p. 64; Jordan, *Who Cared?*, p. 228.
195 Belfast Midnight Mission, Minutes, 1944, Records of Belfast Midnight Mission, 1934–1949, D/2072/1, PRONI.
196 See chapter 3.
197 *Irish Catholic Directory and Almanac, 1946–2007.*
198 Smith, *Ireland's Magdalen Laundries*, pp. 81–82.
199 For a detailed analysis and discussion of the cultural representation of Magdalen laundries see Smith, *Ireland's Magdalen Laundries*.
200 For a fuller discussion of the film see, Leanne McCormick, 'Sinister Sisters?: The Portrayal of Ireland's Magdalen Asylums in Popular Culture', *Cultural and Social History*, 2 (2005), 373–381; Smith, *Ireland's Magdalen Laundries*, chapter 5.
201 Smith, *Ireland's Magdalen Laundries*, pp. 153, 158.
202 Ibid., p. 151.
203 Ibid., p. 150.
204 Ibid., pp. xvi–xvii.
205 For more on illegitimacy in the Republic of Ireland, see Earner-Byrne, *Mother and Child*, chapter 7.
206 Luddy, 'Moral Rescue', 801–802.
207 *The Magdalene Sisters* DVD/video sleeve notes.
208 For more on the influence of the Catholic Church, see J.H. Whyte, *Church and State in Modern Ireland, 1923–1979* (Dublin, 1980) and Tom Inglis, *Moral Monopoly: The Catholic Church in Modern Irish Society* (Dublin, 1987).
209 Smith, *Ireland's Magdalen Laundries*, p. xiv
210 See chapters 4 and 6.
211 This was seen particularly in the debate over education and the desire of the Catholic Church to maintain control of Catholic schools and teacher training.
212 Luddy, 'Moral Rescue', 813.

3

'Modesty is the sister of virtue': moral prevention work with girls

The old adage that 'prevention is better than cure' began to be recognised from the end of the nineteenth century, by those engaged in philanthropic work with women involved in prostitution.[1] To try and prevent girls from 'falling' became the aim of a variety of informal and voluntary organisations, rather than focusing solely on the reformation of those who had already 'fallen'.[2] This chapter focuses on the organisations and discourses in Northern Ireland concerned with preserving female moral standards, encouraging the development of good wives and mothers, and guarding against the encroachment of modernity and the dangers it was perceived to hold for young women and girls. Common themes emerge, as women are firmly fixed in positions as both moral guardians of the nation and as those believed to pose the greatest risk to the moral decline of the nation. The links between national identity and female sexual morality illustrate the importance of preserving female purity and female behaviour as a means of strengthening unity and identity. Across the religious divide in Northern Ireland, the shared language, images and ideals of womanhood are also clearly seen.

In common with rescue work, there exists a complex relationship between those women involved in running and establishing organisations and their members.[3] The policing of female sexuality was thus not a simple gender issue, but a more complicated relationship intersected both by gender and class. Organisations and prevention work were not simply run by middle-class women attempting to transform working-class morals to match their own in a straightforward attempt at social control. A clear distinction emerges between the 'respectable' working-class and the 'rough' working-class with different organisations and methods employed for different groups.

As Pamela Cox has argued, the 'modern girl' has 'posed a social threat since at least the early nineteenth century'.[4] The common concern centred on the perceived growing independence of working-class girls which was seen as leading to moral deterioration.[5] While the concern at the heart of attempts to protect and direct young women and girls may not have changed, it is also clear that the social situations and political change within Northern Ireland, combined with wider world events, influenced and affected the measures employed. Urban growth, migration, expanding female employment opportunities, fears over white slavery, the world wars, fears of modernity and the changing position of women in society, all invoked responses and changes in attempts to protect, regulate and direct female sexuality and behaviour.

This chapter will consider the organisations involved, methods employed and the wider social and political context of moral and preventative work. In particular the role of the Girl Guides, Girls' Friendly Society (GFS), and Girls' Auxiliary (GA) will be considered. These organisations were largely based in Protestant churches, and while reference will be made to Catholic organisations, difficulty of access to archival material prevents detailed discussion of them. As well as archival material, interviews were carried out with twelve women who were involved in these organisations before 1945.

Girls' Friendly Society

There has been little historical scholarship, beyond official histories,[6] on the wider issue of girls' youth movements, in comparison with boys' organisations and in particular the Scouts.[7] There has been some work on the relationships between the Guides and the Empire and also the Guides' role during the First World War.[8] Consideration of the role of girls' organisations in preventative work and the protection of female sexual morality has also received limited attention, however both Carol Dyhouse and Paula Bartley have discussed the GFS, and Dyhouse, the Guides, within the context of the wider organisations responsible for the preservation of female morals and the campaign to prevent girls falling into sexual immorality.[9]

The GFS was formed in Ireland in the 1870s. It was associated with the Church of Ireland and although it was mainly attended by girls from this denomination, others were freely admitted. It was claimed that in the first years of the twentieth century there were over 15,500 girls connected with the society in Ireland.[10]

Virtue and purity were prerequisites of membership of the GFS, as the third of the GFS Central Rules explicitly stated: 'No girl who has not borne a virtuous character is to be admitted as a member; such character being lost, the member is to forfeit her card'.[11] The Rules for the Working Associates in Ireland also cautioned that they:

> must be very careful as to the character of the girls or young women they admit as members. In every case a short delay and careful preparation before admission is advised.[12]

The GFS saw itself 'involved in a mission to "purify" womanhood'.[13] As its Constitution stated, the Object of the Society was 'To unite for the Glory of God in one fellowship of Prayer and Service, the girls of the Empire, to uphold purity in thought, word and deed'.[14] It was not involved in rescue work, or trying to reclaim those who had fallen, but in protecting and strengthening those within its ranks to resist the temptations of the world and helping them to become good wives and mothers.

The structure of the GFS was based on a semi-maternal relationship between the higher class 'Associate' and lower class 'Member' and aimed to bring social harmony across class boundaries, with Associates who organised branches being drawn from the upper and middle classes and members from the working class.[15] However, there was no agenda to remove these class boundaries, as an article in the Irish GFS magazine the *Irish Leaflet*, published in September 1921, explained: 'God has put you where you are; don't quarrel with the circumstances of your life'.[16]

The GFS recognised the need to provide for working girls and initially focused on domestic servants, providing 'instruction in the Home Arts' within the Industrial Training Department.[17] A Protestant Servants Home and Registry was also established in Dublin in 1873, which offered a 'comfortable home to every respectable Protestant woman domestic servant, who while temporarily out of employment or on holiday sought shelter under its roof'.[18] As Harrison argues, the GFS realised the importance of making 'virtue feasible for working girls' and thus created a variety of benefits and assistance for the virtuous such as registries and homes, convalescent homes, protection for travellers, hostels and seaside holidays. The importance of these should be recognised as they occurred during a period when state intervention or assistance was minimal.[19] An Emigration Department assisted with emigration mainly to Australia, Canada or the United States, with 63 girls being assisted in emigrating, from Ulster in 1904.[20] A GFS Lodge in Belfast was established at the end of the nineteenth century and catered mainly for girls coming from the country for work. At Rostrevor, Co. Down, a Convalescent and Holiday Home was founded.

Girls' Auxiliary

The Girls' Auxiliary (GA) was a Presbyterian organisation established in 1911. Its initial focus was on foreign mission but home mission began to take on greater importance as the organisation developed. While its foundation was not as explicit as the GFS in its concern for purity and the prevention of moral decline, in a variety of ways it offered moral instruction and provided a safe and protective environment for girls. There were four main themes of the organisation: thought, prayer, comradeship and service. The service aspect involved activities such as visiting and entertaining children from local children's homes or visiting the girls in Hopedene House, a home for unmarried mothers.[21] The members were also encouraged to become involved in the Band of Hope (temperance youth organisation) and to help out at girls' clubs.[22] The implication was that those within the GA were of virtuous character and were encouraged to pass on their good example to others. It is estimated that there was an eventual membership of around 6,000 throughout Ireland, although it was strongest in Ulster.[23]

Those involved in the GA were mainly the middle class and 'respectable' working class, whose concern through home service focused on those less fortunate than themselves. It was suggested at the GA Conference in 1923 that there was a class of girl who did not join the GA and which was in need of their help:

> there are lots of girls in our towns who have no home interests, nothing to do in the evenings except perhaps to go to a cheap picture house or walk the streets. Branches in a district might unite to run a club for such girls, teaching them useful crafts and showing them how to make the most of their lives.[24]

A clear division thus existed between those of middle-class or upper-working-class backgrounds who joined the GA and those of the lower working class who did not join but whom it was believed needed to be assisted.

Branches of organisations such as the GFS, GA and Guides met on a weekly basis across the country. The format of the GFS and GA was broadly similar. Activities such as sewing and knitting often featured in weekly meetings, as did singing and musical entertainment. Bible study, prayer and religious talks also played an important role. Within GA meetings there was an emphasis on missionary work, and in particular the missionaries who had been members of, and were supported by, the

GA itself. Funds were raised for this work with activities such as bazaars, cake sales and concerts.[25]

Girl Guides

The formation of the Girl Guides differed from that of the other organisations. The official story records how, in response to the desire of girls to join the Scouts, and when faced with girls dressed in uniform at a Scout rally at Crystal Palace in 1909, Lord Baden-Powell decided there was need for a separate movement.[26] As suggested above, discussion has largely focused on the Scouts, and particularly the importance of militarism in their formation and the role of the movement within wider imperial aims.[27] Located as a subsidiary within this debate on imperialism, has been discussion of the Guides and how far they aimed to train mothers for the Empire.[28] There has also been some discussion of the role of the Guides during the First World War, both in their involvement in the war effort[29] and also, as Richard Voeltz has argued, as an 'antidote for "khaki fever"'. The Guides were seen as the solution to this worrying behaviour of young women and girls, provoked by wartime conditions. The movement provided wholesome alternatives and directed energy into useful activities, such as 'cooking, sewing, laundry work, nursing the sick and childcare'.[30] Added to this, the fact that girls were in uniform acted as a form of 'reverse khaki fever', and their involvement in the war effort ensured that the 'fever abated . . . when women's direct participation in the war effort expanded, giving them regular employment and acceptable outlets for their patriotic emotions'.[31] The Guides, during the war years, offered outdoor activities, camping, a uniform and involvement in war work. This attracted girls who were seeking greater liberation, while as Voeltz argues 'maintaining the pose of acting as a middle-class agent of social control to inoculate the increasing numbers of working-class girls against the flagrant "flapper" and the virulent "khaki fever"'.[32] Tammy Proctor tempers this assertion of social control by arguing that while the Guides may have appeared like a safe alternative for women, in reality the movement also 'fashioned a space for girls and women to experience independence and freedom from the restrictions of home life during World War I'.[33]

Guiding was established in Northern Ireland in the aftermath of the First World War, with 95 companies registered by 1921. While 'khaki fever' was not as virulent in Northern Ireland as it was in mainland UK, there was still grave concern with the behaviour of young women and girls, and organisations such as the Guides were seen to play a vital role in the provision of alternative entertainment. While Agnes Baden-Powell, Robert's sister, was anxious in the initial years of Guiding to maintain the feminine aspect of Guides, the influence of Olave Baden-Powell, Robert's wife, encouraged a more adventurous programme: the importance of outdoor activities markedly contrasted with the more sedentary organisations such as the GFS and the GA.

Those who joined the Guides, rather than the other organisations, often did so because of the 'exciting' activities they offered. They saw themselves as being more adventurous and pioneering and dynamic than those who joined the more sedentary and indoor-based organisations. Several interviewees commented on the fact that the attraction of the Guides was that they offered an exciting alternative and catered for those girls considered 'tom-boys'.[34] However, the organisation itself was keen to distance itself from accusations of encouraging tomboyishness and unwomanly behaviour.[35] As the Ulster Chief Commissioner explained, as she presented a cup for needlework in 1931:

> in the earlier days of guiding it had been said that the new movement would cause girls to neglect learning 'home' subjects such as needlework but this competition proved it to be otherwise.[36]

Nonetheless, with their emphasis on practical skills and outdoor activities such as camping, cooking and knot-tying, in conjunction with games, drill and badge work, the Guides needed to tread a fine line between providing for the outdoor and activity based demands of those girls keen to advance female opportunities and activities, and presenting a respectable impression of an organisation which was seen as offering girls training as homemakers.[37]

Protection from city life

Whilst the Guides may have encouraged resourcefulness and self-reliance, it was also felt that, in keeping with the GFS and GA, 'benevolent, protective adult authority' was needed, particularly for those girls who were living outside their family units.[38] Young women living outside the family home and earning a wage aroused most anxiety. This was of particular relevance in Belfast, where the availability of female employment led to large numbers of young women moving to the city from rural areas. In 1911, nearly half of the female labour force in Belfast was under twenty-five, and over ninety per cent of those between fifteen and twenty-four were single.[39] The independence of working girls was seen as dangerous and the assumption emerged that financial independence and sexual immorality were closely related.[40]

As work patterns changed, with domestic service no longer being the main employment for working-class girls, concerns grew about the unhealthy influences that girls were exposed to. Factory work in particular was seen as damaging for both bodies and minds, as girls were believed to be exposed to the low tone of a factory floor. Furthermore, it was believed that these jobs provided no training for what was seen to be a woman's primary role as homemaker and mother. Concern was also expressed over the fact that many factory, warehouse and mill jobs were laborious and monotonous, and it was felt that these girls had little opportunity to 'let off steam'. This increased the desire to elevate boredom and escape after work and encouraged involvement in dangerous entertainments.[41]

These anxieties were articulated at the Annual Meeting of the GFS Diocesan Lodge in 1900, where it was felt that:

> many of these young women had very laborious lives to lead, both those who worked in factories, and those who worked behind the counters of shops and it was as well there should be a place of rest for them where they could receive the guidance which they so needed.[42]

In 1912, the *Irish Citizen*[43] carried a report about the Belfast Girls' Club Union (BGCU), explaining that most of its members worked in mills and factories for twelve hours a day and then had to return home to clean the house. It was then no surprise that they sought 'a little excitement after the long day's monotony, by walking the noisy, crowded streets, gazing into the flaring shop windows, or visiting low-class picture saloons'.[44] Similarly, in 1917, the Presbyterian magazine the *Witness*, reporting the opening of a new girls' club explained how this was:

> one way in which young girls who are either strangers to the city or who find little comfort in their drab lives or association can be most carefully guarded or guided.[45]

Changing work patterns also caused consternation amongst those working in rescue homes as the ready availability of work without references was seen as removing girls from the care and protection of rescue homes and their subsequent reformation.[46]

The concern over the monotony of jobs and the outside pleasures that this pushed girls to seek was a common theme. Mrs Macaualy, the

President of the Presbyterian Women's Union and Girls' Club in 1932, explained that:

> almost all of these girls go out daily to their work and work is so exacting and often so terribly monotonous in these busy days that the reactions may be a serious danger.[47]

In response to these concerns about girls coming to Belfast, a variety of organisations were involved in attempts to provide guidance and protection, by establishing hostels and clubs. Girls coming from the countryside were seen as naive and unaware of the dangers of city life. They were seen to be at risk of being led astray and were easily distracted by unsuitable entertainments and amusements and in need of guidance and stabilising influences. As the Bishop of Down, Connor and Dromore, Rt. Revd Thomas Welland, explained with reference to the GFS Lodge in Belfast:

> young women coming up from the country to a great city like Belfast, perfect strangers, were of course at a great disadvantage especially if those girls had to find suitable lodgings and companions . . . the more the city increases the more temptations and dangers increased and the more need for such a shelter.[48]

The concern was that girls arriving in Belfast would end up living in unsuitable accommodation. The Bishop further explained that 'they might have recourse to lodgings of a very inferior, uncomfortable and sometimes disreputable character'.[49] Lady Dufferin reiterated the point explaining that the:

> fundamental idea of the GFS is the protection of girls and more especially the safeguarding of those who from a change of residence are thrown amongst strangers and into temptations hitherto unknown to them, as in the case of country girls coming for the first time to town.[50]

Those recorded as staying in the GFS Lodge in April 1911 clearly show that it was indeed utilised by those from country areas. Only four of the twenty-nine boarders were from Belfast itself, with seven coming from Co. Armagh, four from England, three from both Counties Donegal and Derry, two from Counties Tyrone, and Down and one each from the King's County, Co. Antrim, Dublin and Scotland.

The age of the boarders was also recorded and it is interesting to note that they cover the age range from 17–40. There were six women aged 17–20; six aged 21–24; six aged 25–28; four aged 29–32; three aged 33–36 and four aged 37–40.[51] It is clear that as with rescue homes, it was not simply young girls who stayed at this hostel but also women in their thirties and forties. While the rhetoric may have been directed towards young women leaving home for the first time, the reality was that women of all ages needed to find suitable lodgings and made use of these hostels.

It must also be recognised that, although the hostels and clubs were aimed at working-class women, a distinction is apparent within this class itself. As Judy Giles suggests, both middle-class and working-class observers could 'confidently distinguish between the "respectable" poor and the "rough" or the "residuum".[52] Working-class 'respectability', she argues, was a 'complex cluster of values', which embraced 'female sexuality, material security, respect for authority and behaviour appropriate to this and a certain emotional and moral outlook'.[53] However, within the 'respectable' working class further divisions may be seen. There were, for example, separate hostels which catered for 'business' girls, that is those who worked mainly in offices or shops, and hostels for 'working' girls who were employed in mills or factories.

The minutes of the Annual Meeting of the GFS Lodge in Belfast in 1898 record forty-five boarders of varying occupations such as governess, dressmaker, milliner's apprentice and typist.[54] The 1911 Census records a similar variety of occupations, seventeen in total, including handkerchief ornamenter, photo artist, fancy box maker, office assistant and nurse. The most popular occupations were dressmaker, shop assistant and occupations connected with the linen industry.[55] This was in contrast to the occupations recorded in the 1911 Census of those in the Magdalen Asylum close to the GFS Lodge on Donegall Pass. The women in the asylum were mainly laundresses, domestic servants and mill workers, which reflects the class differences between it and the lodge.

The variety of provision of establishments for young women also reflects a hierarchy of morality. The asylum was for those who had 'fallen' into sin and who were seen to be in need of reformation; whereas those who had not 'fallen', but who it was felt needed positive influences and a safe place to stay, were provided for at the lodge. The terms used to describe those staying in both the lodge and the asylum also indicate how their situations differed: while those in the lodge were referred to as 'boarders', those in the asylum were regarded as 'inmates'. Methods of gaining entrance to the various establishments also differed. In contrast to the rescue and refuge homes discussed above, entrance to a hostel such as the GFS Lodge required references of good character and girls would be turned away without these, or if their appearance suggested otherwise. As the Dowager Marchioness of Dufferin and Ava explained in 1913:

members of the GFS are required to be girls of good character and therefore it was not possible to admit to lodges those who came without reliable references or whose appearance or account of themselves was not
satisfactory.[56]

Those who could not give a satisfactory account of themselves may well
have gone to the Magdalen Asylum.[57] Hostels, such as the lodge, also
charged the women who stayed in them, while being an 'inmate' of a
rescue home was free. As the Rev Cameron Bristow clarified, the lodge
was 'not a charity but a business, girls had to pay for their lodgings'.[58]

A Presbyterian hostel was opened in Belfast in 1908. Over the first
year more than thirty young women resided there, with their occupations
recorded as 'mostly dressmakers and saleswomen in warehouses' but 'a
few typists, post office clerks and students for the civil service availed
themselves of the accommodation'.[59] The hostels not only provided
accommodation, but aimed at providing guidance and in the early years
some form of advancement and improvement. Various classes were held
in the GFS Lodge such as arithmetic and writing and drill, with a Bible
class on Sunday.[60]

As it was middle-class women who organised and ran the hostels and
clubs the hope was that such contact would provide models of moral
conduct and a refining influence.[61] For example, the work of the GFS
Lodge was seen as a 'potent influence for the good of the class for whom it
was specifically designed': namely the working-class.[62] The help that was
given to the girls in the lodge was from 'their sisters who were in better
positions of life, not assuming over them a position of superiority but
acting as friends'.[63]

The Catholic Church had similar anxieties about the numbers of
Catholic young women arriving in Belfast for work and living outside the
care of their families. This was reflected in the establishment in 1901 of
St Vincent's Home for Working Girls in Clonard Gardens in West Belfast.
This home provided accommodation at seven shillings and sixpence per
week for girls who were mainly employed in the nearby linen mills.[64]
The class divide within the provision of accommodation for women may
also be seen across the religious divide with the changing of the name
of St Paul's 'Home for Working Girls', which was established in 1900 in
Ballymacarrett, under the care of the Sisters of the Most Holy Cross and
Passion, to a 'Home for Business Girls' in 1916.[65]

Similarly, the hierarchy of morality seen in the GFS Lodge and the
nearby Magdalen Asylum existed in a similar manner in the establishments

run by the Catholic Church. The Good Shepherd Sisters, who ran the Good Shepherd Magdalen Home and laundry on the Ormeau Road, also had under their care a Sacred Heart Home for 'orphans and friendless girls of good character where they receive religious instruction and are trained for domestic service'.[66] Those who were considered to be of 'good character' went to one institution, while those whose behaviour was questionable went elsewhere.

The Catholic organisation the Legion of Mary, which had been actively involved in work with women, and purity campaigns in Dublin from the 1920s, began work among the women of Belfast in the 1930s. They initially established the Sancta Maria Home for Girls on the Crumlin Road in 1934 and began a home for destitute women, the Regina Coeli, on the Falls Road in 1936. In 1942, the Mater Dei Hostel was opened on the Antrim Road and catered for expectant single mothers and their babies.[67]

In the main, as with rescue homes, Protestants and Catholics stayed in hostels run by their own denomination. The Protestant hostels, though often run by a particular denomination, did not restrict entrance to that denomination, although the GFS Lodge did give preference to those who were GFS members, or came with a letter of introduction from a GFS Associate. The Census Records for the GFS Lodge indicate that, while 20 of the 29 boarders were Church of Ireland, there were also seven Presbyterians and two Methodists.

Another feature of note is that a number of the hostels provided holiday homes for the girls who stayed there. The GFS had a Convalescent and Holiday Home in Rostrevor and St Vincent's Home had a rest home in Whitehead and a holiday home in Bangor, which was 'largely availed of by the Belfast mill-workers and others who for 12 shillings a week got an enjoyable holiday by the sea-side'.[68] While it may be argued that these holiday homes ensured that, even in their holidays, the girls were being kept under surveillance and 'protection', it must be contended that for most young women working in the mill this was the only way in which they would have been able to afford a holiday. For girls who were ill, in a time when the health service or social security did not exist, convalescent homes provided an affordable place of rest and recuperation.

Girls' clubs

In addition to hostels, there were a variety of girls' clubs that met weekly in Belfast. The initial aim of these clubs was to protect the purity and innocence of girls and to provide an alternative to less desirable activities and the attraction of the streets.[69] Many of the Protestant-run clubs were united under the auspices of the Belfast Girls' Club Union (BGCU), formed around 1910. It linked various girls' clubs, sewing and drill classes and choirs and was particularly aimed at working-class girls, many of whom 'were halftimers in heavy black shawls and [who] could neither read or write'.[70] The Presbyterian Church also provided a room in Church House, where girls employed in mills/factories or in domestic service could attend a Sunday Bible Class or a club during the week where cooking, handcraft and singing classes were provided. This concern about working girls and their need for guidance is also reflected in the activities of the Alpha Club. This was a society of middle- and upper-class women who saw themselves as 'progressive' and met to discuss contemporary issues, and established a Sunday Club for female servants. It was reported how the girls:

> meet in a bright, warm room and have tea, sing, read or tell stories. It is to help lonely girls who come into the city and find it difficult to make friends that the club was formed.[71]

Marcus Collins has detailed the emergence of mixed clubs in the Second World War in England.[72] Although the BGCU was not quite as progressive, it did have social evenings with boyfriends as guests during 1943.[73] As the state became more interested and concerned in the issue of leisure and youth as the Second World War progressed, so the BCGU found itself adjusting to the changing situation.[74] The 1943 Annual Report explained how it 'now finds itself one of many other agencies created to deal with the problem of the young girl growing up'.[75] However, while circumstances might have changed they still felt that 'the one-night-a-week club staffed by voluntary leaders makes a valuable contribution towards solving the problem of the normal adolescent girl especially in a large city'.[76] Even at the end of the war this statement from the 1947 Annual Report reflects how, while the girls attending the clubs may have gained freedoms and changed attitudes, the initial aims of the BCGU to guide and protect still existed:

> Present day clubs with their membership of chattering, eager vivacious young people (in some cases, perhaps a little too sophisticated for their years) but always friendly and usually cooperative present different problems from those met with in earlier days. Changed conditions however, do not alter human nature and the need to provide outlet and wise guidance is still the same. The union is fortunate in having a splendid staff of Leaders

and young Helpers who give of their best to help and teach these rather unstable people and pilot them over the difficult transitional years between girlhood and woman hood.[77]

A number of Catholic organisations made similar provision, one such being a club for 'country girls in domestic service in the city who were often very lonely and had little opportunity to make friends within the Catholic community'.[78] This was based at St Brigid's Hostel Convent of Mercy on the Crumlin Road. The Catholic Church appears to have become increasingly concerned about the leisure activities of girls in the 1920s and 1930s: this is reflected in the increasing provision of clubs for girls in this period. St Brigid's Club was opened in 1922 and a club under the auspices of the Good Shepherd Sisters on the Ormeau Road was established in 1932. Furthermore, two clubs were established by the Legion of Mary in 1934 in north Belfast, and one in Derryvolgie in South Belfast in 1940.[79]

The White Slave Trade

Concerns generated by young women alone on the streets at night were given added impetus by the threat believed to be posed by white slave traders. Fears about white slavery had initially arisen in the 1880s. It was believed that there was an organised international traffic in women and that young British girls were abducted and forced into a life of prostitution. Campaigners such as Josephine Butler and Alfred Dyer agitated for changes in the law, and a Parliamentary Committee was set up to investigate and examine the extent of juvenile prostitution. The Committee reported in 1882 and recommended the age of sexual consent be raised from 13 to 16.[80] Following much campaigning, the age of consent for women was raised to 16 in August 1885 under the Criminal Law Amendment (CLA) Act. The concerns did not end there and perhaps influenced by a lack of success in curbing prostitution or by support from the suffrage movement, the National Vigilance Association (NVA) continued agitation for further reforms.[81]

In December 1912 a new CLA Act was passed, commonly known as the White Slave Act. It revoked the clause that allowed men to claim that they believed a girl whom they had had sexual intercourse with to be over 16, and thus escape criminal prosecution. Amongst other clauses it also increased the fines for brothel owners to £100.[82] While the realities of the White Slave Trade are questionable, it clearly aroused public concern and strengthened the cause for tighter 'protective' controls on young women, particularly in travel. The publicity and public outcry concerning the White Slave Trade reflects, as Bristow suggests, 'fears generated by the changing role of women, domestic and international migration and rapid urban industrial growth'.[83] The idea that young women were being taken against their will created the image of women as helpless and in need of protection. It maintained the idea of women being seduced and forced to engage in sexual activities and increased the need for vigilance and social control of those felt to be at greatest risk.[84] The idea of men as 'predators' was consequently re-emphasised.

These fears were increasingly expressed in Belfast, particularly during 1913, and often at the annual meetings of voluntary organisations. At the Annual Meeting of the GFS Diocesan Lodge the Revd T.G. Collins articulated the view that:

> it was appalling to think that girls might come up from country parts without knowing the dangers of a great city. They were placed within reach of unscrupulous men or women who would bring them to lodgings where they would soon fall into bad company to say the least of it.[85]

The Dowager Marchioness of Dufferin and Ava expressed similar concerns at the same Annual Meeting. She hoped that 'revelations about the White Slave Trade would urge their own workers to greater efforts in promoting welfare and safety of their members'.[86] Similarly, at the Annual Meeting of Belfast Midnight Mission, Lady Dufferin, discussing the White Slave Trade, explained that:

> few had any idea of the widespread nature of this evil, or often callous cruelty, ingenuity or wickedness with which the trade was carried on. It was with perfect horror that they thought of those inhuman men and woman who, influenced by greed, entrapped innocent girls and forced them into a life of misery ending in an early death.[87]

She felt that it was therefore of the utmost importance that in Belfast they should 'strive to cleanse the streets to purify their little corner of the world, to save girls from falling and rescue those that had fallen'.[88] The Committee of the Edgar Home also recorded its support of the bill to stop the White Slave Trade. It was felt that 'much more might be done by those in authority in the State to prevent innocent girls being decoyed away and ruined'.[89]

For some within the female suffrage movement, the issue of the White Slave Trade and raising the age of consent were intrinsically linked to the extension of the franchise to women. Frank Mort describes the divisions and contradictions which emerged within feminism in the first decades of the twentieth century, especially between those who supported the social purity movement and those who regarded purity feminism as a 'repressive moral code based on ignorance and punitive condemnation'.[90] While there may have been divisions amongst feminists about coercive police powers and female regulation,[91] the suffrage movement in Ireland appears united in its view that women needed protection from male exploitation and that this was intricately related to further extension of the franchise.[92]

The belief of many of the suffragists was that women 'were morally superior to men and would be an asset to the political system as they would clean it up'.[93] Mr Joseph Clayton, speaking at a meeting of the Irish Women's Suffrage Society in March 1912, urged the government to pass the CLA Bill and the extension of the franchise to 'women on the same terms as it is or may be granted to men as the shortest cut to the abolition of the white slave traffic'.[94] He explained that even though Belfast was a 'highly-civilised community, the most civilised in the country, and he believed the most progressive', this 'cancer' of the White Slave Trade was still present there.[95] Similar meetings were held across Ireland, North and South in 1912, under the auspices of the Irishwomen's Suffrage Foundation. The central theme of the meetings was that to prevent such immoral activities, women needed to become involved in the political process. At a meeting in Warrenpoint, the speaker used the example of the White Slave Trade to illustrate that 'all efforts to ameliorate evil social and moral conditions are practically useless, and have been useless in the past, owing to the political helplessness of women'.[96]

The discussion of the issue in Ireland exposes a familiar theme: the belief that there was a higher moral standard pertaining in Ireland as opposed to other parts of Great Britain. This was a source of concern for some, however, in that 'regulations and precautions against this evil are less strict over here than in English towns, and consequently the agents of this nefarious traffic find . . . their happy hunting ground'.[97] The *Irish Citizen* also expressed concern that the supposed greater purity of Ireland caused problems, as people were 'hypnotised by cant about our exceptionally purity' and girls grew up with no awareness of the dangers of the outside world and were more susceptible to the white slavers.[98]

Articles concerning the White Slave Trade appeared frequently in the *Irish Citizen* in 1912 and 1913. They urged women to take responsibility for their 'sisters' who needed protection, and claimed that the only way in which this protection could begin to take place was through the power of the vote.[99] Criticism was also lodged against the magazine the *Irish Catholic*, which had apparently expressed concern that the Vigilance Committee set up in Dublin to stem the white slave traffic had 'sinister motives of proselytism' behind it.[100] One writer in the *Irish Citizen* argued the point that as the *Irish Catholic* carried appeals for help for Magdalen Homes, it should surely feel that 'prevention is better than cure'.[101]

The First World War

The disruption to society caused by the First World War combined with the greater freedom that women were perceived to have, brought fears that this would cause moral decay.[102] This was largely related again to the increasing independence experienced by the large numbers of women who were being employed in jobs left by men who had gone to war, a development necessary to maintain essential war production. It was felt that with money, independence and the heightened war conditions, standards of female moral behaviour would decline. Concerns were also heightened by fears of 'khaki fever' and the presence of greater numbers of young women on the streets in the evenings.

Work patterns, and the numbers of women employed in Northern Ireland during the First World War, were not as radically altered as other parts of the UK. Belfast had a high percentage of women in employment before 1914, with women making up over forty per cent of the workforce in 1911, compared with thirty per cent in England.[103] This high rate of employment was largely due to the linen industry. 23,000 women were employed in some capacity in the linen trade in 1911, compared with 6,500 in domestic service.[104] Female employment opportunities in the linen industry grew during the First World War as demand from the military for tents, haversacks, hospital equipment and aeroplane fabric increased. The added numbers of women employed in industrial work increased the anxieties concerning the suitability of this type of work for women. Industrial manufacturing was always seen as a threat to female morals compared with the more suitable occupations of, for example, domestic service, where women were protected from bad influences.[105]

Concern for the moral welfare of the nation and women specifically led to increased supervision of female behaviour whether in the form of health visitors, factory supervisors or Women Patrols.[106] These patrols were organised by two separate organisations, the National Union of

Women Workers (NUWW, which became the National Council of Women in 1919), and the Women Police Volunteers (WPV, renamed the Women Police Service (WPS) in 1915).[107] Conflict arose between the various groups organising the patrols, as some desired a professional female police force rather than voluntary patrols and the historical debate has focused on how these wider aims were compromised or altered as the war progressed.[108] These differences of opinion may be seen in the arguments of the *Irish Citizen* concerning the setting up of patrols in Ireland. It was felt that as the situation in Ireland regarding 'khaki fever' was not as severe as in England, they could resist the hasty establishment of patrols and hold out for the organisation of professional female police. The *Citizen* contended that as Ireland was not:

> so directly under the influence of the militarist wave as in England, this country has not manifested any such scenes of pernicious 'enthusiasm' for the troops on the part of the girls as was seen in England.[109]

The fear was also expressed that if the patrols failed they would be used as an example of female incapacity and would hinder further advances.[110] Regardless of these fears, Women Patrols were established in both Belfast and Dublin and by 1918 there were also two uniformed 'trained and appointed' policewomen on the streets of Belfast.[111]

The work of the Women Patrols raises issues concerning the policing of women by women. Woollacott contends that the patrols should not be regarded as being 'engaged in control or oppression', but rather as 'agents of cultural hegemony', who were in their own way challenging the gender order.[112] The co-operation with the forces of law and order was in contrast to previous feminist movements such as the campaign against the Contagious Diseases Acts, and the militant suffrage movement where activists fought against the police and military. Woollacott further argues that this change reflects the 'primacy of . . . class identification and . . . ambitions', and that as women were kept on in policing capacities after the war this was an illustration of how middle-class women were penetrating the professions.[113] However, as in other areas of female advancement during wartime, the end of the war saw a return to pre-war status.[114] As Louise Jackson has illustrated, the number of women involved in policing fell from over 6,000 during the First World War to a few hundred in the 1920s.[115] Increasingly the arguments for the need for women police became focused on gender differences and particular female roles they were useful for.[116] This specifically female role in policing may be seen in a description of the work of the Women Patrols in Belfast:

making the world beautiful, bringing into everything the sweet harmony of order and cleanliness is woman's highest work . . . women are seeing more and more where their duty lies and entering vast areas of work from which they were in the past stringently debarred.[117]

While both the NUWW and WPS differed in how they saw the role of women in the police force, they did agree on the need for properly trained women officers and a distancing from voluntary charitable work.[118] However, while the NUWW 'disclaimed rescue work in an attempt to dissociate itself from female philanthropy', there existed in Belfast close connections between rescue and reform work and the Women Patrols, particularly in the personnel involved.[119] One of the organisers of the Belfast patrols was a Miss Curran who was also involved in the Church of Ireland Rescue League before the war and her involvement in moral reform work continued in the post-war years. The methods employed were also similar: as the patrols had no powers to arrest or caution they relied on persuasion, giving advice and the 'sheer persistence of their presence'.[120] As Levine suggests, 'in many respects they were tactically and ideologically closer to the . . . Salvation Army than to the police'.[121]

The rhetoric employed in Belfast concerning the patrols reflects this language of Christianity and purity, expounding ideas of rescue and redemption, where 'a bright, patient, all-forgiving hopefulness [is] brought to bear upon even the "black sheep". Another chance, a gentle word of warning, and untiring watchfulness are the methods employed.'[122] There were also close associations with the Churches and Miss Curran, at a Conference held under the auspices of the Presbyterian Church Social Service Committee in 1918, appealed to the ladies of the Church 'to give them all the assistance in their power because this was truly a woman's work'.[123] What was needed were 'women of tact and judgement with kindly sympathetic powers of discrimination and observation with some experience of work amongst girls'.[124] The hope was:

> through kindness and sympathy to be a help to young and innocent girls whose only faults may be high spirits and love of fun which they seek in our streets, having nowhere else to go and therefore may be in danger.[125]

The importance of clubs and societies in preventing moral decline was clearly seen as putting girls in touch with such organisations was regarded as 'one of the direct ways of helping them'. It was felt that in time, and as the patrol workers became better known, girls would actively come and seek help and guidance.[126] The aim was to prevent any misbehaviour taking place. Girls who might be tempted to lower their standards would see the patrols, realise the error of their ways and would be saved from harm.[127]

Whatever their motives for becoming involved in organisations such as the Women Patrols, women clearly felt that they were working for the protection and care of those they were policing, believing they were working to help society and the girls they came in contact with from 'going into the abyss of utterly wasted lives'.[128] The patrols were engaged in protecting not only the vulnerable victims of male lust, but also those whose behaviour ensured they needed protecting from themselves and from whom society also needed to be protected.[129]

Whether young working women did in reality experience great changes as regards their freedom during the First World War is questionable, and it is arguable that these freedoms simply led to more policing and supervision.[130] However, for many social commentators, religious representatives and some women's organisations the behaviour of some young women was cause for concern. As Woollacott contends in her discussion of 'khaki fever', the perception of young working-class women's sexuality was changing from that of vulnerable innocents to 'wilful, expressive of sexual desire . . . autonomous social agents'.[131] Concern was also voiced that immorality was increasing among the respectable classes: it was not simply working-class girls who were challenging the importance of female chastity and respectability.[132]

These concerns were identified by George Armstrong, writing in the *Irish Presbyterian* in 1917, in an article entitled 'After the War, What?'. He explained that:

> The war has brought about the emancipation of women. The hosts of women and girls with money in their pockets, smart clothes, the lure of the cinema before their eyes; the eternal parade in newspapers of the gay lively doings of finer people, particularly of the dramatic and bohemian classes, is an object of profound thought and a tremendously serious factor in the future of the nation.[133]

The freedom that women were seen to have gained during the war was regarded as a threat, not only for the women themselves, but also for the future of the race. The concern with future generations and the harm young women were seen to be causing with their seemingly reckless behaviour was a feature of a wider discussion that perceived women to be the 'guardians of the race'. The ideas of the Social Hygiene movement, and particular concerns during the war years about VD, further fuelled worries that racial decline would precipitate from the immoral behaviour of young women.[134]

Appearance and leisure

Concern about a moral decline that had generated anxiety during the war
years continued in the interwar period. It was assisted by the growing
identification of places frequented in leisure time, such as cinemas and
dancehalls, as morally dangerous and unsuitable places for respectable
young women to visit.[135] Alcohol featured prominently in the debate
about moral behaviour, with both Catholic and Protestant churches supporting temperance movements. Public houses were absolutely out of
bounds for any young woman, as it was only women of dubious character
who would be seen in such places. However, there were places that were
less obvious in their danger that also caused concern.

One such place, which prompted worry during the 1920s, was the
ice-cream parlour.[136] Francis McKee, discussing ice-cream parlours in
Glasgow, describes the campaign that took place in the 1900s against
the parlours. He argues that while initial complaints concerned Sunday
trading and the conduct of the patrons, the real root of the fear expressed
by the conservative forces of power in the city was ice-cream itself. The
shops 'provided an exotic luxury which had overtones of the forbidden'.[137] Furthermore, the 'foreignness' of the product was exhilarating
and it appeared to be undermining the work ethic of the 'Workshop of
the World', and brought an element of sexuality to public eating.[138] On a
practical level, however, the fact that ice-cream parlours were open late
at night, allowing both sexes to mingle freely without control and often
had booth seating that prevented clear views of the occupants and their
activities, was an immediate worry.

Added to the temptations of ice-cream parlours were cinemas, where
many of the films, it was felt, were not fit for young people to see.[139]
Particular concern was generated in the 1930s about films with a sexual
content and working-class adolescent girls 'were seen as especially susceptible to the temptations provoked by sex pictures'.[140] Throughout
the interwar period the Catholic Church in particular was strong in its
condemnation of not only cinemas, but a variety of other forms of entertainment.[141] As the Lenten Pastorals of 1924 exemplify, the areas of greatest concern were, in addition to cinema exhibitions, 'indecent dances,
unwholesome theatre performances, evil literature, drink and women's
immodest fashions'.[142]

The 'disedifying fashions' which women were wearing drew particular
condemnatory attention from the hierarchy of the Catholic Church.[143]
They were seen as negative foreign influences and a League of St Brigid

was formed in 1920 to 'protest against the inroad of foreign immodest fashions'.[144] The Lenten Pastorals of that year were also particularly condemnatory about female dress, with the Revd Dr McHugh, Bishop of Derry, describing the 'dangers from the growing depravity of the age, the contaminating influence of bad examples, the want of Christian modesty in dress'.[145] As Cardinal Logue explained, the Pope had condemned immodest dress and he himself felt such dress was 'an index of the degeneracy and corruption of the age'.[146]

The cause of such immodest dressing according to the Catholic Bishop of Dromore was that 'Irish girls were trying to please the world'. Speaking in Lurgan, Co. Armagh, he explained that while 'he did not believe that Irish girls were immodest . . . there was immodesty in their dress, which was a cause of scandal'.[147] He further appealed to mothers in a separate confirmation service to 'see that their daughters were at all times modestly dressed and so preserve the tradition for modesty among Irish women which had been so endangered lately'.[148]

Those women who were transgressing the ideal and behaving and dressing in a seemingly unsuitable way were also condemned in no uncertain terms by the *Irish Presbyterian*:

> Even in Ireland we have some women who display their persons in this shameless manner. As a rule they are brainless, heartless and characterless . . . the women of the African worlds are modest compared with the corrupters of the growth of both sexes. They should be ostracised by all decent people. How unfitted are these women for the sacred task of motherhood and for the training of immortal souls for heaven.[149]

Dress was perhaps the most obvious feature of the modern young woman, who epitomised for both Catholic and Protestant authorities impurity and declining morals. It was the 'modern girl' who was seen as threatening the 'order, stability and community of a nation'.[150] As the writer of an article for the GFS magazine, the *Irish Leaflet*, explained in 1924, 'to be "modern" and indulge in those things often considered "smart" may not in itself actually be wrong, or prompted by any deeper feeling than that of youthful effervescence', but it nonetheless 'denoted a wrong idea of the values of life'.[151] The article went on to suggest that:

> anything that does not tend to beautify life is superfluous, and anything that may become injurious to a girl's modesty is not only risky, but wrong. Modesty is the sister of Virtue, and these are a girl's dearest possessions . . . Never by word or deed, should a girl weaken men's respect for the ideal of womanhood. This is a duty she owes to herself first and afterwards to every

other woman in the world. Let us as Irish women, keep on high the banner of pure and noble womanhood.[152]

The theme of modernity, and female responses to it, was also dealt with in a sermon by Revd John Waddell at the GA Communion Service during their 1926 Conference. He reflected on the changes that had taken place in the past few decades, particularly since 1914 and the outbreak of the First World War, and the new freedom women had achieved. He was anxious that the 'modern spirit of emancipation' would not degenerate into a 'disease of restlessness and sensationalism such as some girls seem to suffer from these new days'.[153] He reiterated the idea that while women may have extended the boundaries, they still needed to remain within certain limits to retain their true femininity and to exert this influence to the good.[154]

In 1923, the Catholic Bishop of Derry was also unequivocal in his condemnation of the 'modern' woman:

> for a girl to be called modern today is another way of saying she is pagan. She must use the dress of the pagan, disfigure her young face with the paint of barbarism and pretend to take delight in the dance of the savage! She must be prepared to take drink, even to excess, to flaunt her cigarette, and to stifle all the maidenly instincts of modesty. What a contrast this is to the Christian womanhood whose perfection was found in Mary, the Mother of God.[155]

The image and the role model for young women was Mary, the Mother of God. As Andrea Brozyna demonstrates, the image of Catholic womanhood bore a 'notable similarity to the construction of an ideal woman presented in Protestant literature'.[156] The image of the Virgin Mary, which is most often identified as a Catholic image, was also held up by the Protestants as how the ideal woman should behave.[157] While within the Protestant tradition it was felt that the Catholic 'cult of Mary' was blasphemous, they had, however, 'reclaimed' her as an important role model for women.[158] Speaking in 1926, Revd John Waddell explained that the 'ideal of womanhood – was the same as Mary - no doubt she was full of charm as every young girl should delight to be'. However, his concern was that when a girl recognised the charm she had and her power over men she should take care not to exploit this but to set a high standard of behaviour.[159]

Within this Christian ideal of womanhood, the role of wife and mother was most important. It was in this role that women were most effective as moral guardians for both men and their children. It was necessary to restate this high calling in the light of female emancipation in the interwar years as the 'modern girl' was seen by some to be a 'sign of gender upheaval and rebelliousness on the part of female youth'.[160] Revd Waddell explained that while he 'rejoiced' in the new emancipation gained by women, it needed to be recognised that a woman was 'fulfilling the highest ends of her being' when she was 'making her home beautiful and sacred for her husband and children'. He concluded that:

> in the eyes of the Master there is no nobler service, no grander career than that of home-making and . . . those who lightly abandon its privileges and its opponents are despising what God has blessed.[161]

Sex education

While there was much concern and discussion of the role of women as wives and mothers, the need to maintain female purity, and references to the need for moral education, there was a marked lack of activity in this area. Recent work on sex education in England, Wales and Scotland in the interwar and post Second World War period has identified the concerns about VD during the war as one of the main factors in encouraging official consideration about sex education.[162] As the debate emerged in the post-war period there were divisions between the medical establishment, education authorities and those with moral concerns over how any sex education policy should be implemented.[163] In Northern Ireland there were similar concerns during the Second World War about VD and the need for people to be educated about these issues.[164] However, right through the interwar period there was extreme reluctance to carry out education programmes or issue publicity or propaganda about VD prevention and treatment. Charles Thomson, the Medical Superintendent Officer of Health (MSOH) for Belfast, did, however, use his Annual Report in 1943 and 1944 to argue the importance of educating the young properly about the dangers of VD.[165] There had clearly been some discussion of sex education previously as in his 1944 report Thomson explained that 'sex-education in schools by visiting experts, as well as home teaching by parents has been mentioned, but that is as far as it has gone'.[166] He argued that 'VD will never be stopped: it might be reduced if we took children and young people into our confidence'. He believed that the elements of biology should be taught first and then later 'mothercraft' and human physiology and lastly the 'moral and pathological aspects of the subject'.[167]

The role of the Churches in the issue of sex education in Northern Ireland was of paramount importance. Following a discussion concerning VD propaganda in 1942, the Belfast Corporation Committee of Public Health directed the MSOH to request the heads of the several religious denominations to co-operate by enlightening the youth of the city in their care regarding the matter.[168] Charles Thomson subsequently wrote to the Moderator of the Presbyterian Church, the Methodist President, the Catholic Bishop of Down and Connor and the Church of Ireland Bishop of Down, Connor and Dromore, about the rise in the level of syphilis and informing them of the Committees request that the Churches should become involved in sex and health education.[169] Dr Mageean, the Catholic Bishop of Down and Connor, responded by agreeing with the need for some form of sex education but qualified this by explaining that he felt 'too much knowledge is both unnecessary and dangerous' and that he was opposed to 'any form of sex education which would have as its object to teach young people to safeguard themselves against the unfortunate consequences (i.e. pregnancy or VD) of acts that are morally wrong'.[170] He felt that education could only go so far in solving the problem and that the break up of family life had an important role to play as well.[171]

However, Charles Thomson in 1944 refuted the suggestion that 'the inculcation of high moral teaching on more intensive lines will stop the trouble'. He argued that:

> we have had generations of eminent preachers and the example of countless saintly lives, but we still get VD. Of course we must continue to spread the tenets of religion, but it is not enough. Trust the children, teach them, and don't cheat them out of the knowledge they are entitled to.[172]

There is no evidence that Thomson's ideas were ever put into practice in the following decades. Discussion of sex education, in keeping with other issues of sexuality, was extremely limited and contentious in Northern Ireland throughout the twentieth century.[173] This is no doubt a reflection of the traditional and conservative nature of society and the influence of both Protestant and Catholic Churches. In reference to sex education in contemporary Northern Ireland it has been argued that 'there is a culture of silence, conservatism and tradition in relation to sex and morality. These characteristics derive from the continuing power of the Churches in society'.[174] A segregated system of education has existed from the establishment of Northern Ireland with state-controlled Protestant schools and Catholic grant-maintained schools. Both Protestant and Catholic clergy and representatives play a major part in the operation of schools and education boards and the influence of the Churches has closely informed the sex education provided in schools.[175]

The lack of any comprehensive discussion or debate about sex education in Northern Irish schools was perhaps therefore unsurprising, given the segregated nature of schooling, the conservative nature of the society and the influence of the Churches. The issue of introducing subjects such as hygiene and physiology into the curriculum of schools was raised in the Maternity and Child Welfare Committee of the Belfast Corporation in August 1943.[176] It was resolved that the Education Committee would comment of the question generally and in particular why the subject of hygiene was not on the curriculum of Stranmillis Teacher Training College. There appears to have only been limited discussion in the Education Committee on these issues, clearly prompted by the 1943 advisory pamphlet on sex education issued by the English Board of Education. In May 1944 the Education Committee reported that the principal of Stranmillis Teacher Training College had pointed out that as they were working on a depleted staff due to the war, their syllabus was constrained, but that hopefully in the post-war period new syllabuses would be created. On the issue of sex education the Education Committee agreed that the training college syllabus and also the programme of instruction for public elementary schools were in need of revision and that possibly 'impending education reconstruction would bring this about'.[177] A new Education Act was introduced in 1947. However it contained no substantial discussion of sex education and it was not until 1987 that the aims and objectives of sex education were set out by the Northern Ireland Department of Education.[178]

Conclusion

The consensus of Protestant and Catholic voluntary organisations and church leaders concerning female sexuality and the need to both protect women from corrupting influences and also to protect society from dangerous women, are evident in the measures which were taken across this period. Fears that innocent young women would be tempted or forced into immoral activities were in evidence from the beginning of the century. Hostels, clubs and travellers' protection were all organised to guard and guide these innocents. However, warnings were also given about those who were less innocent and whose behaviour and dress was seen to endanger the whole moral fibre of society. Some women were regarded as unable to protect themselves, while at the same time others were able to cause the moral degeneration of society and were unfit to carry out their duties as wives and mothers. While it may be contended that the organisations involved in work with girls were attempting to regulate and police sexuality, it is equally apparent that in many ways they provided unique opportunities for women at the time.

As mentioned above, at a time where there were few state benefits, organisations such as the GFS or St Vincent's Home provided safe and affordable accommodation, holidays and care when ill. For young women outside the support of their families, the assistance and support that was given by voluntary organisations was invaluable. Working conditions in mills were harsh and days were long and monotonous, so clubs and societies provided a much-needed space for leisure and relaxation.

What was also apparent from the interviews carried out with women involved in girls' organisations in 1930s and 1940s was the consuming nature of their involvement and the passion and fondness with which they spoke of their respective organisations. While recognising the small size of the sample, all of those interviewed were positive about their experiences and felt that they had benefited from their time in these organisations. The friends they made were, for many of the women, friends for life and these enduring friendships were what they remembered most. What was also interesting was that several of those who were interviewed had never married and the organisations to which they had belonged as girls were like surrogate families. Their energies had been poured into them, they had remained as leaders and in those organisations which are still in existence, had retained an interest and involvement.[179]

What may also be argued is that in many ways girls' organisations provided a public forum, opportunities and freedoms, which these women might never have had otherwise. One lady, for example, recorded how she had been President of the GA in Ireland during the Second World War and had been able to travel all around Ireland visiting branches and giving talks, usually on her own. She met girls from all over the country and experienced a freedom of travel that would not ordinarily have been possible.[180] Experience of public speaking, administration, organisation and management were also gained. For those involved in, for example, Women Patrols, a taste of police work was given and it was the only way respectable women would experience being out at night in the city centre.

While such organisations and activities played a role in protecting and guiding women and in encouraging the development of high standards of morality and female behaviour, it is obviously impossible to quantify their success in this endeavour. Those who established and ran organisations and activities may have had lofty ideals, but it is difficult to know how aware those who participated and attended were of these beliefs. Similarly, it is questionable how much they conformed to the ideals or viewed themselves as in need of protection or whether they simply used the facilities and grasped the opportunities which were offered to them.

The class divisions in the provision of protection were clear, with different facilities and organisations providing for those from the middle class, respectable working class and the lower working-class. These divisions were further dissected by issues of perceived sexual behaviour and the risk of leading others astray. The contradictory picture emerges of the innocent naive girl who needed protection and the predatory sexual girl whom others needed to be protected from and who, in turn needed protecting from herself.

Notes

1 Luddy, *Women and Philanthropy*, p. 98.
2 Bartley, *Prostitution*, pp. 73–93.
3 See chapter 2.
4 Pamela Cox, *Gender, Justice and Welfare: Bad Girls in Britain, 1900–1950* (Basingstoke, 2003), p. 3.
5 Ibid., p. 4.
6 Official histories of the Girl Guides include Rose Kerr (ed. Alex Liddell), *The Story of the Girl Guides, 1908–1938* (London, 1976); Alix Liddell, *The Girl Guides, 1910–1970* (London, 1970).
7 Exceptions include, Proctor, *On My Honor*; Harrison, 'For Church, Queen and Family', 107–138.
8 Warren, '"Mothers for the Empire"?' in Mangan (ed.), *Making Imperial Mentalities*, pp. 96–109; Allen Warren, 'Citizens of the Empire: Baden-Powell, Scouts and Guides, an Imperial Ideal', in J. Mackenzie (ed.), *Imperialism and Popular Culture* (Manchester, 1986) pp. 232–257. On Guides and the First World War see for example, Voeltz, 'The Antidote to "Khaki Fever"?', 627–638.
9 Bartley, *Prostitution*, pp. 73–93; Dyhouse, *Girls Growing Up*, pp. 108–114.
10 *GFS Annual Reports 1900–1905*, Records of GFS, 1871–1977, MS 578/19/3, Representative Church Body Library (RCB).
11 Central Rules of GFS, 1900, Records of GFS, 1871–1977, MS 578/19/3, RCB.
12 Constitution of the GFS in Ireland, Records of GFS, Diocese of Down, Connor and Dromore, 1883–1965, D/3271/6/1, PRONI.

13 Dyhouse, *Girls Growing Up*, p. 109.
14 Constitution of the GFS in Ireland, Records of GFS, Diocese of Down, Connor and Dromore, 1883–1965, D/3271/6/1, PRONI.
15 Harrison, 'For Church, Queen and Family', 109, 115.
16 *Irish Leaflet*, September 1921.
17 *GFS Annual Reports 1900–1905*, MS 578/19/3, RCB.
18 Protestant Servants' Home Minute Books, 1910, Protestant Servants' Home, Records of GFS, 1871–1977, MS 578/12/2, RCB.
19 Harrison, 'For Church, Queen and Family', 125.
20 *GFS Annual Reports 1900–1905*, MS 578/19/3, RCB.
21 Interview, Mrs D., 27 February 2002 and Mrs F., 10 April 2002.
22 Alison McCaughan, '"Cherchez la Femme": Women in the Presbyterian Church in Ireland and in Society, 1840–1990', in R.F.G. Holmes and R. Buick Knox (eds) *The General Assembly of the Presbyterian Church in Ireland, 1840–1990: A Celebration of Irish Witness During a Century and a Half* (Belfast, 1990), p. 120.
23 Ibid.
24 Girls' Auxiliary Conference, *Witness*, 26 November 1923.
25 Records of GA, 1911–1945, PHS.
26 Kerr, *Story of the Girl Guides*, p. 13.
27 John Springhall, 'The Boy Scouts, Class and Militarism in Relation to British Youth Movements, 1908–1930', *International Review of Social History*, 16 (1971), 125–158; John Springhall, Anne Summers and Allen Warren, Debate: 'Baden-Powell and the Scout Movement Before 1920: Citizen Training or Soldiers for the Future?', *English Historical Review*, 102 (1987), 934–950.
28 Warren, '"Mothers for the Empire"?', p. 97.
29 Ibid., pp. 103–105.
30 Voeltz, 'The Antidote to "Khaki Fever"?', 633.
31 Woollacott, '"Khaki Fever"', 332.
32 Voeltz, 'The Antidote to "Khaki Fever"?', 635.
33 Proctor, *On My Honour*, p. 71.
34 Interview, Mrs F., 10 April 2002 and Mrs J., 25 April 2002.
35 Proctor, *On My Honour*, p. 24.
36 Minute Book, Belfast Guides, 25/3/1931, Records of Girl Guides, Province of Ulster, 1920–1975, D/3875/1/7/1, PRONI.
37 Proctor, *On My Honour*, p. 25.
38 Dyhouse, *Girls Growing Up*, p. 113.
39 Neil, 'Women at Work in Ulster', p. 267.
40 Dyhouse, *Girls Growing Up*, p. 113; Cox, *Gender, Justice and Welfare*, p. 3.
41 Dyhouse, *Girls Growing Up*, pp. 106–107.
42 Annual Meeting Down and Connor and Dromore Diocesan Lodge, 1900, Down and Connor and Dromore GFS Diocesan Lodge Council Minutes, D/3271/1/2, PRONI.

43 The *Irish Citizen* was a suffrage paper published weekly between 1912 and 1916 and then monthly until 1920. It was designed to cater for both militant and non-militant suffragists throughout the whole of the thirty-two counties.
44 *Irish Citizen*, 13 July 1912, p. 59.
45 *Witness*, 26 October 1917, p. 2.
46 See chapter 3.
47 *Witness*, 10 June 1932, p. 3.
48 Annual Meeting Down and Connor and Dromore Diocesan Lodge, 1900, Down and Connor and Dromore GFS Diocesan Lodge Council Minutes, D/3271/1/2, PRONI.
49 Ibid.
50 Ibid.
51 Census of Ireland, 1911.
52 Judy Giles, '"Playing Hard to Get": Working-Class Women, Sexuality and Respectability in Britain, 1918–1940', *Women's History Review*, 1 (1992), 242.
53 Ibid., 243.
54 Annual Meeting Down and Connor and Dromore Diocesan Lodge, 1898, Down and Connor and Dromore GFS Diocesan Lodge Council Minutes, D/3271/1/2, PRONI.
55 Returns for GFS Lodge, 28 Donegall Pass, Belfast, 1911 Census of Ireland.
56 GFS Annual Meeting Diocesan Lodge, *Northern Whig*, 13 March 1913, p. 10.
57 See chapter 2.
58 Annual Meeting Down and Connor and Dromore Diocesan Lodge, 1900, Down and Connor and Dromore GFS Diocesan Lodge Council Minutes, D/3271/1/2, PRONI.
59 *Report of the Committee on Social Service*, 11 June 1909, Minutes of General Assembly of Presbyterian Church.
60 Annual Meeting Down and Connor and Dromore Diocesan Lodge, 18 March 1903, Down and Connor and Dromore GFS Diocesan Lodge Council Minutes, D/3271/1/2, PRONI.
61 Bartley, *Prostitution*, p. 81; Annual Meeting Down and Connor and Dromore Diocesan Lodge, 18 March 1903, Down and Connor and Dromore GFS Diocesan Lodge Council Minutes, D/3271/1/2, PRONI.
62 Annual Meeting Down and Connor and Dromore Diocesan Lodge, 1900, Down and Connor and Dromore GFS Diocesan Lodge Council Minutes, D/3271/1/2, PRONI.
63 Ibid.
64 *Irish Catholic Directory and Almanac*, 1902; I am grateful to Father P. O'Donnell of Clonard Monastery for providing me with information about St Vincent's Home.

65 *Irish Catholic Directory*, 1916.
66 Ibid.
67 Sancta Maria continued operating as a girls' home into the twenty-first century; Regina Coeli became a hostel for homeless women in 1960 and still operates in this capacity today; Mater Dei operated as a mother and baby home until the late 1990s.
68 Information provided by Father P. O'Donnell.
69 Collins, *Modern Love*, p. 63.
70 Circular letter from leaders of Belfast Girls' Club Union, 22 April 1939, Records of Belfast Girls' Club Union, ED/15/5, PRONI.
71 *Northern Whig*, 17 January 1930; newspaper Cuttings concerning the Alpha Club, Records of Alpha Club, 1929–1962, D/1505/4/1, PRONI.
72 Collins, *Modern Love*, pp. 68–75.
73 Annual Report Belfast Girls' Club Union 1943, Records of Belfast Girls' Club Union, ED/15/5, PRONI.
74 Penny Tinkler, 'Cause for Concern: Young Women and Leisure, 1930–50', *Women's History Review*, 12:2 (2003), 247–251.
75 Annual Report Belfast Girls' Club Union 1943, Records of Belfast Girls' Club Union, ED/15/5, PRONI.
76 Annual Report Belfast Girls' Club Union 1944, Records of Belfast Girls' Club Union, ED/15/5, PRONI.
77 Annual Report Belfast Girls' Club Union 1947, Records of Belfast Girls' Club Union, ED/15/5, PRONI.
78 Legion Adoption Society, Mater Dei Hostel, Historical Background Leaflet (n.d.).
79 *Irish Catholic Directory*, 1922, 1932, 1934, 1940.
80 For more on the White Slave Trade and the campaign to increase the age of sexual consent see, for example, Bartley, *Prostitution*; Lucy Bland, *Banishing the Beast: English Feminism and Sexual Morality, 1885–1914* (London, 1995); Edward Bristow, *Vice and Vigilance: Purity Movements in Britain Since 1700* (Dublin, 1977); Mort, *Dangerous Sexualities*.
81 Bartley, *Prostitution*, p. 170.
82 Ibid., p. 172.
83 Bristow, *Vice and Vigilance*, p. 175.
84 Ibid., p. 189.
85 GFS Annual Meeting Diocesan Lodge, *Northern Whig*, 13 March 1913, p. 10.
86 Ibid.
87 *Northern Whig*, 15 March 1913, p. 11.
88 Ibid.
89 Committee Minutes of Edgar Home, 1913.
90 Mort, *Dangerous Sexualities*, p. 148.
91 Frank Mort, 'Purity, Feminism and the State: Sexuality and Moral Politics,

1880–1914', in Langan and Schwartz (eds), *Crises in the British State, 1880–1914*, p. 221.

92 Louise Ryan, 'Traditions and Double Moral Standards: The Irish Suffragists' Critique of Nationalism', *Women's History Review*, 4 (1995), 498.

93 Cliona Murphy, 'The Religious Context of the Women's Suffrage Campaign in Ireland', *Women's History Review*, 6 (1997), 560.

94 *Northern Whig*, 11 March 1912, p. 5.

95 Ibid.

96 *Irish Citizen*, 26 October 1912, p. 182.

97 Ibid.

98 Ibid., 1 March 1913, p. 1.

99 *Irish Citizen*, 7 September 1912, 2 November 1912, 28 December 1912, 1 March 1913, 19 July 1913.

100 Ibid., 2 November 1912, p. 186.

101 Ibid.

102 Summerfield, 'Women and War in the Twentieth Century', p. 315.

103 Boyle, 'Women and Crime in Belfast', p. 59.

104 Collins, 'The Edwardian City', p. 128.

105 Claire Culleton, *Working-Class Culture, Women and Britain, 1914–1921* (Basingstoke, 2000), pp. 69–70.

106 Deborah Thom, *Nice Girls and Rude Girls: Women Workers in World War I* (London, 1998), p. 20.

107 Lousie Jackson, *Women Police: Gender, Welfare and Surveillance in the Twentieth Century* (Manchester, 2006), p. 18.

108 For more on the establishment of Women Patrols and Women Police and the conflicts between organisations see, Levine, '"Walking the Streets"'; Bland, 'In the Name of Protection'.

109 *Irish Citizen*, 13 February 1915, p. 299.

110 Ibid.

111 *Belfast Telegraph*, 20 October 1918, p. 5.

112 Woollacott, '"Khaki Fever"', 337.

113 Ibid., 338.

114 Margaret Higonnet and Patrice Higonnet, 'The Double Helix', in M. Higonnet *et al.* (eds), *Behind the Lines: Gender and the Two World Wars* (New Haven and London 1987), pp. 33–36.

115 Jackson, *Women Police*, pp. 18–19.

116 Ibid., p. 23.

117 *Belfast Telegraph*, 26 October 1918, p. 5.

118 Jackson, *Women Police*, p. 21.

119 Levine, '"Walking the Streets"', 42.

120 Jackson, *Women Police*, p. 172.

121 Levine, '"Walking the Streets"', 56.

122 *Belfast Telegraph*, 26 October 1918, p. 5; Bland, 'In the Name of Protection', p. 40.

123 *Witness*, 15 November 1918, p. 2.

124 *Belfast Telegraph*, 26 October 1918, p. 5.

125 Ibid.

126 *Belfast Telegraph*, 26 October 1918, p. 5.

127 Women Patrols were re-introduced in Belfast in 1943, following similar concerns about the behaviour of young women on the streets of the city centre.

128 Woollacott, '"Khaki Fever"', 340; *Belfast Telegraph*, 26 October 1918, p. 5.

129 Bland, 'In the Name of Protection', p. 46.

130 Culleton, *Working-Class Culture*, pp. 135–148.

131 Woollacott, '"Khaki Fever"', 326.

132 Ibid., 342.

133 George A. Armstrong, 'After the War – What?', *Irish Presbyterian*, 23 (April 1917), 3.

134 Lucy Bland, '"Guardians of the Race" or "Vampires Upon the Nation's Health"? Female Sexuality and its Regulation in Early Twentieth-Century Britain', in E. Whitelegg et al. (eds), *The Changing Experience of Women in Early Twentieth-Century Britain* (Oxford, 1982), p. 375.

135 For more on young women and leisure in the interwar period, see Selina Todd, 'Young Women, Work and Leisure in Interwar England', *The Historical Journal*, 48:3 (2005), 789–809; Tinkler, 'Cause for Concern', 233–260; Claire Langhamer, 'Leisure, Pleasure, and Courtship: Young Women in England, 1920–1960', in M. Maynes, B. Søland and C. Benninghaus (eds), *Secret Gardens, Satanic Mills: Placing Girls in European History, 1750–1960* (Indiana, 2005), pp. 269–284.

136 Annual Meeting of the Edgar Home, 1921.

137 Francis McKee, 'Ice Cream and Immorality', in Harlan Walker (ed.), *Public Eating: Proceedings of the Oxford Symposium on Food and Cookery* (Oxford, 1991), p. 204.

138 Ibid.

139 Annual Meeting of the Edgar Home, 1921.

140 Sarah J. Smith, *Children, Cinema and Censorship: From Dracula to the Dead End Kids* (London, 2005), p. 56.

141 The Irish Free State appointed a full-time film censor in 1923. For more on this and other aspects of censorship see, for example, Peter Martin, *Censorship in the Two Irelands, 1922–1939* (Dublin, 2006).

142 Lenten Pastorals, 1924, *Irish Catholic Directory*, 1924.

143 For more on the issue of female appearance and acceptable behaviour in the Irish Free State, see Caitriona Beaumont, 'Women, Citizenship and Catholicism in the Irish Free State, 1922–1948', *Women's History Review*, 6:4 (1997) 563–585.

144 *Irish Catholic Directory*, 1920, p. 501.

145 *Derry Journal*, 25 April 1920, p. 5.

146 Ibid.

147 *Irish Catholic Directory*, 1928, p. 488.
148 Ibid.
149 *Irish Presbyterian*, March 1920.
150 Louise Ryan, *Gender, Identity and the Irish Press, 1922–37: Embodying the Nation,* (New York, 2002), p. 53.
151 *Irish Leaflet*, February 1924.
152 Ibid.
153 Revd John Waddell, Communion Service, GA Annual Conference, 1926, Records of GA, PHS.
154 Ibid.
155 *Derry Journal*, 27 April 1923, p. 3.
156 Andrea Brozyna, *Labour, Love and Prayer: Female Piety in Ulster Religious Literature, 1850–1914* (Belfast, 1999), p. 15.
157 Ibid., p. 54.
158 Ibid., p. 55.
159 Revd John Waddell, Communion Service, GA Annual Conference, 1926.
160 Pamela Cox, 'Girls in Trouble: Defining Female Delinquency in Britain, 1900–1950', in Maynes, Søland and Benninghaus (eds), *Secret Gardens, Satanic Mills*, p. 192.
161 Ibid.
162 See for example, James Hampshire, 'The Politics of School Sex Education Policy in England and Wales from the 1940s to the 1960s', *Social History of Medicine*, 18:1 (2005), 87–105; Jane Pilcher, 'School Sex Education: Policy and Practice in England 1870 to 2000', *Sex Education*, 5 (2005), 153–170; Roger Davidson and Gayle Davis, '"This Thorniest of Problems": School Sex Education Policy in Scotland, 1939–1980', *The Scottish Historical Review*, 84:2 (2005), 221–246.
163 Hampshire, 'The Politics of School Sex Education Policy', 87–88.
164 See chapter 4.
165 MSOH for Belfast, *Annual Report of Health*, 1943, LA/7/9DA/28, PRONI.
166 Ibid.
167 Ibid.
168 Public Health Committee Minutes, Belfast Corporation, 8/9/1942, LA/7/9AA/20, PRONI.
169 Charles Thomson to Heads of Churches, 15 September 1942, LA/7/9BB/21, PRONI.
170 Rt Revd Dr Mageean to Dr Charles Thomson, 8 October 1942, LA/7/9BB/21, PRONI.
171 Ibid. For more on the issue of sex education see chapter 3.
172 MSOH for Belfast, *Annual Report of Health*, 1944, LA/7/9DA/28, PRONI.
173 Bill Rolston, Dirk Schubotz and Audrey Simpson, 'Sex Education in Northern Ireland Schools: a Critical Evaluation', *Sex Education*, 5 (2005), 218.
174 Ibid. 227.

175 Ibid. 230–231.
176 Belfast Corporation Maternity and Child Welfare Committee, 20 August 1943, LA/7/9AD/3, PRONI.
177 Belfast Corporation, Education Committee Minutes, 5 May 1944, LA/7/7/AB/10, PRONI.
178 Department of Education, Northern Ireland (1987) Circular No. 45; for more on the issue of sex education in contemporary Northern Ireland, see Audrey Simpson, 'A Sociological Analysis of the Theory and Practice of Sex Education in Post-Primary Schools in Northern Ireland' (unpublished PhD thesis, University of Ulster, 2001).
179 Interview, Mrs D., 27 February 2002.
180 Ibid.

4

'People should keep a grip of themselves': treatment and prevention of VD

The previous chapters have discussed some of the ways in which female sexuality was regulated in Northern Ireland and the importance female sexual purity had for society at large. The identification and labelling of women as immoral, dangerous and in need of control has also been discussed, as have some of the organisations which attempted to prevent such 'falls into sin'. This chapter focuses on venereal disease, considering the establishment of VD clinics in Northern Ireland from 1917 and the debates and discourses which emerged in the interwar and Second World War period surrounding VD treatment and prevention. From within these discourses there emerge several groups who were targeted as being at greatest risk of spreading or contracting VD. These include prostitutes, sexually active working-class women and soldiers.

The targeting of women as sources of venereal infection and discrimination upon which VD legislation was based has been an important area of historiographical discussion.[1] It has been argued that women who did not conform to accepted standards of sexual behaviour were regarded as responsible for the spread of disease and this was reflected in legislation that attempted to control the sexuality of working-class women. It is evident that even when legislation was gender-neutral, women were still largely the focus of the action taken, as was the case in other European countries including Norway, Sweden and Germany.[2] It has, however, become clear that a straightforward patriarchal view of society is unsatisfactory and that gender is also dissected by other factors, such as class and age, which influenced both policies and attitudes.[3]

Discussion of VD in a historical capacity has also often focused on the decisions made at central government level and the legislation enacted to deal with VD during both world wars.[4] However, research on various responses to VD at local and regional levels has demonstrated the importance of specific political, social, religious and cultural settings.[5] As will be contended below, the impact and implementation of legislation in Northern Ireland was influenced by a variety of political, religious and social factors.

Establishment of a VD treatment service

The first official attempt in the twentieth century to consider the problem of venereal disease, its prevalence, prevention and treatment, took the form of the Royal Commission on Venereal Diseases (RCVD) which was set up in 1913. The Commission was made up of representatives from politics, the legal and medical professions and the Churches. It heard evidence from various experts from across Great Britain in the three years that it met, before preparing a report of its findings in 1916. Overshadowing the work of the Commission was the experience of the Contagious Diseases Acts of the 1860s and the repeal campaign that followed. The Acts, which operated in certain port and garrison towns in England and Ireland, forced women suspected of having VD to submit to a medical examination. If they were infected they were kept in 'Lock Hospitals' to be treated. A repeal campaign was organized in 1869 and generated a huge amour of public support, particularly from women, and the Acts were repealed in 1886. Thus decision-making was affected by the awareness that legislation risked provoking these concerns.[6]

Dr Brian O'Brien, Medical Inspector to the Local Government Board for Ireland, appeared before the RCVD in 1913 and was charged with explaining the situation regarding the treatment of VD in Ireland. He explained that there was no Lock Hospital in Belfast and in the Royal Victoria Hospital (RVH) in Belfast, it was 'against the rules' to admit patients suffering from VD. He countered this by suggesting that 'this rule had not been observed of late and a certain number of cases have been taken in, though not freely'.[7] The hospital argued that they did not have the funds and Dr O'Brien claimed he knew 'they [did] not have the beds'. He was of the opinion that hospital subscribers and staff would be very reluctant to refuse admission to general patients in favour of venereal ones. However, when questioned about the availability of treatment for VD in Ireland, he claimed that venereal diseases were regarded in the same way as other diseases in Ireland and that any poor person was entitled to and could expect treatment for their diseases.[8] For those 'poor people' in Belfast, this was to be found at the Union Infirmary in Lock Ward 26 for women and Ward 6 for men.

While the Irish representatives to the RCVD were at pains to suggest that VD was virtually unknown in rural Ireland, the death rate from syphilis for Dublin was an issue of concern for the Commission. The death rate per 10,000 was 0.76 for London and 0.51 for Belfast, whereas the death rate for Dublin was 1.4. It was argued, by the Irish representatives, that the high rate was not a reflection of immorality in Dublin but rather to do with the fact that it was a seaport, had a large military station, and an asylum which admitted patients not only from Dublin but also the surrounding counties. Dr O'Brien also argued that poverty and bad housing were additional factors as 'tenements lend towards immorality'.[9]

Although the death rate for VD in Dublin was worryingly high, it was also contended by those giving evidence that there was very little VD among the rural population of Ireland and that immorality was restricted to the large towns. It was suggested that the morality of the rural classes in Ireland was largely due to the influence of the Catholic priesthood. The anomaly in this record of a high standard of morality was the high illegitimacy rate for Ulster, which at 3.5 per 100 was considerably higher than that of the rest of Ireland. When questioned about this, Dr O'Brien suggested that it was partly due to the fact that Ulster was a manufacturing centre that attracted inward migration, particularly of young women, to work in the textile industry, and was the only province where women outnumbered men.[10] Canon Horsley however, felt that the higher illegitimacy rate reflected the influence of the 'Scottish element' in Ulster, referring to the high illegitimacy rates in Scotland of 7.1 per 100 in 1911.[11]

The overwhelming impression from the evidence given was that it was believed that Ireland was a country of high morals and low VD rates and that the immorality that did exist was restricted to a particular class within towns. This view of Ireland as a particularly moral country, and the reluctance to discuss the issue of VD openly, was criticised in the *Irish Citizen* in 1914. Discussing the evidence presented to the Commission from Ireland and the high VD death rate in Dublin, it stated:

> Dublin has attained an evil pre-eminence. We trust we shall hear no more of the suggestion that venereal disease is a subject not to be spoken about or written about in Ireland.[12]

With the absence of reliable figures for those suffering from VD the Commission estimated that 10 per cent of the urban population across Britain and Ireland was infected with syphilis, and that the number suffering from gonorrhoea was probably higher.[13] The Committee decided that it was necessary for the state to intervene and that the existing facilities for diagnosis and treatment were inadequate.[14] It was recommended that treatment centres should be set up and organised by county and borough councils, that laboratory facilities for carrying out Wassermann tests should be improved, and that Salvarsan or its equivalent should be provided free.[15] Seventy-five per cent of the cost was to be met by central government and the remainder from local rates.[16] The Commission avoided any discussion of the prevention of VD other than moral instruction and medical treatment. They did not discuss the use of condoms or prophylactic packets – chemical disinfecting before or immediately after sex. This reflects the moral dilemma faced by the Commission, that 'any instruction on how to avoid disease was tantamount to encouraging sex with unknown partners'.[17]

In July 1916, the Local Government Board (LGB) of Great Britain issued regulations which required councils to submit proposals for treatment schemes. The regulations took on board the recommendations of the Commission and went even further in compelling councils to establish treatment services.[18] In Ireland this took the form of the *Scheme for the Treatment of Venereal Disease under the Regulations (Ireland –County Boroughs) 1917.*

The establishing of clinics relied on co-operation between local authorities and voluntary hospitals. This was to prove a problematic relationship in the North of Ireland, as in the rest of Great Britain.[19] As the evidence given to the RCVD concerning the RVH suggests, there already existed a reluctance to treat venereal patients and this reluctance extended across the country as attempts were made to implement schemes to treat VD.

While the government in London may have decided on a voluntarist approach to the treatment of VD, county councils in the North of Ireland were unhappy with the decisions taken. The councils were required to submit proposals for treatment schemes for VD to the Local Government Board (LGB) of Ireland. In the County councils of Armagh, Antrim, Down, Fermanagh, Londonderry and Tyrone there was resistance to the establishment of treatment centres for VD. By February 1919 schemes were only operating in Armagh, Antrim and the County Borough of Belfast.[20] Although the regulations had been issued in October 1917, even in Belfast the process was a slow one with Dr Bailie the Belfast MSOH, assuring the Ulster Branch of the National Council for Combating Venereal Disease (NCCVD) in May 1918 that 'the Scheme had been drawn up and that he was only waiting its adoption by the local hospitals in order to submit it to the LGB'.[21] The other county councils had either refused to adopt the legislation or had simply ignored it. In Fermanagh a scheme was adopted in February 1919 but was not approved by the LGB as they felt the council had made no attempt to make any facilities available in the county.[22] Patients had to travel to Belfast to be treated, and in 1920 Belfast Corporation made a claim to the LGB concerning payment by Fermanagh County Council of expenses incurred in the treatment of VD patients from Fermanagh at the RVH.[23] It was decided that, as there was no scheme implemented in Fermanagh, patients from there would be counted under the Belfast scheme.[24] It was not until 1923, when the LGB in Ireland had ceased to exist and the responsibility for implementation of public health regulations had been taken over by the new Ministry of Home Affairs, that pressure was renewed on Fermanagh County Council to adopt a scheme. Even then, the approach from the Ministry was conciliatory rather than confrontational, 'suggesting the Council should formulate a scheme, however tentative'.[25]

The problems are illustrated most fully by the attitude of Londonderry County Council. The Minutes of the County Londonderry VD Committee contain only two entries – firstly, in April 1918 when it was decided that it was:

> inadvisable for the Public Health Scheme for the treatment of VD to be adopted until it was first placed before the medical profession of the effected area for consideration and discussion.[26]

The second entry was just over a year later when it was decided to adjourn the committee until a detailed statement of accounts was presented or until Dr Stephenson, the Medical Inspector of the LGB in Ireland, was present.[27] None of these events must have swayed the council as they declared in June 1919 that the 'authorities of the County and County Borough Infirmary Londonderry are not prepared to undertake the treatment of VD in that institution'.[28] The treatment centres were fixed as being the Union Infirmary in Coleraine and the RVH and Mater in Belfast. The situation in Londonderry County and County Borough was the most extreme of all the Northern Irish counties, and no scheme was implemented until 1943 when the war emergency forced the government to demand that treatment centres be established. However, it still took several years of discussions over finance, staffing and location before centres were established throughout the county and county borough.[29] The opposition raised against the treatment of VD in Londonderry may have been encouraged by the vocal opposition to the scheme by the Catholic Bishop of Derry, Revd Dr McHugh, in 1917, who also opposed any publicity being carried out in his diocese.[30]

For many, particularly in rural Northern Ireland, VD was believed

to be relatively unknown in their area. As one Co. Tyrone councillor
stated, 'it [VD] is a disease almost unknown in this country, and here we
are being asked to take it over as something of a general and common
experience'.[31] Similarly, the minutes of Armagh County Council reported
that 'the number of cases which have been reported is not so far great
enough to cause the slightest alarm'.[32] It fell to medical representatives
on councils, such as Dr Thomson in Co. Tyrone, to present the view that
VD was more prevalent than commonly assumed and that those who
had VD needed to be treated locally. Dr Thomson argued that 'hospitals
are intended to treat people no matter what disease they are suffering'. In
response the Council Chairman, a Catholic priest, questioned the need to
bring those suffering from VD in among innocent people, to which Dr
Thomson responded that:

> they are not so innocent as you think, though Irish people, compared with
> others, are much more moral as a rule. There is a great deal of this disease
> that you know nothing about, but I do.[33]

For a number of councillors the treatment of VD on a voluntary basis
in their local hospital was unacceptable: while the decision had been taken
to treat VD on a voluntary basis, from the outset this met with resistance
from some. As one Tyrone Council member explained, VD should not
be treated at a county hospital, but rather at a central location, 'it should
be dealt with as all diseases of a dangerous character are, by isolation
and centralisation, and not by distribution all over the country'.[34] The
suggestion of isolation was furthered by another council member, who
suggested the government should purchase a plot of land, 'somewhere in
West Africa and these lepers should be deported and treated there'.[35]

Tyrone Council members finally accepted that they would have to
provide a new scheme for the treatment of VD, having rejected previous
ones in December 1918 and April 1919. The acceptance was more to do
with the inevitability of the legislation rather than any enthusiasm for the
scheme. The Council Minutes record that:

> while admitting that at present, VD in all its active forms is practically non-
> existent in our County, yet we have come to the conclusion that it is always
> well to be forearmed against a possibility which is now looming large in the
> eyes of experts.[36]

There were further attempts to discontinue the scheme when it came
up for annual renewal but these were defeated, usually by only a small
majority.[37]

This debate reflects wider issues concerning VD. There was ignorance about the diseases, and their causes, symptoms and results. For example, there was an unwillingness to allow those suffering from VD to travel to hospital on public transport for fear of contamination.[38] County councils felt that these proposals had been forced upon them. They did not feel involved in decision-making and were unhappy about the decisions made by the government to treat the disease. The demand for a more interventionist approach and compulsory notification and treatment of VD reflected not only a belief that only a small number of people actually had VD, and that it would be a simple matter to isolate them and wipe out the disease, but also that treatment should be carried out by others, elsewhere. County councils did not want to have to deal with something which they believed did not impact on their rural communities and that, if found anywhere, it would be in an urban environment such as Belfast. The proposals, it was felt, were an implied slur on the moral standards of communities and, by setting up treatment centres, immoral behaviour was being condoned.

Given the other more pressing issues on the Northern Ireland government in the early 1920s, it is perhaps unsurprising that county councils were not forced into implementing the treatment schemes. Another factor in this situation was partition itself, and its impact on health provision. The LGB in Ireland ceased to exist in its original state with the Department of Local Government and Public Health being established in the Irish Free State, and the Ministry of Home Affairs assuming responsibility for health in Northern Ireland. This disruption undoubtedly contributed to the ability of councils to ignore legislation or to procrastinate about its implementation. Luddy has described a similar situation in the Irish Free State in the 1920s with a 'considerable apathy' shown to the implementation of the treatment scheme and a lack of interest in the issues from the medical profession.[39]

There were of course some treatment centres established, and by 1922 treatment clinics were advertised as operational in Belfast and across the country in Armagh, Ballymena, Downpatrick, Kilkeel, Newtownards, Dungannon, Lurgan, Newry and Lisburn. Most of these clinics operated separate clinics for men and women and advertised specific times for irrigation treatment for gonorrhoea.[40] The Board of Guardians of the Belfast Union also co-operated as part of the Venereal Disease Treatment Scheme and subsequently changed its practices in line with the scheme.[41] Dr McLeish, the visiting Medical Officer at Belfast Union, came before the Board of Guardians committee to explain that, in order to comply with the provisions of the VD scheme, the wards in the Union Infirmary allocated for patients suffering from these 'special diseases' should no longer be considered 'Lock' wards. He went on to explain that the wards should be 'open in every respect in a similar manner to the other Infirmary wards, as it is desired to encourage patients suffering from VD to obtain special treatment and that they should be able to receive some in the most confidential manner'. It was recommended that the Wards in future should be known simply as 'Men's Ward Number 6' and 'Women's Ward Number 26'.[42] It was also recommended that consideration be given to the removal of the restriction of visitors to these wards.

In the RVH, the new clinic was established in the King Edward Building under Dr John Rankin in 1919.[43] In the first year there were 578 new cases for treatment, which Richard Clarke argues were mainly ex-servicemen, with a total attendance of 3,277.[44] The laboratory carried out fifty to sixty Wassermann tests for syphilis weekly.[45] The clinic was accessed from an outside door on the Grosvenor Road to ensure 'invisibility of the patients and to keep them separate'.[46] The desire to minimise the social stigma attached to the diseases was an important concern in the design of treatment centres.[47] Dr Rankin writing in 1932 described how men and women had 'widely separated entrances' to the clinic and that as there were always 'a sprinkling of non-venereal patients who receive injections for various infections nobody can know that a case is venereal because he is in a particular room'.[48] He went on to stress the importance of attracting patients and retaining them until they were cured 'as many are afraid that if they are recognised they might be stigmatised or lose employment'.[49] A similar concern had been raised a number of years earlier by Dr Murphy from Lisburn who explained how they had workmen carrying out renovations on the hospital and this prevented some people coming in as they were embarrassed and afraid that they would be seen.[50]

Difficulties and debates

As discussed above, those county councils who did not implement their own treatment schemes sent patients to be treated in Belfast. This arrangement did not always run smoothly and was an issue of much concern for the Belfast Corporation. This was similar to the situation faced by the authorities in urban centres in Scotland, who feared an influx of patients from rural areas.[51] The Belfast Corporation received appeals from Counties Antrim, Fermanagh, Londonderry and Tyrone to arrange treatment of patients from these areas, and agreed terms on which to do so.[52] However, receiving payment for this treatment was not always easy, as a deputation from the Corporation and the MSOH explained to the Assistant Secretary for Home Affairs in December 1922.[53] The issue was clearly not resolved, as in 1926 the Minutes of the Belfast Corporation Public Health Committee recorded a submission from the Corporation to the Ministry of Home Affairs and Department Commission on Local Government Administration. It demanded that county councils who denied their liability and refused to pay for treatment of people from their area, be forced to do so.[54] That suspicion over claims from both parties existed was illustrated when the Executive Sanitary Officer from Londonderry requested a list of the patients from Londonderry who were being treated in Belfast, to be sent in confidence to the MSOH so that he could check that the account could be vouched for.[55]

In Northern Ireland the conflict that arose between the local authorities and the hospitals was largely over financial matters and the money available to pay staff and fund treatment.[56] The payment of those working in VD clinics generated much discussion and disagreements arose between the RVH and Mater hospitals and Belfast Corporation. From the establishment of the clinics in 1919, Staff Minutes from the RVH record that it was unanimously agreed that the salary suggested for the medical officer responsible for the treatment was inadequate, and that the sum of not less than £250 per annum, subject to annual revision, be requested.[57] It is not clear from the Corporation Minutes whether they agreed to this salary or not, but a request from the RVH for increased investment is recorded again in 1921, suggesting that the Corporation had not previously been forthcoming in their payments.[58] At the same meeting, Dr McSporley and Dr McSparran from the Mater hospital also applied for increased funding. They requested that the payment of medical officers in the treatment centre be fixed at the same level as the RVH, which suggests that there was some discrepancy in the amounts paid to different hospitals.[59]

The Corporation appeared to be attempting to cut the costs of VD treatment wherever possible. It was suggested that a charge should be made to practitioners for the drugs used to treat VD, which were supplied free of cost. However, when the MSOH approached the Ministry of Home Affairs about this, he was instructed that the drugs had to remain free under the regulation made by the LGB in 1917.[60]

The unwillingness of the corporation to increase payments, and their apparent frugality, were part of wider financial difficulties faced by the Stormont government. It was financially strapped and the amount of money available for spending in areas such as health and social services had remained virtually unchanged from 1922 to 1944.[61] This resulted in the failure of these services to develop at a similar rate to the rest of the United Kingdom.[62] As Greta Jones has shown, tuberculosis services were similarly restricted in the interwar period in Northern Ireland due to financial difficulties and the reluctance of local authorities to increase their financial commitments.[63] It is clear that if TB treatment was restricted due to financial difficulties, the treatment of VD, which was often regarded as a moral rather than a medical condition, was not going to be first on the list for financial consideration. The combination of financial constraints and the moral conservatism of society were contributing factors in the reluctance of the authorities to advertise treatment centres or to publish information on the causes and consequences of VD.

Publicity and propaganda

The role of publicity and propaganda concerning the dangers of VD in Britain was given to the National Council for Combating Venereal Diseases (NCCVD) which included several members of the RCVD and followed the view of the commission on the issue of VD prevention.[64] The stance taken by the NCCVD was influenced by the views of its members and also fears of a public outcry founded on arguments similar to those directed at the Contagious Diseases Acts (CD Acts), that women were targeted by regulationary controls and that prophylaxis condoned the double standard.[65]

A branch of the NCCVD was formed in Belfast in January 1917 and supported by both the Church of Ireland and the Presbyterian Church.[66] Their first efforts at educational work involved inviting a Mrs Kingsley Tarpley from the London NCCVD over to engage in propaganda work for six weeks.[67] The cost of this work was estimated at £50, and donations of £5 were requested from the members to cover the cost.[68] In her six weeks' work, Mrs Kinglsey Tarpley addressed 20 meetings including the GFS, Women's Patrols, working men, social workers, the Conference of Protestant Clergy, teachers and the Belfast Chamber of Commerce. Other members of the committee also addressed meetings at Ballykinler and Randalstown military camps and the Women's Royal Naval Service (WRNS) in Kingstown, Larne and Buncrana.[69]

However, even though the Ulster NCCVD appeared to have made an early start in terms of propaganda, by 1919 their efforts had not been embraced by the authorities. The general secretary of the NCCVD, in

London, Mrs Neville-Rolfe, wrote to Dr Bailie, the MSOH for Belfast, in May 1919 to explain that a branch of the NCCVD had been in existence for the past two years in Belfast and suggesting that the Health Committee might adopt the branch as their propaganda agent for Belfast.[70] The letter went on to explain that the LGB regulations allowed the acceptance of such a decision and would sanction payments for these educational activities, if the Health Committee approved.[71] In his reply Dr Bailie reported how he had approached the Committee and had been instructed to ask what the proposed programme would be and went on to explain that their VD Treatment Scheme was in operation and 'a very large amount of work is being carried out, which is increasing rapidly'.[72]

Clearly some accommodation was reached and in October 1919, Professor J.A. Lindsay,[73] Revd Dr Purvis and Dr Irwin, the representatives of the Ulster Branch of the NCCVD, attended the Public Health Committee of the Belfast Corporation to ask the committee to take up the question of propaganda.[74] At a subsequent committee meeting a sub-committee was appointed to report on propaganda work.[75] However, as Dr Bailie himself acknowledged, the activities in regard to propaganda were very slow.[76] He defended his own actions by explaining that 'we have had very few opportunities of pushing this matter forward as rapidly as we wished with so many other things engaging the attention of the Committee and Council'.[77] One step which had been taken was the search for a suitable candidate for the role of Organising Secretary for Propaganda. The interviews for the position was one of the first jobs the sub-committee undertook and the only criterion was that the post would be given to an ex-serviceman.[78]

A Mr Garner was subsequently appointed in January 1920, at a salary of £300 per annum.[79] He was to go to London to be trained by the NCCVD but this training never took place. Dr Bailie subsequently explained that while all the arrangements had been made for him to travel to London in June 1920, the LGB only confirmed his appointment to September 1920 and 'owing to the limited period of the confirmation of this engagement with us it became a question of whether it was worthwhile spending money to have him trained for propaganda work . . . and it was decided not to do so'.[80] While he was employed, Mr Garner was involved in a range of activities 'visiting various works and arranging talks and lectures to the workmen connected therewith'.[81] He had apparently been very favourably received and if mangers of companies were not willing for him to talk to the workforce, as they were afraid that such talks would not be favourably received, they were happy for him to leave suitable literature to be

distributed to the workers.[82] Between 6 May and 28 August 1920 he had
been granted 67 interviews, given 28 talks and provided 14 companies
with literature.[83] While it was suggested that a successor for Mr Garner
be appointed, there is no record of this ever taking place. There appear
to be a number of reasons why no successor was appointed: it may be a
reflection of financial constraints or of the Corporation's view that it was
unnecessary to employ someone solely for the purpose of propaganda. Dr
Bailie explained to Mrs Neville-Rolfe of the NCCVD in April 1921 that
'owing to the large volume of work carried out at the clinics my committee do not see the necessity for further propaganda work at present'.[84] Mrs
Neville-Rolfe replied that 'propaganda does not only increase the attendances of those who are infected at the Clinic but it also has a very definite
affect in reducing the extent to which individuals expose themselves to
the risk of infection and therefore prevents the spread of VD'.[85] However,
another contributing factor to the lack of a successor to Mr Garner
emerges from a discussion on VD propaganda within the Department
of Health in Éire in the 1940s. In support of its decision not to advertise
facilities available for VD treatment, the Department of Health referred
to the situation which had occurred when a publicity campaign was
launched in the North of Ireland by the NCCVD after the passing of the
1917 VD legislation. They contended that the campaign of lectures and
distribution of pamphlets by a paid organiser received scant support
from local authorities or the public. Open opposition occurred when the
lecturer visited Londonderry County Borough, with the Catholic Bishop
of Derry, Revd Dr McHugh, publicly declaring his objection to NCCVD
propaganda in his diocese. The result was that 'a subsequent proposal to
carry out lectures in other parts of the country was not encouraged by the
LGB and the matter ended'.[86]

The issue of advertising treatment centres and the displaying of posters
concerned with VD treatment and prevention was also particularly
contentious. Dr W.R. Davidson of Waveney Hospital in Ballymena was
particularly critical of the poster designed to advertise VD treatment
centres in Belfast. He felt it savoured 'of hysteria and the gutter' and that
he had 'always found patients who supposed they had contracted VD
quite frightened enough so that I do not think even the red ink is necessary. I would not come to read the Belfast poster twice and would be sorry
to see it anywhere.'[87] Six months later and Dr Davidson's wish not to see
the posters had come true. Addressing the Public Health Committee of
Belfast Corporation in May 1920 Dr Bailie, MSOH, explained how the
posters he had prepared for use in Belfast had 'failed to obtain permission

to use owing to some old local Act'.[88] This 'old local Act' was Section 58 of the Belfast Mains Drainage Act of 1887 which prohibited the affixing on lavatory walls of such notices. This legislation continued to cause problems throughout the interwar period and was an area of contention in the VD propaganda debates in Scotland as well.[89]

The importance of placing posters in toilets was stressed by Dr Murphy from Lisburn writing to Antrim County Council in 1921.[90] He felt that advertising in public lavatories would mean people would seek help before their cases became intractable. The issue arose again in June 1933 when Charles Thomson, the MSOH, explained to the Belfast Corporation Public Health Committee that 'in many Cross Channel cities notices were erected in public lavatories drawing attention to the dangers of venereal diseases and the necessity for persons suffering therefrom receiving prompt treatment'.[91] He went on to recommend that steps be taken to erect such notices in public lavatories in Belfast and it was resolved that he would communicate with the Improvement Committee, who were responsible for the issue.[92]

In his communication with the Improvement Committee, Charles Thomson argued that 'since the distant date of 1887 when the existing section forbidding such notices on urinal walls was made, public opinion has very strongly changed and it is felt throughout the kingdom that tactfully worded notices should be placed on such walls with a view to eliminating as far as possible this scourge which has wrought such havoc in the past'.[93] The following year saw renewed requests from the Belfast Corporation Public Health Committee to the Minister for Home Affairs to approve of the Corporation erecting posters identifying the dangers of VD and the need to get medical treatment.[94] No solution was reached and the issue of changing the legislation arose in the Public Health Committee Meetings in both 1937 and 1939.[95] It was only with the growing concerns which followed the outbreak of the Second World War that renewed interest in the need for greater publicity arose and efforts were once again made to have posters exhibited.

Following the revelation that the number treated for syphilis at the RVH had increased from 181 in May 1941 to 418 in May 1942, Dr Thomson explained that due to this 'appalling increase . . . it was decided, although it is still illegal in Belfast, to put up bills in certain places of public resort which would inform people of the places where the diseases could be treated'.[96] A satisfactory legal solution was evidently reached the following year as the MSOH was asked to prepare a draft notice for display in public lavatories.[97]

In terms of other areas of publicity and propaganda one of the largest events that took place in Northern Ireland was the showing of the film *Damaged Lives* in Belfast in September 1934. *Damaged Lives* was a Canadian film about a rising young executive who caught syphilis following a 'one night stand' just before he got married. He subsequently passed the disease on to his wife and unborn child. His wife, fearing that her life was over, tried to kill herself, only to be rescued by her husband who explained how the disease was curable. At the end of the film there was a lecture from a doctor about the dangers of VD.[98]

The preparations for the showing of this film began in 1933 when Mrs Neville-Rolfe of the British Social Hygiene Council wrote to Charles Thomson extolling the benefits of the film.[99] In his reply Charles Thomson was not overly enthusiastic, explaining that Belfast had already had a health week attended by over 25,000 people with films, lectures and exhibits and that the year before they had had the Royal Institute of Public Health Congress. He did go on to say that the British Social Hygiene Council was 'practically the first society to which I would turn for material' as the people of Northern Ireland 'have not been educated, as have the people of Scotland and England to the necessity of seeing such films and the realisation that such things exist'.[100] It was subsequently decided to show the film in the Ulster Hall for twelve days starting on 24 September 1934. In correspondence concerning the film, Mrs Neville-Rolfe made the mistake of referring to the Ulster Hall as a cinema, to which Charles Thomson responded that she 'might as well suggest that St Paul's Cathedral had been let for a fortnight for rag-time dances. The Ulster Hall is the holy of the holiest in Northern Ireland . . . we like to regard the Ulster Hall almost as holy ground'.[101] He went on to explain that she should therefore understand that the Belfast Corporation 'in granting the use of this hall have done their best for you'.[102] The showing of the film was not without controversy, with Belfast City Councillor Kilpatrick arguing that while the 'film might be all right from a medical aspect he did not think it should be shown under the auspices of the Public Health Committee'. He felt that 'Belfast still rejoiced in being a religious, God-fearing community and a picture like *Damaged Lives* was an insult to the city'.[103] In reply Alderman Midgley countered that he felt that the showing of the picture with the approval of the Public Health Committee 'was one of the finest things ever accomplished. It was a crusade against superstition and a scourge which should have the approval of all sensible and right-thinking people.'[104]

The film was seen by around 24,000 people in Belfast and the publicity it received was largely positive, though it must be noted that discussion of the film appeared in the three mainly Protestant papers (*Belfast Telegraph, Belfast Newsletter, Northern Whig*) and not in the largely Catholic *Irish News*. The *Belfast Telegraph* described *Damaged Lives* as 'admirably produced and acted . . . the most courageous and praiseworthy [film] ever produced for the screen. It deals with the greatest social scourge of this or any age, and portrays the suffering that may ensue through one moral lapse.'[105] The clergy of various religions within Belfast were asked to provide a statement of support for the film, and several were received including one from Rabbi Shachter of the Jewish Synagogue in Belfast and one from the Revd Doherty of the Mission to Seamen.[106] Revd Lindsay, Rector of St Bartholomew's in Belfast, devoted two Sunday sermons to the issue, extolling the youth of Belfast to become 'fully armoured that they would be proof against all temptation'.[107]

Churches and VD

The association of religion with VD legislation and the importance of the Churches in determining attitudes was more important in Ireland, both North and South, than in other parts of the United Kingdom. In the Irish Free State, the Catholic Church had great influence on the state's attitude and actions towards VD and the regulation of sexuality.[108] Its influence in the 1920s and 1930s 'moral purity campaigns' and in the legislation concerning VD has been highlighted.[109]

Whilst the situation in the North was not so rigidly dominated by the Churches, their influence was still very strong and the Stormont government was at pains to uphold the moral values of the Churches, and VD often seen as a moral rather than a medical issue.[110] As the MSOH for Belfast explained in 1929, concerning VD:

> The Public Health Department is at one with the theologians. People should keep a grip of themselves. Unfortunately some depart from the tenets of society. We must help our unfortunate brethren - as much for the sake of the innocent as for the guilty . . . our mission is to prevent and heal. With this earnest ambition your City Health Department stands four square in the knowledge that 'God is in his Heaven and all's well with the world.'[111]

It was to the Churches that the authorities turned to over the issue of education about VD.[112] Religious language and imagery were often used to discuss public health issues and this reflects not only the conflict between medical and moral instruction but also explains the reluctance of authorities in Northern Ireland to develop an extensive propaganda programme.

Publicity only began to be treated as an important issue during the Second World War.[113] This was in response to the war emergency and the greater governmental concern in London that VD should be controlled, particularly for the sake of troops. Demands from London ensured that the Stormont government pressurised local authorities into establishing treatment centres and provided increased funding for propaganda. Adverts were placed in newspapers detailing the opening times of the VD clinics and giving the 'facts' about VD and its transmission. In addition, the Chief Medical Officer at the Ministry of Health approved the displaying of notices on hoardings or suitable walls.[114]

The advertisements in the newspapers apparently generated both interest and inquiries. A letter to the Ministry of Health in Whitehall from its Stormont counterpart declared:

> we have had a large number of inquiries both by letter and telephone and when speaking to a doctor at the Venereal Disease Clinic of the Royal Victoria Hospital he told me that the number of people coming for advice and treatment had increased appreciably.[115]

Not everyone was convinced of the success of the advertising campaign. A letter to the Ministry of Home Affairs criticised the expense of the campaign and suggested that all that was needed was 'a utilitarian ad – a few lines explaining what VD is and then a list where confidential advice can be received'. The letter goes on to suggest that the same idea should apply to posters and that these should not be displayed in shopping centres, as people seeing the large VD would not stop to read them in the presence of others.[116]

As discussed above, Charles Thomson, the Belfast MSOH, was particularly vocal about the importance of education and publicity about VD. In his Annual Report of 1943 he suggested that, as VD had now reached the advertising columns of newspapers, it had 'so to speak, become respectable', and he argued that the public needed more education and information about VD and the results of infection. He explained that, while some people objected to VD education, and claimed that it was putting 'evil thoughts into the minds of the innocent', the reality was that adolescents were already discussing the topic themselves and needed to be educated properly. He felt that the suppression of facts had no benefit and that what was needed was to 'let in a gust of fresh air; knowledge is power'.[117]

There is no record of this 'gust of fresh air' on the education front actually occurring and, in his report of the following year, the MSOH returned to the subject of education. He claimed to be in touch with the Health Education Central Council, in connection with the Corporation re-affiliating itself, and stated that, 'Public Health Propaganda is imperative'. On the issue of sex education, he explained that while there had been some discussion of bringing experts into schools and of parents teaching at home, no action had been taken.[118]

Spreading VD

Having discussed the establishment of VD treatment clinics and the associated publicity and propaganda it is necessary to consider those who were targeted by both legislation and propaganda. While it is apparent that the legislation introduced during both world wars targeted women, as will be discussed below, also of concern were soldiers, both as at risk from contracting VD and also, at the end of the First World War, as those responsible for spreading the disease.

Following the cessation of the First World War, a 'Committee for the Protection of Ireland from Venereal Diseases' was formed, largely made up of members of Irish Suffrage organisations.[119] Their concerns were explained in a letter to the Clerk of the Belfast Union:

> A Committee of Doctors, Nurses and others interested in the welfare of Ireland has been formed to prevent the spread of VD by troops coming back from the front. Unless precautions against syphilis are taken at once, the country, which up to now has been almost free from this terrible plague will be infected, and the sufferers from general paralysis, blindness and insanity will fill the hospitals, infirmaries and asylums . . . attempts must be made to safeguard Ireland from the worst evil that comes in the train of war.[120]

This fear of returning soldiers was also expressed by Sinn Féin in a pamphlet written by Dr Kathleen Lynn and Richard Hayes which claimed that at the close of the war, around 150,000 soldiers would return to Ireland suffering from syphilis. They demanded that all returning soldiers should have blood tests.[121] It has been argued that the British Army, particularly during the First World War, was constructed by Irish nationalists as the main source of VD infection, and the immoral corrupter of Irish womanhood.[122] Ben Novick has argued that the British soldier in Ireland was portrayed as 'a filthy and diseased creature, a sub-human threat to the cleanliness and virtue of women and children.[123] The propagandists conveniently ignored the fact that more than two hundred thousand Irish men had joined the British Army.

While the British were clearly constructed as immoral in comparison with the high moral standards of the Irish, this was not simply a response of the nationalist propagandists, and the fear of returning soldiers was expressed in other quarters. For example a Co. Fermanagh doctor, Dr L. Kidd, wrote to the Divisional Commander in Belfast in 1922 about the treatment of a soldier from the Florencecourt Platoon, who was suffering from acute gonorrhoea.[124] He was of the opinion that the Medical Attendant of the platoon should examine every man at once. He argued that 'many ex-soldiers who have latent or active VD are special constables and are now scattered about the country'.[125] He believed that the solution would be to test the soldiers who wanted to join the Royal Irish Constabulary (RIC) for VD. However, Dr Kidd, in keeping with the view of other contemporaries, was quick to make the point that he had been in practice for over thirty years in the area and VD was very unusual, as it was in other 'rural parts of Ulster away from Belfast and Derry'.[126] He went on to state that in the years during and after the war, when he had been in charge of the central medical hospital of the district and of large numbers of troops, most of the cases of VD were acquired elsewhere. He found the idea of a 'number of men spreading VD amongst the virgin soil of a rural community' too awful to contemplate.[127] In reply to Dr Kidd's concerns, the Cabinet Secretary at the Ministry of Home Affairs stated that extensive enquiries had been made from all the Medical Officers and the number of VD cases known to have occurred in Special Constables was inconsiderable, with no suspicion of concealed cases.[128]

Concern about troops being responsible for the spread of disease was undoubtedly appropriated by nationalists to advance their cause, but it is arguable that they were part of a wider belief in an Ireland, North and South, Protestant and Catholic, that was more moral and more religious than the rest of Britain, and specifically England. In the North following partition there were frequent references by those who had fought to maintain the Union and whose political views were the polar opposite of nationalists, to the fact that Northern Ireland was free of VD and that any incidence of VD must have been brought in from England.[129]

It is arguable that returning soldiers did represent a contaminated 'other' but this transcended political allegiances to represent a wider idea of contagion and contamination and was one which was experienced in all countries with demobilised soldiers, both during and after the First

World War.[130] The fear associated with soldiers and VD had dissipated by the early 1920s. It had been utilised by both nationalists and suffragists but as, Maria Luddy has argued, the issue was only of 'use to the propagandists in a symbolic way'.[131] The blame for the spread of VD and the source of infection remained resolutely female.

During the First World War, concern grew about the spread of VD in the military. The main transmitter was believed to be the 'amateur', who appeared to be younger than the 'professional' prostitute, did not charge for sex, was not restricted to one particular class, and who was believed to be less likely to take precautions against VD.[132] The introduction of the Defence of the Realm Act (DORA) in 1914 permitted the military and the police to introduce measures such as imposing curfews on certain classes of women and banning women from pubs in particular areas.[133] There was huge opposition to the implementing of such legislation, mainly from the feminist movement, and this increased in volume, with the introduction of DORA 40d in March 1918. This legislation was due to the pressure from the Allied forces on the British Government to act to prevent the spread of venereal disease among the troops. DORA 40d made it an offence for any woman suffering from VD to have sexual intercourse with a soldier or to solicit a member of the forces to have sex with her. Any women suspected of this could be detained for examination and treatment, and imprisoned.

This legislation was regarded as a return to the CD Acts of the nineteenth century, with women again penalised for the sexual behaviour of men and female behaviour and freedom curtailed.[134] The *Irish Citizen* in August 1918 recorded how the first prosecution of a woman in Ireland, under DORA 40d had taken place.[135] The woman was sentenced in Belfast to six months' imprisonment with hard labour for 'communicating the disease to a Canadian soldier'. Letters calling attention to the affects of this regulation on female 'liberty and honour' had apparently been sent to three Dublin newspapers who had suppressed them. The article went on to argue that the regulation was merely an attempt to reintroduce the CD Acts and that:

> it largely increases the danger of disease by giving men a false sense of security, while it constitutes an outrage in the honour and self-respect of women, and is the gravest possible menace to their individual liberty. It also gives enormous power for blackmail and intimidation and the real object of its promoters is to make the practise of vice safe for men by degrading and befouling women. English suffragists are carrying on spirited campaign against Regulation 40D and it is up to Irish-women to fight the evil thing here.[136]

As the article suggests, great opposition was generated and the Home Office was inundated with deputations and petitions from women's organisations that were opposed to the legislation. Mindful of the number of women given the right to vote, DORA 40d was revoked at the end of the war.

An information leaflet on VD published in Ireland in 1919 placed some responsibility for the spread of VD on male behaviour, suggesting that 'if every lad and man would believe, what is a fact, that chastity is consistent with perfect health; and would have the courage to resist temptation to unchastity, these diseases would rapidly disappear from our midst'. It located the initial source of infection among women, and stated that syphilis was 'common among prostitutes, and among girls and women who, while not chaste, cannot be called prostitutes'.[137] As Davidson has suggested, 'even where male culpability *was* emphasised, the prostitute or casual good-time girl remained the constant point of reference as the root source of VD'.[138]

A similar point was raised by Lieutenant Colonel H.C. Donald, writing in the *Dublin Journal of Medical Science*, in 1919. He argued that with the end of the war, VD would begin to increase. The reason for this, he suggested was that during the war:

> women in great numbers have been employed in many kinds of war and other works, consequently they have in many instances been living more or less free or independent lives and have been removed from family influences and home life. As a result of this freedom many have contacted VD.[139]

He went on to suggest that the type of woman believed to be to blame for the spread of VD 'may be classed as an "amateur" and distinct from the "professional" class who receive payment for their traffic'. The 'amateur' was apparently in the majority and would attract the returning soldier. These arguments were backed up by figures from a medical study, which revealed that, 'at present two-thirds of all cases were infected by women of the "amateur" class'.[140]

In VD propaganda, women who did not adhere to the socially accepted role of female sexual behaviour, that of passive sexuality within marriage, were in many cases regarded as prostitutes and potential carriers of VD.[141] The fact that young women who were sexually active and did not charge for sexual intercourse were known as 'amateur prostitutes' exemplifies this. As Annet Mooij has argued, the use of this term bears witness to the fact 'that extra-marital female sexuality has always been defined in the debate on VD in terms of prostitution'.[142] As discussed in previous chapters, women were often labelled and identified in terms of their perceived sexual behaviour.

The interwar years saw a strengthening of the opinion that women were the source of VD and responsible for its spread. Thus, it was their behaviour, rather than that of men, which needed to be regulated and changed. The concern with female behaviour was reflected in contemporary discussions about dress and immodest behaviour, associated with forms of entertainment such as dance halls and cinemas.[143] As Revd James McGlinchy, writing in the *Catholic Bulletin* in 1934, explained, 'chastity is the most beautiful of virtues: but when tarnished the result is loathsome. From sins against chastity the most loathsome and excruciating of diseases have their origin.'[144]

As discussed in chapter 3, the interwar years saw a growing concern about a perceived decline in moral standards and behaviour which was often connected with increased female emancipation in the areas of work and home. This was a widespread experience: as Mooij has described for the Netherlands, concern about female behaviour and particularly the 'amateur', was part of a wider concern with post-war modernisation.[145]

While increased attention was focused on sexually active young women, the view that professional prostitution was still a main source of venereal infection had not totally dissipated. As Mary Sponberg asserts, during the interwar period 'many still believed that policing prostitution was the only way of restricting the spread of VD'.[146] A memorandum, written in the 1920s, which described the measures used in Northern Ireland for combating venereal disease, reflects this opinion. It declared that the legislation had a two-fold aspect: (1) preventive and (2) remedial. The aim of the preventive legislation was the suppression of prostitution. There were three aims of this legislation: firstly the suppression of prostitution on the streets and in public parks; secondly the suppression of premises licensed for the sale of intoxicating liquor where prostitutes would be likely to congregate; and thirdly, the suppression of brothels.[147]

The view that prostitutes were the main vectors of venereal infection was also an area of debate in the Irish Free State in the 1920s and 1930s. An unpublished interdepartmental report on VD in 1926 suggested VD was not spread by prostitutes and that 90 per cent of the men in the Irish army who contracted VD were infected by women who were not prostitutes.[148] This view was strongly contested by Frank Duff, of the Legion of Mary, who had been instrumental in attempts in previous years to clear Dublin's red light districts. He argued that 'behind all venereal disease the prostitute is hidden somewhere' and recommended a crackdown on brothels and illegal drinking houses and prolonged detention under religious influences for young girls who had become involved in prostitution.[149] Frank Duff's influence can be seen in the eventual legislation of 1935, which allowed for the moral reclamation of prostitutes, but did not tackle the related social problems.[150]

The Public Health Committee of the Belfast Corporation was also concerned with the issue of prostitutes in 1935 when two members raised the issue of detaining, examining and medically treating 'professional women'.[151] In a response to this Dr Thomson, MSOH, referred to the failure of the CD Acts of the 1860s and also the situation in Brisbane, Australia where there was compulsory notification of VD. He quoted the Brisbane Commissioner of Public Health who argued 'the professional women is not the worst offender . . . most of these women take care of themselves for business purposes alone . . . the sexually promiscuous amateur is the most frequent source of infection'. This, Dr Thomson argued, should 'kill the ideas that the professional women should be segregated, examined, treated etc'.[152]

During the Second World War, similar concerns emerged as in the First World War about the spread of VD in the military. Under pressure from the other Allies, and in particular the United States, Defence Regulation 33B was enacted. It had begun to be enforced in Northern Ireland by the spring of 1943 and while the language used was gender-neutral it nonetheless impacted more heavily on women.[153] The regulation stipulated that 'special practitioners' had to notify the Medical Officers of Health of the names of any sexual contacts given by patients suffering from venereal diseases when attending clinics for treatment; that is, people from whom they might have contracted the disease. If any contact was named twice, he or she was to be examined and, if infected, was to undergo treatment until free of the disease. If the individual refused treatment he or she was liable for fines or imprisonment.[154]

The discussions surrounding Regulation 33B by Charles Thomson reveal how women were perceived to be to blame for the spread of VD. In his 1943 Annual Report Thomson only referred to the 'suspected female infector'. He went on to explain that of the thirty-seven entries on the register in the Public Health Department in Belfast, only nineteen included the 'suspected female's' full name and address, but even these provided no further details about the women in question. He believed that the lack of detail about the women on the register was due in part to the fact that 'male adventurers have already fortified themselves with more or less copious draughts of wine', and that when they began to display the symptoms of disease the 'gay Lothario was unable to give a helpful statement as to who, how, when or where!'.[155] Thomson's choice of words is noteworthy. Women were 'suspects' or 'infectors' and a 'grave source of danger', whereas the men involved were merely described as 'adventurers' or 'gay Lotharios'. The implication was that male sexual activities were simply pleasure-seeking, normal and acceptable aspects of natural male behaviour, while sexually active women were predatory, dangerous and a source of disease

That women were to blame was further emphasised in October 1944 when Thomson drew the attention of the Belfast Corporation Public Health Committee to an article in September's *Public Health Journal* by Fergusson Ross about VD in Liverpool. He reproduced a paragraph for the committee on the causes of promiscuity that, while referring briefly to men, was focused on women and made the point that it is 'not the prostitute who comes to the clinic for treatment, but the wife, the sweetheart, and the so-called goodtime girl'.[156] A throw-away comment at the end of a letter from Charles Thomson to Dr Rankin at the VD department at the RVH, also highlights his belief that women, and specifically working-class young women, were to blame for the spread of VD. In response to an increase of syphilis since 1941 Thomson asked Dr Rankin 'What sort of people are these patients? Are they servant girls or what?'[157]

Compulsory notification

As described above, Charles Thomson was very dissatisfied with the implementation of Regulation 33B and was keen to obtain greater powers of notification and compulsory treatment of VD sufferers. However, this was a marked change in attitude from less than ten years earlier when he had been strenuously against compulsory notification. In comparison with, for example Scotland, and in particular Edinburgh Council, the debates in Northern Ireland amongst the medical profession or the Belfast Corporation or other councils were very limited. Edinburgh Corporation had gone so far as to submit a bill to the House of Commons in 1928 that, if it had been passed, would have instituted compulsory notification and treatment of VD.[158] In Northern Ireland no such public debates were generated and even within in the medical community discussion of VD in any form appears to have been relatively muted. The *Ulster Medical Journal* only published three articles on the treatment of syphilis between 1917 and 1923, one in 1928 and two on the treatment of gonorrhoea in 1936 and 1940.[159]

Charles Thomson's correspondence, statements and annual reports in the 1930s and 1940s reveal an extreme reversal of opinion about how to approach the treatment of VD and a growing awareness and interest in the tactics used throughout the world to prevent VD. In 1935 Dr Thomson explained how 'inspection, segregation and regulation are difficult, if not impossible, to carry out and public sentiment is bitterly opposed to this plan'.[160] He discussed the operation of compulsory notification in Brisbane and also the system of limited notification in Bradford. Interestingly, Thomson comments that 'no other authority in the country has attempted to get similar powers',[161] seemingly unaware of the 1928 debates in Scotland regarding compulsory notification.[162] However, by 1943 Thomson had changed his mind completely and used the example of the efforts made in Scotland to bolster his argument for compulsory notification.[163] As early as October 1942, using the example of regulations in place in New York, Dr Thomson advised the Belfast Corporation Public Health Committee to ask the Minister of Home Affairs to frame regulations making it compulsory for general practitioners to notify the MSOH of all those with VD, who would then be compulsorily treated.[164] He returned to this theme in his 1943 Annual Report, arguing that Regulation 33B was a failure, pointing to the lack of notifications he had been given and also to how the information was too vague to be of any use.[165] Similarly, in September 1943, after it was clear that the Ministry was not prepared to support the idea of making VD notifiable, Thomson wrote to the Venereal Disease Sub-committee of the Public Health Committee further outlining his position.[166] At this point Thomson introduced the Swedish example of compulsion and explained how VD rates had been reduced there. In arguing for a change in the legislation Thomson explained why he felt that Regulation 33B had been a failure in Northern Ireland. In the first instance he revealed that there had been a lack of notifications received from the Special Practitioners and explained how the few notifications he did receive came from the army practitioners.[167] Even then, the information received was very vague and very few people were named twice. Thomson hoped the sub-committee might appeal to the Ministry to consult the Imperial Authorities to amend Regulation 33B to allow the MSOH to act on one intimation rather than two. He returned to the theme in his Annual Report of 1944, once again using the examples of compulsion in Sweden and New York and asking 'How long, then are we to put up with our weak voluntary system?'[168]

In December 1943 the Ministry of Health in Whitehall issued a circular which advised local authorities that they could trace contacts that had only been identified once as possibly having VD, rather than the twice stipulated in 33B. By October 1944 this had been adopted in Northern Ireland: as Dr Thomson explained to the Public Health Committee, 'it has become custom . . . to take action on receipt of one notification . . . no compulsion can be brought to bear upon those who have only been notified once, but at least they are appraised of the fact that they are probably suffering form VD in a communicable sense'.[169]

VD rates

As discussed previously the attitude which prevailed through Northern Ireland was that numbers suffering from VD were inconsequential. This remained the case through the interwar period to the Second World War. In 1943, the Ministry of Home Affairs stated:

> we get frequent returns of the number of cases [of VD] amongst the troops, contracted in Northern Ireland and the number of them is negligible. The area . . . is in a very satisfactory state so far as it is concerned.[170]

Similarly, with the planned extension of VD regulations to Northern Ireland during the Second World War, it was felt that:

> while the trouble is not that serious in Northern Ireland, as we cannot prevent the English people making this regulation applicable here, there would be no point raising any difficulty about it.[171]

The extent to which it was believed that Northern Ireland was free of VD, even by the 1940s, is revealed in a question in the Northern Ireland Parliament in 1942, to Sir Dawson Bates, the Minister of Home Affairs. He was asked whether:

> in the view of the existence of VD in Great Britain he will take steps to ensure that every person coming to Northern Ireland from Great Britain will be subject to a medical examination at the port of embarkation?[172]

The answer was in the negative!

The incidence and prevalence of VD in Northern Ireland is difficult to estimate. There was very little discussion in contemporary sources concerning rates of venereal disease in Northern Ireland, with the finding of the Royal Commission on Venereal Diseases in 1916 that 10 per cent of urban populations were infected with syphilis used as a general guide. There are several sources of figures which have been used elsewhere to build up a picture of infection. These include numbers of Wassermann

Reactions carried out, and mortality rates from locomotor ataxy and general paralysis of the insane (GPI), which were, in the main, caused by syphilis.[173] For Northern Ireland, the figures for Wassermann Reactions are incomplete and the mortality rates recorded for GPI are much lower than would be expected considering comparative populations, raising questions over the accuracy of the figures recorded. However an attempt to determine rates can be made based on the records from treatment centres and clinics.[174]

The numbers attending VD clinics in Northern Ireland are incomplete, but available figures record the number of new cases (both with and without VD) attending VD clinics between 1924 and 1945. For those with VD numbers rose from 2,645 in 1924 to peak at 4,023 in 1932 before a fall to 2,150 in 1941, and then a slight rise to 2,615 in 1945.

What is interesting to note is the high proportion of those attending VD treatment centres who were not suffering from VD. For the whole of Northern Ireland this was, on average, 40 per cent between 1924 and 1931, and then rose to 55 per cent during the war years of 1939–1945. For Belfast, between 1932 and 1945, the average was substantially higher at 67 per cent. This high proportion may be evidence of the success of publicity, which increased awareness of the diseases and encouraged people to seek treatment. Conversely, it arguably reflected the failure of publicity and propaganda to provide the public with a clear understanding of the symptoms or causes of the diseases. Official opinion was that the high numbers of those attending clinics who were free of the disease reflected an appreciation of the value of the treatment centres to people who felt they might have been exposed to risk of infection.[175]

The more detailed figures available for those treated at the RVH and Mater hospitals in Belfast identify both new cases treated as well as total attendances.[176] The incidence of VD, as shown by the figures of the new cases attending the RVH and Mater suffering from VD, shows a gentle downward trend from 1,277 in 1932 to 1,247 in 1935 and 1,006 in 1939 before a rise in the 1940s to 1,393 in 1946.[177]

A steady growth in the prevalence of VD is shown by the total attendance at the RVH and Mater, from 3,774 in 1932 to 6,377 in 1935, 8,287 in 1938, 12,080 in 1942 and 13,116 in 1946.[178] This is in contrast to the Irish Free State where the total number of patients attending treatment centres was 2,589 in 1935 and in Dublin the number of patients in the 1930s and 1940s was not more than 2,600 per annum.[179]

The importance of Belfast as a centre for the treatment of VD is also clearly seen from the available figures. For the nine years between 1932 and 1945, on average 60 per cent of new cases (with and without VD) were treated in Belfast. During the Second World War, the figure rose to 80–85 per cent of all cases of VD in Northern Ireland being treated in Belfast County Borough. As discussed already, a number of county councils were reluctant to establish clinics and patients from these areas travelled to Belfast for treatment.

While there was a general increase in attendance during the war years, 1939–1945, the most extreme increase was for patients who gave their address as the Port of Belfast. The number attending the RVH or Mater rose from 48 in 1940 to 153 in 1942. During this period, the number of ships in Belfast increased rapidly, with Allied ships and naval fleets docking there. The docks in Belfast were vastly extended, and thousands of ships were repaired and docked there during the war. From January 1942, there was a particular increase in the number of American ships docking in Northern Ireland which may have contributed to the numbers seeking treatment before official US treatment centres for VD were established.

The incidence of syphilis and gonorrhoea in Belfast between 1932 and 1946 followed a divergent pattern to that of England and Scotland in the interwar period. In 1932 in Belfast, 51 per cent of patients treated for VD had syphilis and 49 per cent gonorrhoea. These proportions stayed roughly the same until 1942 when the proportion suffering from syphilis increased to 67 per cent before declining to 44 per cent in 1945. In contrast, the numbers suffering from gonorrhoea fell in 1942 and 1943, before an increase in 1944 when they exceeded the numbers suffering from syphilis. In England and Scotland however during the interwar period, the proportion of patients suffering from gonorrhoea was always higher than that for syphilis.[180]

In terms of the gender division of those treated for syphilis and gonorrhoea in Belfast, other than for the years 1941–1943, male cases of gonorrhoea were higher than those suffering from syphilis.[181] During the 1930s, 95 per cent of all patients treated for gonorrhoea were male. In Scotland in the interwar period a similar situation existed, with the majority of patients treated for gonorrhoea being male, even though it was assumed that the real proportion amongst those infected was relatively evenly divided between male and female.[182]

Thus female cases of syphilis greatly outnumbered cases of gonorrhoea. A major contributing factor is that gonorrhoea in women is often asymptomatic, leading to many women being unaware that they are infected and seeking treatment. The ratio of female patients with gonorrhoea to those with syphilis in the 1930s, treated in Belfast clinics, was 0.14:1. This compares negatively with the assumed real ratio for women of three or four cases of gonorrhoea to every case of syphilis. The ratio of 0.14:1 for Belfast also compares unfavourably with that for Scotland which was itself considered relatively low at 0.9:1.[183] Although the number of women treated for gonorrhoea in Belfast increased substantially in the 1940s, the ratio only peaked at 0.6:1, which still left a large number of cases potentially going untreated and undetected.

It is difficult to know the numbers who had contracted VD and who did not seek medical treatment and also the numbers who could afford to pay for treatment privately and did not attend the free treatment centres. Nonetheless the idea that VD was something unknown in Northern Ireland was clearly untrue. This reflects the common theme throughout this book that the perception of a country of higher moral standards and greater Christian values than the rest of the UK was not the reality. Similarly, as in other areas it was most often believed that women were responsible for the spread of VD, and that men needed to be protected from them. The changing focus from prostitutes to 'good-time girls' reflects the growing concerns through the interwar years and into the Second World War about female sexuality and falling moral standards.

Notes

1 For example, see Walkowitz, *Prostitution*; Bland '"Cleansing the Portals of Life"', pp. 192–208; Mort, *Dangerous Sexualities*.
2 For example, see Blom, 'Fighting Venereal Diseases', 228; Lundberg, 'Passing on the "Black Judgement"', p. 41; Sauerteig, '"The Fatherland is in Danger, Save the Fatherland!"', p. 83.
3 Davidson, *Dangerous Liaisons*, pp. 324–325.
4 For example, see Baldwin, *Contagion and the State in Europe*; Bland, 'In the Name of Protection', pp. 23–49; Hall, '"War Always Brings It On"', pp. 205–223; Hall, 'Venereal Diseases and Society in Britain', pp. 120–137; Roger Davidson, 'Fighting "The Deadly Scourge": The Impact of World War II on Civilian VD Policy in Scotland', *The Scottish Historical Review*, 75 (1996), 72–97.
5 Roger Davidson, 'The Great Scourge: Approaches to the History of Venereal Disease in Modern European Society' (unpublished paper, February 2003); my thanks to Roger Davidson for providing me with a copy of this paper.
6 Towers, 'Health Education Policy 1916–1926', 73.
7 Royal Commission on Venereal Diseases (RCVD), PP 1914, Cd. 7475, vol. XLIX, evidence of Dr Brian O'Brien, Medical Inspector to the Local Government Board for Ireland, 27 February 1914, qq. 7992–8295.

8 Ibid.
9 Ibid.
10 Ibid., qq. 8286–8289.
11 Ibid., qq. 7992–8295.
12 *Irish Citizen*, 3 January 1914, p. 258.
13 RCVD, *Final Report of the Commissioners*, PP 1916, Cd. 8189, vol XVI.
14 Evans, 'Tackling the "Hideous Scourge"', 418.
15 The Wassermann Test is a complement-fixation antibody test for syphilis, named after the bacteriologist August von Wassermann. Salvarsan is an arsenic-based drug discovered by Paul Ehrlich in 1909 and was the most effective treatment for syphilis until the introduction of penicillin in the 1940s.
16 RCVD, *Final Report of the Commissioners*, pp. 84–87.
17 M.W. Adler, 'The Terrible Peril: An Historical Perspective on the Venereal Diseases', *British Medical Journal*, 19 (1980), 207.
18 Evans, 'Tackling the "Hideous Scourge"', 421–422.
19 Davidson, *Dangerous Liaisons*, p. 50; Evans, 'Tackling the "Hideous Scourge"', 424.
20 Tyrone County Council Minutes, 13 February 1919, LA/6/2GA/3, PRONI.
21 Minutes of the Ulster Branch of NCCVD, May 1918, LA/7/9BB/12, PRONI.
22 Fermanagh County Council Minutes, 27 February 1919, 14 July 1919, LA/4/2GA/2, PRONI.
23 Public Health Committee Minutes, Belfast Corporation, 2 December 1920, LA/7/9AA/15, PRONI.
24 Ibid.
25 Fermanagh County Council Minutes, 27 April 1923, LA/4/2GA/2, PRONI.
26 County Londonderry VD Committee Minutes, 30 March 1918, LA5/9AK/1, PRONI.
27 Ibid., 26 April 1919.
28 Londonderry County Council Minutes, 10 June 1919, LA/5/2GA/8, PRONI.
29 County Londonderry VD Committee Minutes, 1942–1946, LA/5/9AK/2, PRONI.
30 Luddy, *Prostitution*, p. 188; *Note on VD Propaganda*, VD Returns of Cases in 1938 and 1943, Department of Health, B 135/12, National Archives of Ireland (NAI).
31 *Derry Journal*, 14 February 1919, p. 4.
32 Armagh County Council Minutes, 25 February 1919, LA/2/2GA/10, PRONI.
33 *Derry Journal*, 16 December 1918, p. 4.
34 Ibid., 14 February 1919, p. 4
35 Ibid.

36 Tyrone County Council Minutes, 11 November 1919, LA/6/2GA/3, PRONI.
37 Ibid.
38 *Derry Journal*, 16 December 1918, p. 4.
39 Luddy, *Prostitution*, p. 204.
40 List of Treatment Centres for the Treatment of VD, 8 December 1922, Correspondence Concerning the Frequency, Provision for and Treatment of Venereal Diseases, 1922–42, CAB/9B/23/1, PRONI.
41 Boards of Guardians and workhouses existed until 1948 in Northern Ireland and the introduction of the National Health Service. This is in contrast to Southern Ireland where the Boards of Guardians were abolished following Independence and replaced by County Boards of Health or Boards of Public Assistance with workhouses becoming either County Homes for the elderly or District Fever Hospitals. In other parts of Britain workhouses closed throughout the 1920s and 1930s.
42 Belfast Union, Report of the Infirmary and Child Welfare Committee, 14 May 1919, Belfast Board of Guardians VD Correspondence, BG/7/BH/11, PRONI.
43 The clinic remained in this location until 1970.
44 Richard Clarke, *The Royal Victoria Hospital Belfast: A History 1797–1997* (Belfast, 1997), p. 104.
45 Ibid.
46 Ibid.
47 Davidson, *Dangerous Liaisons*, p. 54.
48 Dr Rankin to Dr Thomson MSOH, 4 January 1932, LA/7/9BB/17, PRONI.
49 Ibid.
50 Dr Murphy to Secretary Antrim County Council, 16 January 1921, LA/1/3AG/13, PRONI.
51 Davidson, *Dangerous Liaisons*, p. 49.
52 Public Health Committee Minutes, Belfast Corporation, 3 June 1919, 26 August 1919, 23 September 1919, LA/7/9AA/13, PRONI.
53 Ibid., 12 December 1922, LA/7/9AA/15, PRONI.
54 Ibid., 13 April 1926.
55 Ibid., 29 May 1923.
56 For discussion of areas of conflict in Scotland, see Davidson, *Dangerous Liaisons*, p. 50.
57 Medical Staff Minutes, Royal Victoria Hospital, 28 May 1919.
58 Minutes of Special Meeting of Public Health Committee, Belfast Corporation, 7 February 1921, LA/7/9AA/15, PRONI.
59 Public Health Committee Minutes, Belfast Corporation, 22 February 1921, LA/7/9AA/15, PRONI.
60 Ibid., 15 November 1932.

61 Mary Daly, *A Social and Economic History of Ireland Since 1800* (Dublin, 1981), p. 206.

62 Arthur Green, *Devolution and Public Finance: Stormont 1921–1972* (Glasgow, 1979), p. 7.

63 Greta Jones, *'Captain of All These Men of Death': The History of Tuberculosis in Nineteenth and Twentieth Century Ireland* (Amsterdam and New York, 2001), p. 132.

64 The NCCVD was influenced by the eugenic and feminist ideals of many of its members; see for example Joan Austoker, 'Biological Education and Social Reform: The British Social Hygiene Council 1925–42' (unpublished masters thesis, University of London, 1981).

65 Davenport-Hines, *Sex, Death and Punishment*, p. 223; Tomkins, 'Palmitate or Permanganate', 385. It was the refusal of the NCCVD to implement or encourage the use of preventative measures, particularly the use of chemical prophylaxis, which led to the establishment of the Society for the Prevention of Venereal Disease (SPVD) in 1919. For more on the debate concerning the NCCVD and the SPVD, see Tomkins, 'Palmitate or Permanganate', and Towers, 'Health Education Policy 1916–1926'.

66 Luddy, *Prostitution*, pp. 187–188.

67 Minutes of Ulster Branch NCCVD, 13 October 1917, LA/7/9BB/12, PRONI.

68 Ibid.

69 Ibid., 3 May 1918.

70 General Secretary NCCVD London to Dr Bailie, MSOH Belfast, 22 May 1919, LA/7/9BB/20, PRONI.

71 Ibid.

72 Dr Bailie to Mrs Neville-Rolfe, 5 June 1919, LA/7/9BB/20, PRONI.

73 Professor Lindsay was also involved in the Belfast Eugenics Society, further illustrating the close links between eugenics and the NCCVD; for more on Lindsay, see Greta Jones, 'Eugenics in Ireland: The Belfast Eugenics Society, 1911–1915', *Irish Historical Studies*, 28 (1992), 81–95.

74 Public Health Committee Minutes, Belfast Corporation, 21 October 1919, LA/7/9AA/13, PRONI.

75 Ibid., 31 October 1919.

76 Dr Bailie to Mrs Neville-Rolfe, 23 December 1919, LA/7/9BB/20, PRONI.

77 Ibid.

78 Public Health Committee Minutes, Belfast Corporation, 31 October 1919, LA/7/9AA/13, PRONI.

79 Ibid., 13 January 1920.

80 Dr Bailie to Mrs Neville-Rolfe, 19 April 1921, LA/7/9BB/20, PRONI.

81 Ibid., 13 May 1920.

82 Dr Bailie to Chairman and Members of Belfast Corporation Public Health Committee, 25 May 1920, LA/7/9BB/21, PRONI.

83 Report submitted to the Belfast Public Health Committee, 20 September 1920, LA/7/9BB/21, PRONI.
84 Dr Bailie to Mrs Neville-Rolfe, 19 April 1921, LA/7/9BB/20, PRONI.
85 Mrs Neville-Rolfe to Dr Bailie, 21 April 1921, LA/7/9BB/20, PRONI.
86 *Note on VD Propaganda*, VD Returns of Cases in 1938 and 1943, Department of Health, B 135/12, NAI.
87 Dr W.R. Davidson to Antrim County Council, 17 October 1919, LA/1/3AG/13, PRONI.
88 Ibid.
89 Davidson, *Dangerous Liaisons*, p. 138.
90 Dr Murphy to Secretary Antrim County Council, 16 January 1921, LA/1/3AG/13, Antrim County Council, VD, PRONI.
91 Extract from Minutes of Public Health Committee, 27 June 1933, VD Propaganda Work, 1919–1944, LA/7/9BB/21, PRONI.
92 Ibid.
93 Charles Thomson to Chairman and Members of the Belfast Corporation Improvement Committee, 9 August 1933, LA/7/9BB/21, PRONI.
94 Public Health Committee Minutes, Belfast Corporation, 9 January 1934, LA/7/9AA/18, PRONI.
95 Ibid., 12 October 1937, 31 January 1939, LA/7/9AA/19, PRONI.
96 Dr Thomson to Dr Rankin, 1 June 1942, LA/7/9BB/14, PRONI.
97 Public Health Committee Minutes, 30 June 1942, Belfast Corporation, LA/7/9AA/20, PRONI.
98 See www.movies.nytimes.com (accessed 6 January 2009).
99 Mrs Neville-Rolfe to Charles Thomson, 23 October 1933, LA/7/9BB/20, PRONI.
100 Charles Thomson to Mrs Neville-Rolfe, 25 October 1933, LA/7/9BB/20, PRONI.
101 Ibid., 6 April 1934.
102 Ibid.
103 *Belfast Telegraph*, 1 October 1934.
104 Ibid.
105 Ibid., 29 September 1934.
106 Revd Doherty to Charles Thomson, 21 September 1934; Rabbi Shachter to Charles Thomson, 23 September 1934, VD Miscellaneous Correspondence, LA/7/9BB/19, PRONI.
107 *Belfast Telegraph*, 25 September 1934.
108 See for example Dermot Keogh, *The Vatican, the Bishops and Irish Politics, 1919–1939* (Cambridge, 1986); Whyte, *Church and State in Modern Ireland*; McAvoy, 'The Regulation of Sexuality'.
109 Luddy, *Prostitution*, pp. 194–237; Philip Howell, 'Venereal Disease and Prostitution in the Irish Free State', *Irish Historical Studies*, 33 (2003), 338–340.

110 The influence of the Churches is also evident over issues of family planning. See chapter 6.
111 Charles Thomson, MSOH, Belfast, *The Belfast Book, 1929* (Belfast, 1929), p. 96.
112 See chapter 3.
113 The treatment and prevention of VD during the Second World War is more fully discussed in chapter 5.
114 Public Health Committee Minutes, Belfast Corporation, 20 April 1943, LA/7/9AA/20, PRONI.
115 Letter to Ministry of Health, Whitehall from Ministry of Health, Stormont, 16 March 1943, VD Publicity and Propaganda, Ministry of Health and Local Government, HLG/1/2/2, PRONI.
116 J.B. Meehan to Mr Henderson, Ministry of Home Affairs, 16 April 1945, VD Publicity and Propaganda, HLG/1/2/2, PRONI.
117 MSOH for Belfast, *Annual Report of Health, 1943*, LA/7/9DA/28, PRONI.
118 Ibid.
119 Luddy, *Prostitution*, pp. 190–191.
120 Committee for Protection of Ireland from Venereal Diseases to the Clerk of Belfast Union, 16 June 1918, Belfast Board of Guardians Venereal Disease Correspondence, BG/7/BH/11, PRONI.
121 T. Percy C. Kirkpatrick, 'Syphilis and the State', *Dublin Journal of Medical Science*, 145 (1918), 351.
122 Luddy, *Prostitution*, p. 193.
123 Ben Novick, *Conceiving Revolution: Irish Nationalist Propaganda During the First World War* (Dublin, 2001), p. 156.
124 Dr L. Kidd to Divisional Commander, Belfast, 11 July 1922, CAB/9B/23/1, PRONI.
125 Ibid.
126 Ibid.
127 Ibid.
128 Cabinet Secretary Ministry of Home Affairs to Dr L. Kidd, 30 December 1922, CAB/9B/23/1, PRONI.
129 For example, *Derry Journal*, 14 February 1919, p.4; Armagh County Council, Minutes, 25 February 1919, LA/2/2GA/10, PRONI; Tyrone County Council, Minutes, 11 November 1919, LA/6/2GA/3, PRONI.
130 Ann Taylor Allen, 'Feminism, Venereal Diseases and the State in Germany, 1890–1918', *Journal of the History of Sexuality*, 4 (1993), 45–47.
131 Luddy, *Prostitution*, p. 191.
132 Bland, 'In the Name of Protection', p. 28.
133 Ibid., pp. 28–29.
134 Ibid., p. 32; Woollacott, '"Khaki Fever"', 334.
135 *Irish Citizen*, August 1918, p. 617.
136 Ibid.

137 Government Leaflet, 'Information on the Dangers of Venereal Disease and on Facilities for Treatment', 1919, Antrim County Council, General Correspondence, LA/1/3AG/13, PRONI.
138 Davidson, *Dangerous Liaisons*, p. 149.
139 Lieutenant Colonel H.C. Donald, 'The Diagnosis and Treatment of Syphilis', *Dublin Journal of Medical Science*, 142 (1919), 77.
140 Ibid.
141 Davidson, *Dangerous Liaisons*, p. 149.
142 Mooij, *Out of Otherness*, p. 125.
143 See chapter 3.
144 Revd James McGlinchey, 'Maxims and Counsels for the Christian Family', *The Catholic Bulletin*, 24 (1934), 1004.
145 Mooij, *Out of Otherness*, p. 135.
146 Mary Sponberg, *Feminizing Venereal Disease: the Body of the Prostitute in Nineteenth-Century Medical Discourse* (New York, 1997), p. 181.
147 Memorandum on the Measures Available in Northern Ireland for Combating Venereal Diseases, February 1926, CAB/9B/21/1, PRONI.
148 Unpublished Interdepartmental Report on VD, 12 February 1926, VD Interdepartmental Committee of Inquiry 1925, Department of Health, B 135/13, NAI; For more on this report see Howell, 'Venereal Disease and Prostitution', and Susannah Riordan, 'Venereal Disease in the Irish Free State: The Politics of Public Health', *Irish Historical Studies*, 34 (2007), 345–364.
149 Frank Duff, Report to VD Interdepartmental Committee of Inquiry, VD Interdepartmental Committee of Inquiry 1925, Department of Health, B 135/13, NAI.
150 McAvoy, 'The Regulation of Sexuality', p. 263.
151 Dr Thomson to Public Health Committee, Belfast Corporation, 12 February 1935, LA/7/9BB/19, PRONI.
152 Ibid.
153 Cox, 'Compulsion, Voluntarism and Venereal Disease', 97.
154 Davidson, *Dangerous Liaisons*, pp. 210–216.
155 MSOH for Belfast, *Annual Report of Health, 1943*, 2–5, LA/7/9DA/28, PRONI.
156 Charles Thomson to Belfast Corporation Public Health Committee, 27 October 1944, LA/7/9BB/19, PRONI.
157 Charles Thomson to Dr J.C. Rankin, 1 July 1943, LA/7/9BB/14, PRONI.
158 Susan Lemar, '"The Liberty to Spread Disaster": Campaigning for Compulsion in the Control of Venereal Diseases in Edinburgh in the 1920s', *Social History of Medicine*, 19:1 (2006), 83–85
159 *Transactions of the Ulster Medical Society*, 1917–1929, becoming the *Ulster Medical Journal*, 1929–1945.
160 Charles Thomson to Public Health Department, Belfast Corporation, 18 February 1935, LA/7/9BB/19, PRONI.

161 Ibid.
162 Lemar, "'The Liberty to Spread Disaster'".
163 MSOH for Belfast, *Annual Report of Health, 1942–43,* LA/7/9DA/28, PRONI.
164 Charles Thomson to Belfast Corporation Public Health Committee, 6 October 1942, LA/7/9BB/21, PRONI.
165 MSOH for Belfast, *Annual Report of Health, 1942–43,* LA/7/9DA/28, PRONI.
166 Charles Thomson to Belfast Corporation VD Sub-committee, 14 September 1943, LA/7/9BB/19, PRONI.
167 Ibid.
168 MSOH for Belfast, *Annual Report of Health, 1944*, LA/7/9DA/28, PRONI.
169 Charles Thomson to Belfast Corporation Public Health Committee, 27October 1944, LA/7/9BB/19, PRONI.
170 Ministry of Home Affairs, Stormont to R. Gransden, Cabinet Secretariat, Stormont, 16 April 1942, CAB/9B/23/1, PRONI.
171 Ibid.
172 Mr McGurk, Northern Ireland Parliament, House of Commons Debates, 21 April 1942.
173 Davidson, *Dangerous Liaisons*, p. 158.
174 The numbers attending the RVH and Mater Treatment Centres are available in detail from 1932-1947. The annual totals are calculated from 31 March–31 March each year.
175 *History of the Second World War: United Kingdom Medical Services* ed A.S. Macnalty, (London, 1955), p. 353.
176 Total attendances are the number of cases which at the beginning of the year were under treatment for VD, which includes those who had previously attended the centre, those who had stopped attending and had returned, plus the number of new cases.
177 MSOH for Belfast, *Annual Report of Health.*
178 Ibid.
179 Luddy, *Prostitution*, pp. 204–205.
180 Davidson, *Dangerous Liaisons*, p. 163.
181 MSOH for Belfast, *Annual Report of Health.*
182 Davidson, *Dangerous Liaisons*, p. 170.
183 Ibid.

5

'One Yank and they're Off':[1] interaction between US troops and Northern Irish women, 1942–1945

The first American troops came to Northern Irish shores on 26 January 1942. Their numbers peaked at one hundred and twenty thousand in December 1943, which represented the equivalent of one-tenth of the total population before the start of the second World War, and in some areas, even more.[2] Troops were stationed all over Northern Ireland. The US Air Force was based at Langford Lodge, on the shore of Lough Neagh, with airbases across the province, including at Toome, Greencastle near Kilkeel, and Maghabery. Londonderry served as naval headquarters and was the main US communications base in Europe during the war as well as being the largest convoy escort base in the UK. Finally, the army was stationed all over Northern Ireland, often in rural areas.[3] The arrival of these troops was code-named Operation MAGNET.[4]

The stationing of US troops around the world during the Second World War and the subsequent interactions with the local public has generated much scholarly discussion.[5] The involvement of women in both Britain and Australia with US troops, for example, has been located in a wider debate surrounding changing female sexual identity and its impact on citizenship and international relations.[6] The subject of US troops in Northern Ireland, however, has been discussed in a rather uncritical way by official war histories, local historians, or those writing their wartime memories, with no real discussion of the nature of the relationships or involvement with local women.[7] Yet it is important to consider the particular and unique situation in Northern Ireland as it impacted the interaction between troops and local women and within the wider contemporary debates concerning female sexuality. The impact of the troops arriving in Northern Ireland was immediate and the excitement that they generated in young women was undeniable. American troops were conspicuous on the streets, as were the girls and young women who accompanied them. The arrival of American troops in the UK saw the intervention of ordinary soldiers and sailors in the construction and implementation of new patterns of female sexuality, and the techniques of parents, priests, religious organisations and local police and doctors intended to control women's behaviour were, without a doubt, mightily challenged.

Rural Northern Ireland

In Northern Ireland prior to the Second World War, female sexual purity and chastity were regarded as being of the utmost importance. There was no general acceptance of female sexuality expressed outside marriage and a variety of measures were employed to enforce the dominant code of behaviour. Preventative measures, such as hostels and girls' organisations, were used to guide and protect young women. Rescue homes and institutions were used to secure women's reform if they transgressed acceptable social norms. In both Protestant and Catholic communities, women were contradictorily regarded as both moral guardians and as those most likely to lower moral standards.[8] Female behaviour was placed under added scrutiny with the arrival of US troops, as it was feared that women were 'losing their heads'[9] and endangering the high moral standards upon which both communities in Northern Ireland prided themselves.

Scholars have attempted to understand the relationship between war and fears concerning female sexual behaviour. Using the example of Britain during the Second World War, Sonya Rose argues that war 'exaggerates the significance of the nation as a source and object of identity', and that during war public attention is focused and directed to ideas of what the nation represents.[10] Rose adds that under these conditions and in a society which has a tradition of constructing female sexuality as dangerous, 'women who were perceived to be seeking out sexual adventures might well be defined as subversive'.[11] In short, sexual propriety and control constituted central concerns to national stability in Britain during the Second World War. Positioned against the images of Britain as a brave and stoic nation, united in adversity and willing to sacrifice personal interests for the collective good and to show good humour in the face of bombings and shortages, there was no place for the moral laxity as embodied by pleasure-seeking, sexually expressive young women. Such women were perceived to be a threat to the imagined, unified, self-sacrificing community.[12] It is a persuasive argument concerning the issue of national identity and those whose behaviour was perceived to threaten it, especially during wartime. When the presence of an external enemy combined with the influence of propaganda, both worked to strengthen national identity.

It is, however, difficult to apply this theory without reservation to Northern Ireland, where ideas of national identity were and still are problematic. During the Second World War, while Northern Irish society was united in suffering under wartime restrictions, it was not fully united in support of the war. Northern Ireland was deeply divided politically and religiously, and the country was not united in support of the war effort. In other words, there was no unified national identity from which to exclude those who were a threat or who failed to conform to the accepted standards of behaviour.

The relationship of Northern Ireland to the independent nation of Éire added a unique dimension to Northern Irish politics during the war.[13] Éire was officially neutral, although its president, Eamon de Valera, openly declared his opposition to the basing of American troops in Northern Ireland, that is, in what it considered part of its rightful territory. Northern Ireland was thus the only place in the UK bordering a neutral state. It was therefore perceived to be particularly susceptible to enemy infiltration via its border, which was both long and easy to cross. The IRA followed Éire's lead in the war, and even while the government of Éire opposed the IRA in this period, there remained a constant threat of IRA activity against the American troops.[14] Parker Buhrman, the American Consul in Belfast, reported to the American Embassy in Dublin, that 'individual American soldiers have been subjected to threats by IRA partisans ever since they arrived in the North of Ireland. Quite a number have been assaulted under the cover of darkness.'[15] In his report, he also qualified the situation and explained that not all nationalist groups in Northern Ireland were hostile and that 'while on the face of it the troops were received with good will only by the Unionist groups, actually they were received just as heartily by Nationalist groups.'[16]

The presence of Irish-Americans in the American Army further complicated this political issue, since many of them had families and relations living in Éire who often held strong anti-British views. As Buhrman also pointed out 'there is a disposition on the part of those who have religious and kinship ties with the Catholic population of Ireland to espouse the so-called Irish point of view. They are susceptible to IRA influences.'[17] There was, therefore, a political dimension to the interaction between US troops and the local population in Northern Ireland that was absent on the British mainland.

The society of Northern Ireland also differed markedly from the rest of the United Kingdom. The relatively small population as compared to the rest of the nation meant that the impact of US troops was immediate and dramatic. The Northern Irish population was also largely rural with strong religious adherence and high church attendance. Both the Protestant and Catholic Churches exercised considerable influence on attitudes and behaviour, an influence reflected in the more conservative ideas and stricter standards of sexual conduct than those that existed in many other parts of the United Kingdom.

For both American troops and Northern Irish civilians, the cultural and social differences were starkly visible. Troops from large American cities, who were used to a wide variety of entertainment and 'dating', found the situation in Northern Ireland very different. As the US Military *Pocket Guide to Northern Ireland* explained, 'there is virtually no nightlife. Pubs close early and the floorshow and juke joint are non-existent'. With reference to women, the Guide explained that Northern Ireland was

> an Old World country where a woman's place is still, to a considerable extent, in the home. In the cities, to be sure, modern trends and the pressure of the war itself have liberalised social attitudes. But in the rural sections – and it is quite possible you will be billeted in areas that are rural beyond your expectations - the old ideas still exist.[18]

Although no unified national identity existed, therefore, there was nonetheless unity across religious and political divides regarding female behaviour. Female virtue was central to the identities of both Protestant and Catholic communities in Northern Ireland, and the importance of female moral standards and sexual behaviour transcended other divides, indeed, were perhaps magnified because of the absence of other common markers of Northern Irish identity. As one magistrate explained, as he pronounced sentence on a woman in Londonderry who had been charged with indecent behaviour after being found with a sailor behind an air-raid shelter, 'we Irishmen are rather proud of the purity of our Irishwomen, just like the purity of our racehorses'.[19] If the leaders of Northern Ireland could agree on one thing, it was that women were responsible for the breeding of a new generation, and like horses, their mating was to be carefully contained and their purity preserved.

Hollywood idols?

Fraught as the relations between Americans and the Northern Irish were, it is also apparent that the women of Northern Ireland were particularly interested in the arrival of US soldiers. They not only socialised with them and engaged in sexual relationships with them, but in a number of cases, even married them. More than simply reflecting a desire for the exotic, Northern Irish women's sexual encounters with American men reflected the social changes in Northern Ireland during the war years and especially changes in women's status.

The Americans in Northern Ireland enjoyed a certain erotic and exotic appeal. A major contribution to the desirability of the US troops was their smart outward appearance, in particular, their uniforms. Compared with the British soldiers, the American servicemen were much better dressed and groomed. One woman who worked with the American Red Cross in Belfast during the Second World War described the 'lovely' uniforms the Americans had, how well pressed they were, and how they looked so much more professional than their British counterparts, whose uniforms often did not match. In her opinion, British soldiers seemed part of a less efficient and less organised outfit.[20]

Another factor in the process of turning American troops into objects to be desired was the role of Hollywood in, as Marilyn Lake argues, 'coding American men as lovers, as sexual, as men to be looked at'.[21] Ideas about Americans in general were largely based upon national stereotypes, which in turn were derived mainly from American films.[22] Like the rest of the United Kingdom, cinema-going was a huge pastime in Northern Ireland. The American vice-consul in Belfast, John C. Fuess, prepared a report on cinema-going habits in Northern Ireland for the Psychology Division, Research and Analysis Branch of Strategic Services in the US. He stated that it was estimated that the average individual saw a film twice a week. Young people attended the cinema more than the older generations, and more women than men attended. Members of the working class were more likely to go to the cinema than those of the upper class, and city people more than those from the country. His research also indicated that 'American films are unquestionably the most popular films shown and constitute ninety-five per cent of all exhibitions'.[23] Gangster films were 'crowd pullers' and as such constituted a major part of the films shown. However, vice-consul Fuess warned that

> while they [gangster films] are unquestionably popular, there is little question that the export of these films is highly detrimental to the United States in giving a completely distorted picture of American life. Film exhibitors have remarked upon their effect in spreading slang words among children. This type of film should be curtailed, if not totally eliminated.[24]

The Report also referred to the fact that realistic films such as *The Grapes of Wrath* were considered sordid by the film-going public and not appreciated. Educational films were also unpopular and vice-consul Fuess maintained that propaganda had to be thoroughly disguised if it were to prove successful.

Into this social and cultural atmosphere entered thousands of young American troops. Pamela Winfield writes that 'they strutted into pubs, cafes and local dance halls looking straight off the silver screen in their well cut uniforms, doubles of the film stars the girls adored'.[25] Therefore, for many women the ideal romantic hero came with a 'silver screen' American accent, and this status was greatly assisted by the fact that the US troops had access to a range of scarce material goods such as chocolates, stockings, chewing gum, fresh fruit and cigarettes. Rationing had made goods of this kind very desirable and raised the status of those with access to them. American soldiers thus took on an almost mythical status, and were, for a number of women, objects of desire to be actively pursued.

Anxiety arose because it was Americans and not local men who were the objects of desire.[26] As one air-raid warden in Londonderry commented, 'we were getting our eyes wiped, left, right and centre'.[27] Another local commentator explained that while the women of the city developed quite a rapport with the US troops, 'Derry men were not too pleased . . . and thought it grossly unfair competition for the affections of the city's womenfolk'.[28]

Behind these concerns lay other, more hidden concerns about women's sexual freedom. Both Protestant and Catholic communities worried about the behaviour of young women. In particular, many more women had gained employment that required them to live outside the family home and entailed a greater measure of independence. It is difficult to determine total figures of women employed during the Second World War, but the number of insured women workers in Northern Ireland increased from 111,900 in 1939 to a peak of 118,600 in 1943. There also existed growing opportunities for women in occupations that had previously been male dominated, such as engineering. Before the war there were fewer than 300 women employed in engineering, but this figure rose to 12,300 by 1943.[29] During the war more women moved from rural areas to larger towns and cities to undertake various types of war-related work. Their new jobs and living situations removed a measure of parental control and many in society shared the fears expressed by the *Armagh Guardian* in 1943 that the break-up of home life would have disastrous consequences.[30] In 1943, the Church of Ireland's Moral Welfare Association also expressed concerns about the impact of war on Northern Ireland. They feared that, for both young men and women soldiers, the realisation that many of the people they knew might go off to war and never come back ensured they 'lived largely in the present . . . thinking neither of the past or the future'. It was felt that young people wanted to 'grasp life while they had it', and the inevitable result of this conduct would be a 'lowering of [moral] standards'.[31]

Women's financial and personal independence meant that it became more acceptable for young women to go out at night on their own, and socialising in peer groups often took the place of the family environment. It was women's presence and conduct in public that led to demands for women police such as those employed during the First World War.[32] In June 1943, the Reverend Neil, delivering the Home Mission Report to the General Assembly of the Presbyterian Church, stated that 'the number of girls running through the streets of Belfast and Derry today is staggering'.[33] Catholic priests expressed similar concerns. The Bishop of Derry stated at a confirmation service in Co. Donegal that 'I wish I could take some of the people to see the conduct of their girls in Derry – girls from Donegal and Inishowen. It would be better for them to live on potatoes and salt'.[34] He appealed for stricter parental control, as 'Irish parents have always regarded the purity of their daughters as a very important thing'.[35] The presence of American soldiers and sailors in Northern Ireland made the enforcement of parental, community, or even governmental control much more difficult.

Women, alcohol and entertainment

Women's newfound freedom caused considerable anxiety for community leaders in Northern Ireland, especially since women participated in illicit and even illegal sexual activity with the American men they found so attractive. To be sure, some of the concerns expressed simply reflected typical worries about military personnel stationed in a foreign country. Still, Northern Irish leaders revealed great uneasiness over how illicit sexuality betrayed women's deficiencies.

Criticism of the sexual behaviour of US troops was kept relatively muted in the public domain. However, reports from censored letters reveal some of the complaints that were made about Americans. While the mail censored from Northern Ireland concerning US troops was often more favourable than that coming from other parts of the British Isles, the main areas of complaint about US troops in Northern Ireland were similar to those in the rest of Britain. They concerned the troops' treatment of women, especially accosting them in the streets, having too much money and spending it on alcohol, disorderly behaviour, and general boasting about America.[36]

The relative wealth of US troops enabled them to purchase large amounts of alcohol and their heavy drinking was often criticised. One censored letter declared that 'it will be a red letter day in Ireland the day the Yankee Army clears out . . . They are the worst set of drunkards ever was imported into any place'.[37] During the court case of a young woman charged with drunkenness and indecent behaviour for having been found in an air-raid shelter in Londonderry with an American soldier (the girl was drunk and the soldier sober), the resident magistrate asked the military and police authorities to control the price of alcohol, as it was 'common knowledge that the Americans with their big pay could buy bottles of whiskey at £3'.[38]

Likewise, the ability of the American troops to buy large amounts of alcohol and other goods was the cause of a great deal of jealousy from local men and British troops who were not able to do so. Consequently, some of them felt that they were being outdone by the Americans on all fronts when it came to female attention and it was, unsurprisingly the cause of a number of fights and disturbances. One fight in Londonderry was precipitated by three British soldiers challenging an American soldier sitting with some girls at a dance with the taunt 'these bloody Yanks get all the girls around here'.[39] It was also alleged that in Ulster towns British servicemen roamed the streets nightly as they could not afford to frequent the same places of entertainment as the Americans.[40]

Women, alcohol, and entertainment were what Americans were believed to desire most, and it was their nocturnal searches for them that provoked most criticism.[41] Some of the rowdiness was blamed on boredom. Louise Farrand, Assistant Director of the American Red Cross in Belfast, explained that her organisation was trying to relieve the problem of American troops on the street by providing entertainment. She went on to state that 'if American troops were drunk or going around with the wrong sort of girls, remember they had nothing else to do'.[42] It was suggested that in Belfast the 'crowded conditions, lack of entertainment facilities and a shortage of hotel accommodations were reflected in numerous cases of drunkenness and disorderly conduct'.[43] Circumstances were to blame for the troops' bad behaviour rather than the men themselves.

It was eventually deemed necessary to restrict the places to which US troops could go. Across Northern Ireland, many places were made off limits to Americans. These included pubs, hotels, cafés and some residential properties. Some were placed off limits because they were located in areas known for IRA or Republican sympathies and may have been physically dangerous places for the troops to visit. Public houses, some of which had been discovered selling alcohol at inflated prices and in excessive amounts to Americans, were also placed on the restricted list. Places that prostitutes or women deemed unsuitable were known to frequent were also placed out of bounds. Consequently, US troops were forbidden to enter a number of houses occupied by women in towns and villages across Northern Ireland.[44] All of Amelia Street in Belfast, which was infamous for prostitution, was placed off limits. In Londonderry, amusement centres also caused much concern. The senior US Shore Patrol officer believed that one particular amusement centre on Williams Street was second only to the Criterion Dance Hall as far as disorderly behaviour and fighting was concerned. He also believed that it was a favourite spot for 'prostitutes to work their pickup racket'.[45]

It was perhaps inevitable that bored and frequently drunken American soldiers would seek sexual encounters with local women. Some women clearly considered these men an unwanted menace. One Wren (as members of the Women's Royal Naval Service were known) commented in a letter, 'it's not safe for us to be out unless we go together. I'd hate to be out in Derry alone after dusk believe me. These Yanks are positive fiends for women and should all be in homes (mental ones)'.[46] Another letter referred to the fact that the Americans have 'got themselves a nasty name here as far as girls are concerned'.[47] Americans were reputed to be particularly persistent when pursuing women and at times harassed them. As one woman from Warrenpoint wrote, 'I have missed you these last three months and more so now at nights, for if you go down the street at all there is a Yank after you all the time and as soon as we get shot of one lot another lot is at our elbow – it doesn't make any difference to them whether you say you are married and don't want them or not'.[48] This experience was shared by a writer from Coalisland, Co. Tyrone, who described how around twenty US soldiers had arrived in the village on a course, got drunk, and 'went about the streets chasing girls around until the police had to intervene'.[49] One letter-writer declared that 'if things go as they are, there will be more Yankee babies here than in America'.[50]

The prime concern for the authorities in both Northern Ireland and the rest of the UK was to keep US troops and, consequently, the US authorities happy and healthy. Criticism was silenced through censorship, and friction or conflict between troops and civilians was resolved quickly and quietly. These included cases where troops were accused of break-ing the law, usually destruction or damage of property. Compensation was quickly paid to ensure no further complaint. It is apparent, however, that women who made accusations against US troops and whose moral conduct was questionable were treated as untrustworthy. If a situation arose where Irish women pressed charges against American servicemen, these charges were often ignored. Two sisters accused an American sailor of sexual assault in Londonderry. The sisters gave similar statements, as did civilians who had helped them, and they identified the sailor. The sailor denied the charges. The Senior Patrol Officer added an addendum to the statements that had been taken, and noted that the sailor in ques-tion had not been put on report, explaining that he had apparently been seen by the women making the accusations at the police barracks the night before the incident, and also that the 'local police have stated that both girls are of a questionable character'.[51] The appended statement from the Shore Patrol Officer on duty that night also explained that the two girls had seen the sailor for 'a few minutes the night before' and he felt they could easily have remembered him. He also stated that he too had learned from the police that both the girls were prostitutes.[52] The sexual reputation of these women was therefore an important factor in whether or not the authorities believed they were telling the truth. As the police believed them to be prostitutes, their statements and identification of the sailor subsequently carried no weight and were not taken seriously.

While there were complaints about the behaviour of the American troops towards women, then, blame was more often placed on the women who were involved with them. They were accused of loose morals and pursuing and 'throwing themselves at soldiers'.[53] A 1943 letter to the editor of the *Belfast Newsletter* expressed disgust at having seen 'some nice-looking American soldiers being pursued by two very undesirable young women, who were causing them great embarrassment by trying to talk to them and force their companionship on them'.[54] It was felt that 'there is a bad element who leads them on', and that while 'their [American troops'] conduct is disgraceful, a lot of our girls are 100% worse'.[55] Some went even further in their condemnation of the girls, whom they felt were 'all after the Yanks for a good time . . . It would make you feel ashamed of Northern Ireland.' The Americans were seen as 'a lot of kids only acting the fool and dirty girls hitch hiking them away and leaving them without a cent'. Another writer from County Antrim opined, 'I do not blame the men, the girls throw themselves at them because they have plenty of money and can give them a good time'.[56] As the Royal Ulster Constabulary's Inspector General reported, the locals, particularly the women, got on well with the troops as long as they 'lavished money on them'.[57]

The redirecting of attention towards female sexual behaviour rather than misbehaviour of American troops is further illustrated with the case of a US sailor who had broken a window in a house in Londonderry and assaulted two men. The case was straightforward as the police caught the sailor on the same night that the offence occurred. However, the report from the Shore Patrol Officer involved in the case suggested that the woman whom the soldier had gone to see that night was a prostitute. The report went on to say that the woman was pregnant, had plans to marry a British sailor, and did not have a residence permit for the City of Derry. She was also a Free State subject and was to be charged and sent back to Éire by the police. Information about the woman and her personal life received greater attention than the assault and damage caused by the American sailor.[58] The crime perpetrated by the US sailor was considered less serious once knowledge about the character of the woman in question came to light. Female sexual sin was perceived as being much worse than male drunkenness, violence and damage to property. It is apparent that this actively applied double standard, combined with the 'needs of wartime diplomacy', ensured that American servicemen were largely free from blame for the 'presumed breakdown of the moral standards of women and girls'.[59] It was clearly women and not men who were to blame and who would subsequently 'pay the price of sexual transgression'.[60]

The numbers of girls who consorted with troops publicly and without supervision alarmed the authorities and caused outrage from members of the public: being seen in the company of American servicemen at night was simply not what 'decent' girls did. It was generally assumed that these women engaged in sexual relationships with the American men. The postal censorship report recorded a letter from Lisburn that declared, 'you wouldn't hardly meet a decent girl over here now . . . They are ruined by the Yanks, one is not safe going out with any of them. You know young CW, she has disgraced her mother . . . She is going out with Yanks all day long and I hear she has got that bad disease.'[61] Furthermore, the magistrate at the Londonderry trial of a woman charged with disorderly and indecent behaviour explained that the police had great difficulty when they saw women speaking to sailors. His advice was that 'any woman who has respect for herself isn't to be strolling the streets of Derry at night'.[62]

Steps were taken to try and control the problem of girls consorting with soldiers on the streets at night. Beginning in September 1943 a Women's Patrol took to the streets of Belfast, and in Londonderry there was a crackdown by the police on women and girls believed to be involved in immoral activities. However, being seen talking to American troops in the street was sometimes enough to prompt an arrest.[63] Furthermore, women arrested for disorderly conduct were usually in the company of US troops at the time of arrest.[64] Relatively small fines were imposed for obstruction and disorderly behaviour. Trespassing on the American Naval Camp was punished more severely, either by a large fine or by imprisonment. Three women from Belfast, aged eighteen and nineteen, were sentenced to three months in prison after being found in a hut on the Naval Base in Londonderry. They had met the sailors in Belfast, travelled to Londonderry with them, and then stayed the night in the hut.[65]

While some of the sexual interactions between local women and troops may have been impromptu and informal, more organised forms of sexual entertainment for soldiers were evidently also available. Newspaper reports of court proceedings indicate a number of prosecutions for keeping what was referred to as a 'disorderly house'.[66] Three women, previously convicted for leaving nine children alone in the house while they went dancing, were convicted three months later for keeping a disorderly house.[67] The court was told that the police had been keeping a watch, and during eleven days forty-three persons had visited the house, the majority of whom were soldiers and sailors. When they entered the house at two o'clock in the morning, they found sailors and women in various states of undress.[68] In Londonderry, a man and his wife were sentenced to three months' hard labour for the same crime, along with two women accused of aiding and abetting them. The police reported that between 25 January 1943 and 5 February 1943, sixty American and Canadian sailors, marines, and civilians left the house smelling strongly of drink.[69]

Women who were accused of neglecting their children while they went out at night with servicemen were particularly condemned by the magistrates trying their cases.[70] As one newspaper headline declared, 'Soldier's Wife Sentenced. Neglect of Children. Out to 2 a.m. A Sailor Escort. Disgrace to Irish Womanhood'.[71] The resident magistrate, in summing up the case in court, stated that,

> this is as shocking a case as I have ever heard in this court in view of the fact that we pride ourselves on the high standard of the purity of Irishwomen. I hope there is no soldier or sailor or airman's wife in Derry or County Derry

or anywhere in Ireland who has committed this horrible crime . . . It has dishonoured the name of Irishwomen.[72]

Neglect of children by a mother seemed to many authorities to represent the extremes to which women's sexual freedom and the abandonment of their traditional roles might lead.

The companionship of nice girls

How to occupy and entertain large numbers of American servicemen in legal and licit ways when they were off duty, on leave, and off base was a major and immediate concern for the civilian and military authorities. Indeed, the issue of hospitality for the troops received much more official attention in Northern Ireland than in mainland Great Britain. This regard has been attributed to the fact that the American presence in Northern Ireland had a political sensitivity that was largely absent on the mainland. For this reason, the leisure time of American troops needed to be carefully organised in order to prevent any physical risk to the troops and to prevent adverse publicity from those opposed to their presence. Of course, the organisation of hospitality could take place more easily in Northern Ireland than on the mainland as it was a small and tightly run state, replete with its own devolved local government.[73]

In February 1942, it was agreed that the American Army would take care of soldiers' welfare on base, and the American Red Cross (ARC) would look after soldiers off base in local towns.[74] The first American Red Cross Club opened in Londonderry in 1942. These clubs were centres of entertainment for off-duty troops and were regarded as little bits of America in Britain. They provided accommodation, entertainment and American foodstuffs such as doughnuts. In September 1942, a Northern Irish Committee on troop welfare and hospitality was also established under the leadership of Basil Brooke, the minister of commerce. Local Hospitality Committees were then established in the autumn of 1942 and were organised by the Women's Royal Voluntary Service (WRVS) under their chairwoman, Lady Gladys Stronge.[75]

One of the most popular forms of entertainment organised by the ARC were dances. The *Londonderry Sentinel* recorded that 'thousands of Irish girls have abandoned Irish jigs and reels for American square and country dances to say nothing of the famous "jitterbugging"'.[76] However, disquiet soon arose concerning the girls who attended these dances. It was felt that contact between US troops and local women needed to be controlled, as the soldiers were not able to differentiate between 'bad' and 'good' girls.[77] Louise Farrand, Assistant Director of the Belfast ARC Club, explained that 'we have also attempted to have a date night twice a week, permitting the men to bring in their own girls. The result was not particularly desirable and we have decided to abandon that in favour of working up our own hostess list.'[78] She went on to describe how this list was made. Firstly, the personnel managers of various large organisations and businesses were contacted and asked to recommend groups of desirable girls. The girls would then be interviewed and checked by the authorities for security reasons. If deemed suitable they were issued with a permanent pass.[79] If a soldier wanted a particular girl on the hostess list she would have to be registered and comply with the same regulations. Miss Farrand explained the success of the scheme and the need for properly vetted hostesses more fully a month later, in August 1942:

> We are building up our Dance Hostess list very slowly, as we feel we must be very cautious in this matter. The city is teeming with undesirables, and while we are holding no brief for soldier morality, we feel that we wish to maintain a certain high standard of atmosphere in order that the boys will feel that we are trying to give them the thing they want most, the companionship of nice girls.[80]

It is thus obvious that there was a concern by the US authorities over the possibilities for sexual involvement between Northern Irish women and American men, even at licit entertainment establishments. It was hoped that by providing 'nice' girls for the American soldiers, moral standards could be more easily maintained.

Appeals for respectable hostesses were frequently made in the press. For example, in 1943, the 'young ladies' of Londonderry were called on to help with the reorganisation of the Red Cross Club in the city.[81] The *Londonderry Sentinel* explained that although the Club offered excellent catering facilities as well as dances these were 'hardly enough to keep lively young men away from undesirable places in the city'. It was felt that if local girls were in attendance, young men would be more inclined to frequent the club. Consequently, it was suggested that each of the city churches would nominate a party of girls and volunteer workers who would be interviewed and their 'special talents' noted. The Americans, it was claimed, had already thought up a 'snappy name' for them, such as the 'Maiden City Lassies' or the 'Derry Maids'. The article encouraged girls to sign up as hostesses, declaring that, 'the best types of girls from all sections of society are wanted'.[82]

While the rhetoric may have not been class specific, the methods of control and their implementation were often targeted at lower-class women. Rose suggests that class was seen as a measure of respectability and that lower-class women were considered to be more prone to 'promiscuity and sexual licentiousness'.[83] Of course, it is clear that generalisations with respect to class are flawed, and the idea that all working-class women held or were perceived to hold different standards of morality than their middle-class counterparts cannot be accepted without question. The working-class cannot be seen as an homogenous entity. For example, there is an important distinction between the 'respectable' working class and the 'residuum' or lower working class. It is equally evident that class did not necessarily define acceptable standards of behaviour. For example, many working-class women in Northern Ireland, particularly from rural areas, would never have attended dances, particularly if Americans were in attendance.[84] It is also apparent that it was perfectly acceptable for many middle-class women to attend dances, and subsequently meet and even marry US troops.[85] Nonetheless, those who generated most concern among the authorities, and whose activities were most tightly regulated and policed, were women from the lower working class.

Licit entertainments thus fulfilled an important function in regulating class in wartime Northern Ireland. The authorities were better able to regulate and control those who attended official dances and events, and chose 'suitable' hostesses. Attempts to restrict contact between the troops and local women on the streets were not so easily managed. The fear was that 'undesirable' women largely from the lower working class posed a threat to troops and were deliberately trying to accost and seduce the men. The authorities condemned and severely punished these women as convenient scapegoats in their campaign to preserve the social status quo.

Race relations

An added complication to relations between Northern Irish civilians and the US military was the arrival of African-American regiments. Racial tensions between white and black American soldiers caused great concern in general for American and British military authorities alike, but these tensions were also felt in sexual interactions with Northern Irish women. One American corporal based in Northern Ireland wrote, 'the people over here make absolutely no distinction between the races as we do in the States and when the black and the oranges meet, well I can't say what a coloured race it will be. It is not uncommon to see a white woman and a black man walking down the street together.'[86] For most Northern Irish women these men were the first black people they had ever seen and some were captivated. A black private wrote, 'the Irish people treat us just as if we were Irish. Before we came here there wasn't any coloured people and from that you know the kind of questions we were asked when we landed. The girls over here are right in there, if you dig what I mean.'[87] Two other black soldiers recorded how 'all the girls are going crazy about us' and 'get a load of this. I am loaded down with these Irish girls. I mean I have found my Rose.'[88]

For white Americans, especially those from racially segregated states in the south, the social mixing of races was abhorrent, let alone the sexual mixing. As one Private, writing from Northern Ireland, complained, 'I have see nice looking white girls going out with a coon. They think they are hot stuff. The girls are so dumb it is pitiful. Wait 'til Georgia gets those <u>educated</u> Negroes back there.'[89] Another letter described how 'those from the South want to go out and carve up the colored boys immediately. The civil war has started among the American troops in Ireland.'[90] The threat of physical violence was very real and numerous fights broke out between black and white soldiers in pubs and dance halls. The American Consul in Belfast, Parker Buhrman, explained in a letter to David Gray, the American Ambassador in Dublin, how there had been 'some friction around Londonderry between our Negro Navy personnel and our troops, arising out of the fact that our troops objected to the American Negroes dancing with the Irish girls, which precipitated a good many fights in the local dance halls.'[91] The result was a separate dance hall for African-American personnel.

Loose women, loaded with disease

Of particular concern in Northern Ireland as elsewhere was the incidence of sexually transmitted diseases among American troops. Venereal disease had long been associated with prostitution, and concerns about both social problems were clearly linked. In Northern Ireland as a whole the prosecutions for prostitution increased from ten in 1941 to 171 in 1942, peaking at 185 in 1943.[92] While this increase may reflect an increased concern by the authorities about such activities, it is likely that actual numbers of women engaged in prostitution also rose. At the same time, women's increased sexual freedom gave rise to new concerns about women as sexual predators and infectious agents. Longstanding discourse had portrayed women who had engaged in premarital sexual relations, who had become pregnant outside of marriage, or who had become prostitutes, as victims, and understood their 'fall' into sexual sin as the result of betrayal, male exploitation, ignorance, innocence, alcohol, bad parents, bad companions, or 'feeblemindedness'. These ideas gave way to concerns that women were purveyors of disease and a threat to male health.

Contemporary prosecutions of sexually active women demonstrate the new and harsher attitudes. In February 1943, a newspaper report in the *Londonderry Sentinel* headlined 'Filthy Little Girls' outlined the problem.[93] Two women from Co. Tyrone had been charged with 'wandering abroad without any visible means of support' in Londonderry and had been seen by the police going into a boarding house with US Marines. The Head Constable commenting on the charge stated that there had been

> a very big increase in the number of that type of girl coming into the city. They came in penniless and paraded the city in the hope of picking up servicemen and getting money from them. They got drunk and very often caused malicious damage. They were very objectionable and degraded the city.[94]

Detective Inspector Dobbin concluded that 'these filthy little girls were becoming a pest'.[95] Similarly, the Resident Magistrate in Londonderry, after placing two fifteen-year-old girls on probation and instructing them to keep outside Londonderry at night, warned householders to be very careful when employing maids, 'having regard to the present loose and disgraceful state of affairs amongst young girls and women in the city'.[96] Four more cases were reported in the news a month later, in March 1943. They involved girls who had been found guilty and fined five shillings for obstruction. The girls claimed they were innocent of the offence and that the sailors in question had simply stopped them to ask for directions.[97] Detective Inspector Dobbin again declared that 'girls of this description gave a lot of trouble and if they went home at a respectable hour members of the service would not give as much trouble'.[98]

Discussions of sexually transmitted diseases seldom focused on the actions of the servicemen themselves but instead on the way in which women responded to them. This focus is similar to that of other discussions happening around the world. Large numbers of American troops were also based in Australia during the war years, for example, and a similar cause for concern arose from the undeniable fact that Australian women were not always innocent victims of seduction, but in many cases 'actively initiated' their sexual encounters with American troops.[99] Furthermore, female sexuality in general began to be seen as active rather than passive, with women seen as more capable of controlling their sexual lives.

Concern was also firmly directed towards maintaining the health and welfare of the troops rather than that of the women with whom they were involved. As one interviewee explained, 'the men were most important, as long as they were entertained and happy that was all that mattered, the girls, well they had to look after themselves, they weren't considered important.'[100] The aim of the military was to ensure that the troops were happy and remained healthy. This involved ensuring that respectable female company that would not debilitate their troops was readily available.

The military authorities were extremely concerned about the contraction of sexually transmitted diseases by troops during the Second World War, as they had been in previous conflicts. As Lesley Hall argues, war has traditionally been associated with an increase in venereal infection.[101] The MSOH for Belfast explained that in the city 'there was an increase [in sexually transmitted diseases] - there always has been in war-time'.[102] Concerns about the spread of such diseases in Northern Ireland and across the UK as a whole were heightened following the arrival of US soldiers.

There was a wide variation in the way in which the British and US governments approached and dealt with the issue, and this difference was to cause considerable friction between the military and governmental authorities of both countries. The British government was reluctant to introduce too harsh legislation because it feared a public outcry would occur if it introduced stringent legislation that targeted women specifically. This concern was directly related to previous experience of the consequences of the CD Acts in the 1860s and legislation passed in the First World War, in particular, the law known as DORA 40d. Campaigning by women's organisations in particular about the injustice of the legislation, its condoning of a sexual double standard, and its unfair treatment of women, had led to the repeal of previous legislation. The British government during the Second World War was understandably anxious not to provoke a similar situation.

However, as in the First World War, there was growing pressure on the British government from the other Allied nations to implement strict legislation to control the growing problem of sexually transmitted diseases.

For Americans, coming from a country where prostitution was actively suppressed and attention was focused on 'promiscuous' women and ways of preventing the spread of venereal diseases, the lack of action taken by the British caused considerable anxiety. The concern felt by the British military was as much about the effect on Anglo-American relations as about the health of the troops. As Lieutenant-Colonel Rowe, Secretary of the Anglo-American Relations Conference of the War Office, explained to the Foreign Office, the 'problem' of the accosting of US soldiers by women on the streets and the subsequent spread of disease risked affecting long-term Anglo-American relations.[103] He believed that American soldiers would 'naturally conclude that, as a nation, we are extremely lax in our morals and when they see that vice flourishes openly in our streets, they conclude that it is accepted by the public and that our Government is powerless, or unwilling to deal with it.'[104]

Further concerns arose over the fear that women's organisations in the States would react badly to the stories of accosting and their outrage would be used to further anti-British propaganda. The spread of venereal disease was an additional concern, with US army statistics claiming that 30 per cent of such disease among their army in Britain was contracted there. It was believed that the idea that Britain was rife with venereal disease would not sit favourably with the American families of soldiers sent to Britain.[105] The British government worried that unfavourable reports might even encourage the US to return to its isolationist stance in world affairs after the war. As seen in chapter 4, pressure from the other Allies eventually convinced the British government of the necessity of legislation and in November 1942 Defence Regulation 33B was passed, requiring practitioners to notify the MSOH of the names of sexual contacts given by people receiving treatment for VD.[106] As observed, this legislation while officially gender-neutral, was clearly focused on women as the source of infection.[107]

It was not only legislation but also official pronouncements about sexually transmitted diseases that were on a very different footing in Northern Ireland as compared with the US, and this provided another source of tension. In Northern Ireland, sex was not a topic readily discussed in public. In 1943, the *Armagh Guardian* suggested that in rural areas any 'mention of the subject was to tread on very dangerous ground, rendering the speaker liable to be charged with indecency'.[108] To try and prevent the spread of sexually transmitted diseases amongst their troops both at home and abroad, the American military produced a great deal of propaganda and publicity advising troops about the dangers of the diseases.

A *Guide to VD Control for Non-commissioned Officers* was published in 1941 by the US Social Protection Division, in an attempt to dispel some of the myths concerning the diseases. Myth number twenty-eight of the *Guide* stated that 'it is honourable to conceal the identity of the contact'.[109] The reply to this myth was as follows:

> The girl has burnt you. She has not been concerned with your health. She is likewise causing other men, with whom you are living and fighting for your country, the same trouble she is causing you. You should try to help protect your friends from a girl who is not interested in anything but the money or the drinks she can get from you and your friends.[110]

Another pamphlet, *So You've got a Furlough Coming Up*, published by the US War Department in 1944, illustrates how blame was - in American fashion - apportioned to all sexually active young women. It advised against sexual relations outside marriage as the most important protection against venereal disease. It then went on to state:

> Avoid prostitutes, Pick-Ups, Push-Overs and 'Easy-Women.' Prostitutes, practically without exception, are infected with venereal disease. They are not and cannot be made safe. Pick-Ups and other 'Easy Women' are by all odds likely to be infected too. Another thing to remember is that a girl, free of infection at one time, may now have VD and can easily pass it on to you.[111]

Similarly, the posters published by the US authorities warning against venereal disease portrayed sexually active young women as infectious agents. One poster displayed a gun with the word 'LOADED?' written beneath it. Underneath the gun were three young women dressed in a glamorous fashion, one woman winking suggestively. The caption read, 'Don't take chances with Pickups! Loose Women may also be Loaded with Disease'.[112] Another poster pictured an elegantly dressed woman smoking a cigarette, with the slogan, 'You may think she's just your "gal," But she may be Everyone's Pal'.[113] A third poster showed a woman standing at the corner of a wall, wearing a knee-length skirt, heavily made-up and smoking a cigarette. Above her were printed the words: 'Easy to Get' and below: 'Syphilis and Gonorrhoea'.[114] The implication of the posters was that because these women were 'easy to get' it was very likely they would be infected with venereal disease. In short, while the women may have looked clean, this did not guarantee that they were not infected. All women were, in effect, seen as potential sources of venereal disease, and these images produced by the military 'remained associated with the traditional images of male victim and the female seductress'.[115]

Much of wartime American campaigning concerning sexually transmitted diseases emphasised the fact that they assisted the enemy. In effect, by contracting such a disease one was 'putting a man off the team' and damaging the overall effectiveness of the army.[116] The propaganda appealed to the patriotism of American troops stationed in the British Isles. It warned that it should be a matter of pride to avoid infection, as it reflected 'not only on your own intelligence, but also on the state of discipline and morale of our troops'.[117] Men were also reminded that they would have to return to America, and that 'it will be unpleasant to report that you spent your war service in a GU hospital'.[118] The implication that contracting a sexually transmitted disease was a failing and thus something to be ashamed of challenged the previously held view of contraction as a 'concomitant of militarism'. Such a disease was certainly no longer to be considered a rite of passage into manhood or a sign of virility.[119]

The methods used to prevent venereal disease, particularly the issuing of prophylactics to US troops at the American Red Cross clubs, met with substantial opposition in Northern Ireland. The US authorities referred to the 'prejudice amongst the civil population' in Northern Ireland that prevented the usual establishment of a prophylactic station at US bases there.[120] Indeed, instead of using the term 'prophylactic', a sign saying 'Aid Station', in conjunction with a green light, was used. Evidently, at least some of the US troops were making use of these stations. One contemporary observer, Derrick Gibson-Harries, reported that an Armagh newspaper described how troops were employed in the city with spiked sticks to walk round and pick up the litter of condoms, particularly when the American troops were leaving.[121] Littering of condoms was a problem wherever troops were stationed and was a frequent cause of complaint. A Home Office Circular, issued on 17 July 1944, described how 'contraceptives are left in public places, private gardens, shop fronts, shelters etc., where they cannot give but offence to decent people'.[122]

There were conflicting reports about the levels of VD amongst the troops based in Northern Ireland during the Second World War. A report from the British Troops in Northern Ireland (BTNI) in February 1942 told how the daily number of cases for VD in hospital was about 100 for all three services. The BTNI recorded the weekly average as between 40 and 50, of which two-thirds came from the army. The report went on to explain that these totals were 'somewhat higher than in the rest of the UK', due, it argued, to men being far away from home, and the lack of entertainments and sports grounds.[123] Similarly, Revd T. Gordon Ott, Anglican Chaplin, attached to the Royal Canadian Navy (RCN) in

Londonderry, noted in March 1945 that 20 per cent of RCN personnel in hospital were suffering from VD.[124] Keith Jeffery contends that while it is possible the sailors may have contacted the disease elsewhere, 'it seems likely that the majority of contacts were in Northern Ireland'.[125] However, the US command in Northern Ireland commented in its General Orders, that for British troops in Northern Ireland the venereal rate was low, due, it believed, to the 'high moral standards of the inhabitants' and that the number of prostitutes, 'both public and clandestine', was very low, with no 'red-light district' in any of the towns and cities.[126] Colonel J.H. McNick, the US Medical Corps Historian, also suggested that the 'VD rate for US Army troops in Northern Ireland compared favourably with other sections of the British Isles'.[127]

While it is difficult to make any definite assumptions about the rate of VD amongst the troops, the relatively high civilian rates and the increase during the war years would suggest that it was very likely that the rate for troops was high. Furthermore, the lack of publicity and public discussion of VD can only have contributed to the levels of infection and would have had obvious consequences on the spread of disease amongst the troops. However, the need for the US military authorities to maintain good relations in Northern Ireland both during and after the war may have influenced their positive comments about the low levels of VD and morality of the population.

The efforts of the US, British, and local governments and their medical and military authorities on this matter were considerable. Increasingly these efforts focused on promiscuous girls and women considered sexually deviant. They found agreement in the belief that women were the source of sexually transmitted diseases and responsible for its spread.[128]

War brides

Not all of the sexual contacts between American men and Northern Irish women ended in legal or medical complications. Just weeks after the arrival of American troops in the British Isles came the first requests for marriages with local girls, and the first marriage in Northern Ireland involving an American serviceman took place just over two months after the first troops arrived. On 13 April 1942, twenty-year-old Private Herbert W. Cooke from Cleveland, Ohio, married Thelma Smith, daughter of a Belfast café owner at a local Presbyterian church. The officiating minister felt that as long as the license was in order he was not obliged to secure permission from the groom's commanding officer.[129] American military authorities decided permission was needed, however, and began to warn troops in the UK against marrying local women. In Northern Ireland, newspapers reported the warnings and suggested the reason for this advice was concern for potential brides, since these women would not be given allowances from the US authorities and would have no legal guarantee of maintenance in the future.[130]

Warnings against international marriages became even more forceful. A headline in a 1942 edition of the *Londonderry Sentinel* ran 'US Soldiers and Irish Girls. Marriage Problem. Official Warning'.[131] The official warning issued by the US military was read in the churches of the Catholic Diocese of Down and Connor by request of the bishop. It reiterated the point that US citizenship was not conferred through marriage and that any woman who married an American serviceman could find herself in a very difficult position. However, the warnings clearly did not have the desired effect and in July 1942 European Theater of Operations (ETO) Circular 20 was issued by the US military. It stipulated that marriages could only take place with the US commanding officer's permission, and after written notice of three months.[132]

Marriages were discouraged for a variety of reasons. It was felt that it would be bad for morale if some soldiers had wives with them while others did not. It was also argued that it complicated Anglo-American relations, with the belief that Americans were 'grabbing off' with British girls while their own men were overseas.[133] Likewise, it was believed that such marriages were a 'passing fad with post-war complications'.[134] US marriage allowances were much higher than those in the British Army and this bonus, it was believed, 'constitutes a certain lure for the worst kind of girl'.[135] Furthermore, there were fears that British gold-diggers would target American troops. A cable from a concerned American mother to the commandant of the Londonderry Naval Base expressed similar concerns as her son 'plans to marry [an] Irish girl . . . I do not approve please stop marriage plans [as] boy is my heir to considerable estate [and] possibly girl knows this'.[136]

For those who decided to marry despite the warnings, gaining permission was a complicated process designed to weed out those whose motives may have been questionable. Written requests for permission had to be submitted to the prospective groom's commanding officer by both parties. The prospective bride had to fill in a personal history form that provided details of her family background. The girls were then checked out by the local police and by the authorities in London and interviewed by the Chaplain. A medical examination followed if it was suspected that the woman was pregnant. In the cases where pregnancy was suspected this waiting period was usually waived as it was felt that a speedy wedding was necessary for respectability's sake. As one request for marriage to the Commandant of the Naval Base in Londonderry stated, 'I respectfully request permission to marry immediately because of the physical condition of my prospective bride. This request is made in an effort to relieve the nervousness which a long delay would cause and to save my prospective bride as much embarrassment as possible'.[137]

The American forces relied on local information concerning women who wished to marry US servicemen when making their decisions about permission to marry. This information was provided in a variety of ways. In Belfast, the American Red Cross seconded a local woman to assist the Commanding Officer in vetting those who applied for marriage. She interviewed girls and decided if they were suitable. Letters of reference were provided from priests or ministers. Requests were also sent from the Commandant at the Naval Base in Londonderry to the Police County Inspector's Office. The requests asked if they would have 'Miss X' investigated as to her loyalty and other pertinent factors. The return letters asked whether the girl concerned was a 'person of good character and loyal'.[138] In the majority of cases the women involved were not known to the police. However, there were those whose prior behaviour or reputation led to an unfavourable report. For example, the County Inspector of the RUC in Londonderry wrote concerning one woman that 'it is common knowledge. . .that this person and her sister are regarded as of low moral character by the majority of citizens of this city'.[139] The issue of loyalty obviously took on greater concern in Northern Ireland, where the neutrality of Éire, the nationalist opposition to the war, and the threat of violence towards US troops were of prime importance. It was thus necessary to know whether the woman concerned had any connections with the IRA or anyone engaged in anti-unionist activity.

Even if the marriage was considered to be acceptable, a number of techniques were employed to prevent it from taking place. These included 'advice from all echelons of command and chaplain, transfer of personnel, persuading civilian registrars not to issue licenses'.[140] Nonetheless, permission was granted for the majority of the requests for marriage. Indeed, around 1,800 women from Northern Ireland married members of the US forces during the war years.[141] There is no available information concerning how many of these marriages were successful. However, in 1946, following a campaign by the *Belfast Telegraph* claiming that Northern Irish girls who married US troops were being neglected, the

US government provided three ships which took over 1,000 brides and children to the United States.[142]

A considerable number of women were already pregnant when they submitted a request for permission to marry. Pregnancy outside marriage was a great cause for concern in Northern Ireland. The shame that it carried was just as great in wartime as it had been at other times. The stigma of illegitimacy cut across the class divide. For example, a letter written from a woman in Londonderry to Colonel Ladd at the Naval Base in the city illustrates that not only working-class women were involved. The letter-writer begged for permission to get married and stated that the marriage was not for personal gain or intended as a means to get to America. She went on to explain that 'through a slight mistake I have become pregnant', and that her condition was of great concern because 'my family have a very high reputation and owing to my father holding a government position I do not wish any scandal to be fallen on them'.[143] It is significant that it was only the women who desired to marry who were vetted, interviewed and whose suitability was questioned; men were not put under the same scrutiny. They simply had to declare they had no dependants in the United States and could support a wife.

Mutual, warm and genuine?

In spite of the multiple tensions regarding sexual relationships involving US troops stationed in Northern Ireland, there was also a great deal of warmth expressed towards the Americans. It was felt that there was a great connection between Ulster and America. When the first American troops arrived in Northern Ireland, a *Belfast Telegraph* editorial pointed out that 'our ties with the United States are long established. From this land went the forebears of the Fathers of the Republic, of 13 Presidents, and down to the present day every town and hamlet here has its American links of kinship'.[144] Unionist newspapers such as the *Belfast Telegraph* and *Belfast Newsletter* were in general very positive when discussing American troops, and often spoke of their generosity, especially to children, since American troops held Christmas parties for local children at their bases.[145] It was this generosity which is remembered with fondness by many who recorded their wartime memories, especially after rationing was enforced.[146]

American sources reveal a similar goodwill. The official history of the American Forces Liaison Division referred to the close link between Northern Ireland and America, claiming that it was 'small wonder that these young and eager soldiers from America should find it easy to mingle with the good natured and hospitable people of Northern Ireland'.[147] The weekly regional intelligence reports recorded that the regard between Americans and the people of Northern Ireland was 'mutual, warm, genuine and deep rooted'.[148] Censored letters from soldiers themselves also recorded how some seemed to enjoy their time in Northern Ireland.[149] It has even been suggested that the American troops themselves felt more at home in Northern Ireland than in any other part of the United Kingdom.[150] The American Consul in Belfast described how well the troops were received in Northern Ireland, but that 'the initial hospitality accorded to our troops was much greater than expected. In fact if anything it was a little too much because it set much too high a standard'.[151]

The arrival of US troops clearly had a great impact on Northern Ireland, a conservative and mostly rural society. They brought with them the glamour of Hollywood and generated new forms of entertainment. They also had an important impact on female behaviour and ideas about female sexuality, and previously held assumptions slowly began to change. The established rules of courtship were disregarded under the new, heightened wartime conditions, and the US troops had something to offer to Northern Irish women. The variety of encounters with US troops illustrates the impact on all sections of the community. Respectable upper-, middle-, and working-class girls could become Red Cross hostesses and meet servicemen under the controlled conditions of official dances. Similarly, US troops often attended local churches and could meet respectable girls in a supervised environment. These relationships often led to courtship and marriage. At the other end of the scale were the illicit meetings on the streets or in air-raid shelters, the visiting of houses of ill-repute and unofficial dances in unsupervised dance halls. The girls involved in these encounters were in the main lower-working-class women, whose behaviour was not as closely supervised. These were the women who caused the authorities most concern and who were prosecuted in the courts for their public associations with US troops.[152] More widely, it is evident that women were often blamed for the bad behaviour of the troops. There was clear gender discrimination which saw the transgressions of the troops through a prism of female responsibility. The fears generated by the perceived lowering of moral standards impacted on wider concerns of community identity. Within the divided society of Northern Ireland and under the conditions of war, these fears and concerns about female sexuality were of heightened importance.

Notes

1 Popular Second World War joke: 'Have you heard about the new utility knickers? One yank and they're off!'
2 Reynolds, *'Rich Relations'*, p. 11. The comparison is with 1937. In more sparsely populated Co. Fermanagh, US troops represented the equivalent of one-fifth of the pre-war population.
3 For more on the arrival and stationing of troops in Northern Ireland see Francis Carroll, 'United States Armed Forces in Northern Ireland During World War Two', *New Hibernia Review*, 12:2 (2008), 15–36.
4 A number of other nations had troops based in Northern Ireland. After the Americans, the Canadians were represented in greatest numbers. The ports of Belfast and Londonderry were host to naval and other ships from a wide number of countries.
5 Gardiner, *'Over Here'*; Longmate, *The G.I.'s*; Reynolds, *'Rich Relations'*.
6 Lake, 'The Desire for a Yank'; Sturma, 'Loving the Alien'; Rose, 'Girls and GIs'.
7 See for example Blake, *Northern Ireland in the Second World War*; Doherty, *Post 381*; Gibson-Harries, *Life-Line to Freedom*; Hughes, *Toome's Wartime Airfield*. A recent exception is, Carroll, 'United States Armed Forces in Northern Ireland'.
8 See chapter 3.
9 Cardinal Joseph MacRory, 'Lenten Pastorals', *Armagh Guardian*, 25 February 1944, p. 4.
10 Sonya O. Rose, 'Sex, Citizenship and the Nation in World War II Britain', *American Historical Review*, 103 (1998), 1147–1176.
11 Ibid., 1164.
12 Ibid.
13 Known as the Irish Free State until 1937 and as Éire from 1937 to 1948, before becoming the Republic of Ireland.
14 Six members of the IRA were executed by the government of Éire and over one thousand were imprisoned during the Second World War.
15 Report to Embassy, 'Developments in Northern Ireland', Parker W Buhrman, no. 65, 8 September 1942, File 800, Confidential Reports, Belfast Consulate General, 1936–1942, RG 84, National Archives Building, Maryland (MD NAB).
16 Ibid., 26 September 1942.
17 Ibid., 11 September 1942.
18 *A Pocket Guide to Northern Ireland* (Washington D.C., 1942), p. 17.
19 *Londonderry Sentinel*, 13 January 1944, p. 2.
20 Interview, Mrs M., 5 September 2001.
21 Lake, 'The Desire for a Yank', 629.
22 Reynolds, *'Rich Relations'*, p. 30.
23 Report on Categories of Current Information on Motion Pictures Abroad

of Interest to Psychology Division, Research and Analysis Branch Office of Strategic Services from John C. Feuss, 2 May, 1943, File 840.6, General Records, Belfast Consulate, 1943, RG 84, MD NAB.

24 Ibid.

25 Pamela Winfield, *Sentimental Journey: The Story of the GI Brides* (London, 1984), p. 4.

26 Rose, 'Sex, Citizenship and the Nation', 1150–1151.

27 Brian Lacy, *Siege City: The Story of Derry and Londonderry* (Belfast, 1990), p. 241.

28 Anon., *The War Years: Derry 1939–45* (Derry, n.d.), pp. 41–42.

29 Myrtle Hill, *Women in Ireland: A Century of Change* (Belfast, 2003), p. 119.

30 *Armagh Guardian*, 5 March 1943, p. 3.

31 Church of Ireland Diocesan Meeting, Moral Welfare Association, February 1943, Church of Ireland House, Belfast.

32 See chapter 3; *Belfast Newsletter*, 10 April 1943, p. 2; *Northern Whig*, 27 September 1943, p. 3.

33 *Londonderry Sentinel*, 10 June 1943, p. 3.

34 Ibid., 29 April 1944, p. 4.

35 Ibid.

36 US Troops in Northern Ireland, Postal and Telegraph Censorship Report, 8 December 1943, RG 165, MD NAB.

37 Extracts relative to US troops in Northern Ireland, Postal Censorship report, 8 February 1943, Ministry of Information 12/503, United States File No. 33, FO 371/34123, TNA.

38 *Londonderry Sentinel*, 25 August 1943, p. 2.

39 Statement Concerning Fracas at Clarendon Dance Hall, 5 December 1944, File P 13–1, Misconduct of Personnel, General Correspondence Files, 1944, Naval Overseas Bases, Londonderry, Northern Ireland, RG 181, MD NAB.

40 Letter from Londonderry to Empire News, Manchester, Army Mail Censorship report, 26 July–10 August 1942, File 250.1, Adjutant General's Section Administration Branch, Classified General Correspondence, 1942–1944, RG 338, MD NAB.

41 Hughes, *Toome's Wartime Airfield*, p. 51.

42 *Londonderry Sentinel*, 3 September 1942, p. 4.

43 *A History of the United States in Northern Ireland*, vol. 2, 1 January–20 December 1942, p. 25, File 597, Administration File 1942–1946, ETO Records of the Historical Division, RG 338, MD NAB.

44 List of 'Off limits' Establishments, 2 November 1943 and 13 January 1944, File 225, ETO Historical Division, Administration File, RG 338, MD NAB.

45 Report from Senior Shore Patrol Officer to Commanding Officer, Marine Barracks, USOB, Londonderry, File P 13–1, RG 181, MD NAB.

46 Army Mail Censorship Report, No. 77, 11–25 October 1943, A 9095/33/45, FO 371/32416, TNA.

47 US Troops in Northern Ireland, Postal and Telegraph Censorship Report, 8 December 1943, RG 165, MD NAB.
48 Army Mail Censorship Report, NO. 77, 11–25 October 1943, A 9095/33/45, FO 371/34126, TNA.
49 US Troops in Northern Ireland, Postal and Telegraph Censorship Report for Northern Ireland, Information and Records Branch, London, 1 May 1942, RG 165, MD NAB.
50 Ibid., 8 December 1943.
51 Memorandum from Senior Patrol Officer to the Commandant, USOB, Londonderry, 3 January 1944, File 13.1, RG 181, MD NAB.
52 Statement of Shore Patrol Officer, 27 December 1943, File 13.1, RG 181, MD NAB.
53 Geoffrey Field, 'Perspectives on the Working-Class Family in Wartime Britain, 1939–1945', *International Labour and Working-Class History*, 38 (1990), 15.
54 *Belfast Newsletter*, 10 April 1943, p. 2.
55 Ibid.
56 US Troops in Northern Ireland, Postal and Telegraph Censorship Report for Northern Ireland (No. 27), Information and Records Branch, London, 1 May 1942, RG 165, MD NAB.
57 Inspector General's Report, 1943, Correspondence Concerning Civilian Relations with US Troops, CAB/9CD/225/18, PRONI.
58 Statement of Samuel S. Smith concerning incident on 28 December 1943, File 13.1, RG 181, MD NAB.
59 Rose, 'Girls and GIs', 150.
60 Summerfield, 'Women and War in the Twentieth Century', p. 615.
61 Army Mail Censorship Report, No. 77, 11–25 October 1943, A 9095/33/45, FO 371/34126, TNA.
62 *Londonderry Sentinel*, 11 November 1943, p. 3.
63 Ibid., 2 March 1943, p. 2.
64 Ibid., 23 September 1943, p. 2; 11 November 1943, p. 3.
65 Ibid., 15 April 1943, p. 4.
66 *Londonderry Sentinel*, 14 January 1943, p. 2; 4 March 1943, p. 2; 29 April 1943, p. 2; 13 May 1943, p. 4; *Irish News*, 24 September 1942, p. 3.
67 *Londonderry Sentinel*, 10 September 1942, p. 2; 14 January 1943.
68 Ibid.
69 *Londonderry Sentinel*, 4 March 1943, p. 2.
70 For example, *Londonderry Sentinel*, 25 August 1942, p. 2; 1 June 1943, p. 2; 19 October 1943, p. 2; 11 November 1943, pp. 2–3; 13 January 1944, p. 2.
71 *Londonderry Sentinel*, 1 December 1943, p. 2.
72 Ibid.
73 Reynolds, 'Rich Relations', p. 193.
74 Ibid., p. 154.

75 Ibid., p. 193.
76 *Londonderry Sentinel*, 22 September 1942, p. 4.
77 Elfreda Berthiaume Shukert and Barbara Smith Scibetta, *War Brides of World War Two* (Novato, CA, 1988), p. 11; Reynolds, '*Rich Relations*', p. 263.
78 Monthly Report by Louise Farrand, 10 July 1942, File 900.11/616, ETO, Great Britain, Belfast Club, Records of the American Red Cross, 1935–46, RG 200, MD NAB.
79 Ibid.
80 Letter to Mr Robert Lewis from Miss Louise Farrand, 8 August 1942, File 900.11/616, ETO, Great Britain, Belfast Club, Records of the American Red Cross, 1935–46, RG 200, MD NAB.
81 *Londonderry Sentinel*, 16 September 1943, p. 2.
82 Ibid.
83 Rose, 'Girls and GIs', 150–151.
84 Interview, Mrs W., 30 June 2003.
85 Marriages, General Correspondence Files, 1944, Naval Overseas Bases, Londonderry, Northern Ireland, RG 181, MD NAB.
86 Army Mail Censorship Report, no. 48, 26 June–10 August 1942, File 250.1, Adjutant General's Section Administration Branch, Classified General Correspondence, 1942–1944, RG 338, MD NAB.
87 Ibid., 12–26 April 1942.
88 Ibid., 1–15 September 1942.
89 Ibid., 26 June–10 August 1942.
90 Ibid., 12–26 April 1942.
91 Letter from Parker W. Buhrman to David Gray, 19 May 1942, File 800, Belfast Consulate General, Confidential Reports, 1936–1942, RG 84, MD NAB.
92 *Report on the Administration of Home Office Services, 1939–1946, Government of Northern Ireland* (Ministry of Home Affairs, Belfast, 1947).
93 *Londonderry Sentinel*, 25 February 1943, p. 3.
94 Ibid.
95 Ibid.
96 Ibid.
97 *Londonderry Sentinel*, 2 March 1943, p. 2.
98 Ibid.
99 Lake, 'The Desire for a Yank', 623.
100 Interview, Mrs M., 4 September 2001.
101 Hall, '"War Always Brings It On"', pp. 205–223.
102 Medical Superintendent of Health, Belfast, *Annual Report of Health, 1946*, LA/7/9DA/28, PRONI.
103 Memo from Rowe, 19 February 1943, FO 371/34124, TNA.
104 Ibid.
105 Letter from Richard Law, Foreign Office, to Osbert Peake, Home Office, 5 March 1943, FO 371/34124, TNA.

106 For more on the impact of Regulation 33B see chapter 4.

107 See chapter 4.

108 *The Armagh Guardian*, 3 May 1943, p. 5.

109 *Guide for VD Control for Non-Commissioned Officers*, Social Protection Division Publications, General Records of the Social Protection Division, RG 215, MD NAB.

110 Ibid.

111 *So You've got a Furlough Coming Up?*, 13 January 1944, Social Protection Division Publications, RG 215, MD NAB.

112 Social Protection Division Publications, RG 215, MD NAB.

113 Ibid.

114 Ibid.

115 Sander L. Gilman, *Sexuality, An Illustrated History: Representing the Sexual in Medicine and Culture from the Middle Ages to the Age of AIDS* (New York, 1989), p. 311.

116 'You Don't Think it Could Ever Happen to You', war pamphlet, 9 February 1944, Social Protection Division Publications, RG 215, MD NAB.

117 Memo to all Personnel from HQ Command, US Army Forces in British Isles, 21 May 1942, File 323 Special Observers, ETO Records of Historical Division, Administration Files, 1942–1946, RG 338, MD NAB.

118 Ibid.

119 Hall, 'Venereal Diseases and Society', p. 132.

120 General Orders of Headquarters of the United States Army, Northern Ireland Forces, no. 31, 2 February 1945, Civil Defence, CAB/9CD/225/6, PRONI.

121 Gibson-Harries, *Life-Line to Freedom*, p. 61.

122 'Relationships Between the Civil Population and Members of the Armed Forces', Home Office Circular no. 202/1944, 17 July 1944, CAB/9CD/225/18, PRONI.

123 Appendix 7, War Diary 'A', February 1942, British Troops in Northern Ireland (BTNI), CAB/3A/49, PRONI.

124 Keith Jeffery, 'Canadian Sailors in Londonderry: A Study in Civil-Military Relations, 1942–45' (unpublished paper, n.d.) p. 42. My thanks to the author for providing a copy of this paper.

125 Jeffery, 'Canadian Sailors' p. 43.

126 General Orders of the Headquarters of United States Army, Northern Ireland Forces, no. 31, 2 February 1945, CAB 9/CD/225/6, PRONI.

127 *History of the Second World War*, p. 399.

128 Marilyn E. Hegarty, 'Patriot or Prostitute? Sexual Discourse, Print Media and American Women During World War Two', *Journal of Women's History* 10 (1998), 115.

129 *A History of the United States Army in Northern Ireland*, vol. 1, 1 January 1942–31 December 1942, p. 28, File 597, Administration File 1942–1946, ETO Records of the Historical Division, RG 338, MD NAB.

130 *Londonderry Sentinel*, 2 April 1942, p. 3.

131 Ibid., 16 June 1942, p. 2.

132 Reynolds, '*Rich Relations*', p. 210.

133 Letter from Maj. Gen. R.P. Hartle, USA NIF, to Lt. Gen. Frank M. Andrews, Commander, ETOUSA, 20 April 1943, File 200, ETO Records of the Historical Division, RG 338, MD NAB.

134 Ibid.

135 Ibid.

136 Cablegram from Boston to Commandant Naval Base Londonderry, 18 July 1944, File P-7, Domestic Relations, General Correspondence Files, 1944, Naval Overseas Bases, Londonderry, Northern Ireland, RG 181, MD NAB.

137 File P-7, Domestic Relations, Personnel Officers Files, 1944, Naval Overseas Bases, Londonderry, Northern Ireland, RG 181, MD NAB.

138 Ibid.

139 Letter from County Inspector to Commandant at US Naval Base, Capt. V.L. Kirkman, 27 October 1944, File P-7, Domestic Relations, Personnel Officers Files, 1944, RG 181, MD NAB.

140 Letter, Hartle to Andrews, 20 April 1943, RG 338, MD NAB.

141 Hill, *Women in Ireland*, p. 125.

142 Carroll, 'United States Forces in Northern Ireland', 35

143 Letter to Colonel Land, 20 April 1944, File D-7(I), Marriages, General Correspondence Files, 1944, RG 181, MD NAB.

144 *Belfast Telegraph*, 27 January 1942, p. 2.

145 The nationalist press tended to ignore the presence of US troops. For example, there was no editorial comment on the arrival of the first US troops in comparison with the effusive coverage in the unionist press. The nationalist press did report the pronouncements of the Catholic Church, particularly those of Cardinal MacRory, the Archbishop of Armagh who was opposed to the stationing of British and US troops in Northern Ireland.

146 Gibson-Harries, *Life-Line to Freedom*, p. 59; Hughes, *Toome's Wartime Airfield*, p. 53.

147 A History of the American Forces Liaison Division: Northern Ireland, Ministry of Information, Files of Correspondence, 1942–1945, INF 1/327B, TNA.

148 Home Intelligence Weekly Report 21–28 December. 1942, Ministry of Information A 154/33/45, United States File No. 33, FO 371/34123, TNA.

149 Base Censor Office no. 1, Morale Report 1–15 February 1943, File 250.1, ETOUSA Adjutant General's Section, Administration Branch, Classified General Correspondence 1942–1944, RG 338, MD NAB.

150 Reynolds, '*Rich Relations*', p. 258.

151 Letter from Parker W. Buhrman to David Gray, 26 February 1942, File 800, Belfast Consulate General, Confidential Reports, 1936–42, RG 84, MD NAB.

152 See, for example, *Londonderry Sentinel*, 25 February 1943; 2 March 1943; 23 September 1943; 11 November 1943.

6

'Confused with prejudice and muddled thinking': preventing pregnancy

As the previous chapters have demonstrated there was a great deal of united opinion across the religious and political divisions in Northern Ireland concerning female sexuality and behaviour. This unity can also be seen over issues of birth control. It is further evident that throughout the twentieth century at a local level and at Stormont the authorities were concerned not to provoke opposition from the Churches and in particular the Catholic Church. As with VD publicity and propaganda, the authorities were intent on avoiding controversy at all costs. However, in the case of family planning it is arguable that while the actual opposition from the Churches was relatively muted, it was the fear of potential opposition that hindered the development of a family planning service.

This chapter considers the establishment of the first family planning clinic in Belfast in 1936 and the growth of a family planning service in the 1950s and 1960s. It is of no surprise that services in Northern Ireland grew at a slower rate than the rest of the UK. The first family planning clinic opened in Belfast in 1936, in comparison with 1921 in England, and 1925 in both Scotland and Wales. Governmental legislation was also implemented later in Northern Ireland. The 1967 National Health Service Amendment (Family Planning) Act, which permitted local authorities to provide contraception on social as well as medical grounds, with no restrictions placed on martial status or age, was not introduced until 1969 in Northern Ireland. Similarly, it was not until 1974 that a free family planning service was given official recognition, something which had occurred two years earlier in the rest of the UK. This chapter also considers the issue of abortion, where legislation differs significantly from the rest of the United Kingdom. The 1967 Abortion Act was never extended to Northern Ireland and abortion remains illegal. Attempts to extend the legislation in 1984, 2000 and 2008 have met with strenuous cross-community opposition.[1] The problems created by the lack of clarity over abortion legislation are discussed below.

Marie Stopes and Belfast

The first birth control clinic in Northern Ireland was a Marie Stopes clinic which opened in 1936 and closed just over ten years later in 1947. Marie Stopes opened her first clinic in 1921 in London and through the 1930s and 1940s opened regional clinics in Leeds, Aberdeen, Cardiff, Swansea and Belfast.[2] It is clear that the Belfast clinic lacked a number of the factors necessary for long term survival. It faced religious opposition from the Catholic Church and struggled to gain political support from politicians across the religious divide.[3] A similar situation emerged at Abertillery in south Wales in the 1920s when the clinic established there faced open opposition from local ministers, which is believed to have contributed to its closure.[4] While there was support from some local politicians, such as Harry Midgley of the Northern Ireland Labour Party and also some liberal unionists, there was no one willing to take on the role as champion of the birth control issue.[5] Wives of prominent local men sat on the committee of the clinic, but perhaps restricted by the dominance of Stopes herself, no one individual emerged to ensure the clinic's survival. Although one of those who approached Stopes about opening a clinic in Belfast was Professor Lowry, the gynaecologist at the Royal Maternity Hospital in Belfast, his support was subsequently limited and put under strain due to Stopes' bitter and public conflict with his former pupil Dr Louise McIlory over the use of the cap as a form of birth control.[6]

The success of the clinic was also constrained by the difficulties which arose between the staff and the clinic committee and also between Marie Stopes and the clinic committee. Greta Jones details a dispute between the committee and Dr Eveline McDaniel over the employment of a relative of a member of the committee whom Dr McDaniel did not consider suitable for the position.[7] This, Jones contends, reflects the 'contrast in style and attitudes of women who worked in their leisure time by manipulating social networks and friendships and women who exercised professional skills within rule bound institutions'.[8] Further substantiation that there was a conflict between the committee and Marie Stopes herself is found in a letter from Dr Mary Grove-White of the Singapore Family Planning Association in 1953, which claimed that the clinic in Belfast had closed its doors because the committee 'could not stick Marie Stopes'.[9] Stopes interfered constantly in the running of the clinics, and case sheets had to be sent to her on a weekly basis. This interference, combined with her renowned dogmatic personality, was bound to cause upset with the committee.[10] Clearly the lack of local autonomy and support had a negative effect on the clinic's success.

The clinic also ran at a continual financial deficit during its years in existence. This also contributed to the decision to close in 1947. While numbers attending the clinic rose in the 1940s, Stopes was still disappointed by the numbers and did not consider the Belfast clinic a success.[11] With the closure of the clinic women had to depend on private doctors or the small clinic which had been run by Dr Olive Anderson since 1940 as part of her work as an obstetrician at the Royal Victoria Hospital. Perhaps prompted by the closure of the Marie Stopes clinic in 1947, Dr Anderson in May 1950 was in contact with the Family Planning Association (FPA) in London about the possibilities of establishing a family planning clinic in Belfast.

The establishment process

The establishment of the clinic and the obtaining of premises was not an easy task. In May 1950 Dr Anderson explained to the FPA in London that the 'local authority was likely to be completely unhelpful in providing premises as Roman Catholic opinion is very strong'.[12] The FPA in London subsequently wrote to the Northern Ireland Hospital Authority in June 1950 enquiring about the possibility of obtaining the use of clinic premises in their hospital to run a Family Planning Session.[13] The reply explained that due to the pressure of existing services on the available accommodation the authority was 'unable to facilitate the establishment of a clinic at any of their hospitals'.[14] In further correspondence about the issue with Dr Anderson, Mrs Howard, the FPA Organising Secretary, asked if she could make contact with Mr Jones of the Hospital Authority and find out whether it was really a shortage of premises which led to the negative response or whether there were other objections.[15] After a visit to Mr Jones, Dr Anderson explained that 'it is the religious question which is the stumbling block'; however she offered a glimmer of hope that 'the door is not quite closed and we will go on exploring ways and means'.[16]

The 'religious question' was unsurprisingly of particular importance in Northern Ireland. From its establishment in 1921, there was opposition to the very existence of the state from within the nationalist, mainly Catholic, population. As argued above, the government and local authorities were often at pains to avoid contentious issues that would provoke further opposition from the Catholic community.[17] However, while there appears to have been great concern on the part of the authorities that the issue of family planning and the establishment of family planning clinics would provoke religious controversy and opposition, there appears to have been little organised religious opposition to the work of the clinics. This is a similar situation to that which Fisher describes in relation to south Wales in the 1930s.[18] Nonetheless, as will be seen, the perceived controversy and contention of religious opposition was as difficult to overcome as the reality for the promoters of family planning clinics.

Dr Charlotte Arnold, who had been involved with the Marie Stopes Clinic and continued to see patients privately following its closure, described the attitude towards family planning in Northern Ireland as:

> religious and political, and they only see it as a means of reducing the birth rate. The Catholics are forbidden to have anything to do with it and the Protestants fear that if they reduce the size of their families they will eventually be outnumbered by the Catholics in the six counties and have to go in with Eire. They feel very strongly about it and the Ministry of Health would not be helpful.[19]

Voluntary agencies were also unwilling to help. As Mrs Constance Boyd, who was to become the first secretary of the Belfast Women's Welfare Clinic, explained in March 1951, the Belfast Council for Social Welfare and the After Care Committee had decided it could 'no longer give public support to a project which would lose the measure of cooperation which they now receive from Roman Catholics'.[20] In a bid to avoid antagonising Catholic opinion, Dr Anderson and Mrs Boyd suggested that the clinic could be established in a Protestant hospital. After a year of negotiations, it was agreed in May 1951 that a clinic could be established in Malone Place, which was an all-Protestant maternity hospital attached to the Belfast City Hospital and under the auspices of the South Belfast Management Committee.

As Gayle Davis has argued in relation to Scotland, it was the 'voluntary agencies and lay pressure, largely composed of women, that were the real force of change'.[21] This was also the case in Northern Ireland and organisational support for the establishment and running of the family planning clinic came in the form of an all-female voluntary committee. The correspondence between individuals in Northern Ireland and the Family Planning Association in London illustrates how interested women were put in touch with each other and how female networks developed. For

example, Constance Boyd, the founding secretary of the Belfast Women's
Welfare Clinic (BWWC), was a friend and patient of Olive Anderson,
and yet only became aware of their shared interest in establishing an FPA
branch in Belfast following a visit to the FPA headquarters in London in
August 1950.[22] She subsequently went with Olive Anderson to present the
case to the Secretary of the Hospital Authority, and when Mrs Bosanquet
of the FPA in London paid a visit to Belfast in June 1951 organised a
drawing-room meeting for interested women.[23] Similar meetings were
also held with considerable success in 1930 in south Wales.[24] This idea of
a drawing-room meeting reflects a tradition of middle- and upper-class
female philanthropy, where committee meetings for various organisations were often held in the homes of members. This tradition of female
philanthropy was extremely important in Belfast. From the latter decades
of the nineteenth century women were heavily involved in a variety of
organisations establishing female networks and contacts.[25] This was
clearly still a feature of Belfast society in the 1950s, with women of similar
socio-economic and religious backgrounds becoming involved in the
running of the BWWC. These women were mainly wives of professional
men, often medics or academics. A number had worked professionally
before their marriages and involvement in a voluntary capacity with the
family planning clinic allowed a return to the working world.[26]

In the early years, the clinics were staffed completely by volunteer lay
helpers and even doctors worked on a voluntary basis. As the first clinic
in 1951 was on hospital premises, there could be no membership or
consultancy charges and patients only paid for contraceptive appliances.
This was in contrast to those clinics affiliated to the FPA in London.
These clinics paid an annual per capita payment of one shilling for every
new patient, so patients were charged fees by the clinic.[27] The majority
of family planning clinics established in the UK were, by the 1950s and
1960s, either local authority run or affiliated to the FPA. However, the
BWWC and, from 1964 onwards, the Northern Ireland FPA (NIFPA),
were reluctant to join the FPA and keen to maintain their independence.
The relationship between the FPA in London and BWWC/NIFPA in
Belfast highlights the uniqueness of the situation in Northern Ireland.

Belfast Women's Welfare Clinic

From the outset those involved with the BWWC wanted to keep a low
profile and not attract any publicity. They believed that this would
be difficult if they were members of the FPA.[28] As Constance Boyd

explained in a letter to Margaret Howard of the FPA in June 1951, 'of course we shall have to proceed cautiously and quietly here in Belfast. Dr Anderson is most anxious that we should comply in every reasonable way within the wishes of the hospital management committee and for this reason we think it wise at present not to affiliate to the Family Planning Association.'[29] In response, by return of post, Margaret Howard explained how she felt it would be a great pity for 'your committee to operate as an isolated unit when there is so much to be gained by joining a large and well established organisation which can offer you so much help'.[30] She went on to question how the wishes of the Belfast Hospital Management Committee were contrary to the policy of the FPA and how there would be no immediate need to use their name on stationery.[31] Olive Anderson sought to clarify the issue with the FPA and explained that, 'as we have been loaned premises by the Hospital Authority we feel that we cannot embarrass our friends in the local management committee by giving it more publicity than absolutely necessary, it is very difficult I am sure for you to understand this, but I would like to thank you for the help that you have given us, you have the satisfaction of knowing that one more clinic will be functioning'.[32] While close ties were maintained between Belfast and London, it was not until 1977 that the Northern Ireland Family Planning Association became an official branch of the FPA. It was felt by those in Belfast that unnecessary attention would be drawn to the clinic by official affiliation and that the FPA in London did not understand the uniqueness of the situation in Belfast.

As discussed above, the greatest concern was that the clinic would attract religious opposition. As Constance Boyd explained in 1953, when the clinic had been operational for two years, 'if we can avoid the attention of the Roman Catholic politicians we can go on doing some useful work.'[33] Ten years after the establishment off the BWWC in 1961, the same fears were still evident. Dr Joyce Neill, who became the Chairperson of the NIFPA in 1965, explained to the FPA in London that it was Roman Catholic opposition which prevented publicity for the clinic.[34]

As the 1960s progressed, it became apparent that publicity for the clinic was necessary, though care was taken to try and assuage any Catholic fears about family planning and to emphasise that clinics advised on the safe period or rhythm method, which were acceptable methods to the Catholic Church.[35] In a report in the *Belfast Telegraph* in March 1965, Dr Mary Adams, one of the members of the executive committee of the NIFPA, explained 'we get a proportion of Catholics who come to be instructed in their Church's approved rhythm methods, and also some ask about mechanical forms of contraception'. She went on to say that while 'all the directors of the Association are non-Catholics . . . the patients come from all denominations . . . the Association does not want to alienate itself from the Catholic Church . . . we would like to see them co-operating with us'.[36] This point was reiterated by Dr Joyce Neill at the first public meeting of the NIFPA in November 1965, when she argued that Northern Ireland family planning clinics must be prepared to advise Roman Catholic patients on methods of family planning which were acceptable to their beliefs. Writing in 1965 to Dr McKeown, the Medical Officer for Tyrone, concerning permission to set up a family planning clinic in Dungannon, Dr Neill pointed out that as 'there is a large Roman Catholic proportion in the population, the clinic must be sensitive to this situation, and give advice on methods acceptable to particular patients. In Belfast there is the Catholic Marriage Advisory Council to which we often refer patients, but in the country family planning clinics must, of course, give advice on all methods including the rhythm method.'[37]

Nonetheless, in the mid-1960s there still existed in some circles a belief that the issue of family planning was likely to cause controversy. The BBC refused to mention the NIFPA public meeting held in November 1965 on its local diary programme, justifying its decision by claiming that it did not announce events which it felt to be controversial. In response to this Dr Neill expressed her disbelief that the BBC could really believe that the subject of family planning was still controversial. She went on to declare, 'the need for controlling the size of families is freely admitted by the Roman Catholic Church; the only difference of opinion is on methods approved – a difference which our association has publicly respected.'[38] The BBC clearly had a change of heart as it broadcast an 'Inquiry' programme on family planning in January 1966, on which Dr Neill appeared as one of the contributors. The reluctance in Northern Ireland to discuss issues such as family planning was expounded by one of the programme presenters:

> In Northern Ireland, family planning has a nasty taste – people don't like to talk about it – correspondence from the clinics sometimes has to be sent to an accommodation address in a very plain envelope – even the medical profession, in certain instances are reluctant to recommend that their patient should visit a clinic for family planning service. In fact, we seem to be playing our usual apathetic and inhibited part.[39]

He lamented the shortage of clinics in Northern Ireland: one for every 250,000 people in comparison with one for every 100,000 people in the rest of the UK.[40] Dr Neill in written comments about her interview on the programme, explained that she believed the slow development of family planning in Northern Ireland was due to the Puritanism of both Northern Irish Catholic and Protestant communities.[41] She emphasised this point in a letter to the FPA in London the following month, and explained the slow development of family planning as '. . . an uphill battle. Not only does our government lean over backwards to appease our "oppressed" Roman Catholic minority, but we have a strong Calvinistic element to deal with, to whom we appear as the Scarlet Women in person.'[42]

While it is acknowledged that there may well have been opposition within the Protestant community, it is difficult to find any evidence that this took the form of organised opposition. The Church of Ireland and the Presbyterian Church, the two largest Protestant denominations in Northern Ireland, were supportive of the idea of family planning within marriage. In 1959, the Presbyterian Church endorsed the Resolution adopted by the Anglican Lambeth Conference of 1958 which stated that family planning was a 'right and important factor in Christian family life and should be the result of a positive choice before God'.[43] For the majority of the other smaller Protestant denominations there has been a general acceptance of the role of family planning within marriage. However, opposition has focused on the provision of contraception to the unmarried.[44]

Nonetheless, it is evident that concerns about religious susceptibilities continued into the 1970s and after the Health Boards had taken control of all the family planning clinics. In response to what was clearly a vehement letter from a Dr Patterson of Tyrone County Hospital, Dr Denise Fulton of the NIFPA argued that the need for birth control was accepted by the majority of people and it was only the methods to be used that caused differences.[45] Dr Patterson also suggested that family planning was a 'Protestant Service for a Protestant people'. This horrified Dr Fulton, who explained:

> we deal with all sections of the community and teach the Rhythm Method if that is what they want. There are Roman Catholic doctors and nurses working in the Area Boards Family Planning Service and family planning services are running successfully in Ballymurphy and Suffolk. There is a demand for one in Andersonstown which has been supported by the local parish priest. In fact clinics in Catholic areas are particularly necessary as some of the older R[oman] C[atholic] doctors do not wish to treat their patients directly for birth control.[46]

With a lack of publicity about the clinic, patients were either referred to the BWWC by personal contacts or by their GP. A smaller number were referred through other avenues such as hospital departments, midwives, health visitors, marriage guidance councillors or family planning clinics elsewhere.[47] However, by the early 1960s it was felt that there needed to be a more active campaign to publicise the existence of the clinic. In 1962, a circular letter was sent to 100 heads of departments, hospital staff and consultants in Belfast to whom family planning was thought to be a concern.[48] Earlier in the year, the death of a young woman through an illegal abortion had encouraged Dr Neill to make contact with the *Belfast Telegraph* to ask if one of the female correspondents would write an article about the work of the clinics.[49] This appeared under the title 'Planning the Family' in the *Belfast Telegraph* in May 1962 and demonstrates the publicity constraints that the clinics operated under. The author of the article, Betty Lowry, described the climate of opinion in Northern Ireland towards family planning as 'befogged and confused with prejudice and muddled thinking'.[50] She went on to explain that 'for fear of giving offence, the women who give their time voluntarily [to run the clinics] made me promise not to give the addresses of the clinics'.[51] She reported the concern that both patients and helpers at the clinic expressed, that the women 'in greatest need of advice and practical help don't know about the clinic and run the risk of abortion in back streets'.[52]

Although increased publicity was one of the explicit aims of the NIFPA when it was formed in 1964,[53] it was not until the following year that the decision was taken to list the addresses and opening times of the clinics in the press.[54] This policy proved successful, with twenty-eight adverts being placed in the *Belfast Telegraph* between September 1966 and February 1967, which in turn produced over sixty enquires. Similarly, a letter to the editor of the *Belfast Newsletter* that explained about the work of the clinics produced twenty-seven enquires.[55] By 1970, it was felt that it would be acceptable to place posters advertising the clinics in GP waiting rooms, and baby and health clinics.[56] However, further discussion by the executive committee of the NIFPA about displaying posters concluded that 'such posters are usually resented and torn down' and it was decided to aim at increasing free publicity via the BBC and the press.[57]

When it opened the BWWC held two sessions, a Wednesday evening with Dr Elizabeth Robb and a Thursday morning with Dr Olive Anderson. It was decided to hold a clinic session in the morning as it was felt that this made it possible 'for patients to come from any part of the Province by an early train or bus and return home in the afternoon'.[58] As the BWCC was the only family planning clinic in Northern Ireland at this time, this was of great importance. A survey of patients attending the clinic in 1960, revealed that 56.1 per cent of those attending the clinic were from Belfast with the other 43.9 per cent coming from all over Northern Ireland, some travelling over seventy miles to get these.[59]

A second clinic opened in Belfast on the Newtownards Road in 1961, followed by a clinic in Bangor. By the early 1970s there were NIFPA clinics in Coleraine, Dungannon, Portadown and Rathcoole, Enniskillen, Ballymena, Larne, Lisburn, Omagh, Carnmoney, Ballymoney, Londonderry, and Lisburn Road, Lincoln Avenue, Ormeau Road and Suffolk in Belfast. Gradually these clinics were taken over by the Local Health Authorities (LHAs) and a number of new clinics were opened under their auspices. By 1973, there were thirty-eight family planning clinics, run by either the LHA or the NIFPA in Northern Ireland.[60] From 1 April 1974, the Northern Ireland Area Health Boards took over the running of all family planning clinics and contraceptive advice and supplies became free. This enabled the NIFPA to relinquish their role in running clinics and concentrate on the training and advisory side of their work.[61]

Government involvement

The involvement of the LHAs and the Stormont government in family planning had only developed from the late 1960s. There had been relatively little discussion of family planning at a governmental level until 1967 when the Ministry of Health decided to award a grant to the NIFPA. As discussed above, there was an assumption amongst those working within family planning that the political authorities would be unreceptive and opposed to their cause. However, the reality was one of limited opposition and a general acceptance of the situation.

Following the awarding of a grant to the NIFPA in April 1967 of £500, and up to a further £1,000 on the basis of £1 of grant for every £1 received by the NIFPA from elsewhere, the response from the Northern Ireland House of Commons was largely positive. Mr Phelim O'Neill MP congratulated Mr Morgan on 'being the first Minister who has had the courage and the sense to give a grant to NIFPA'.[62] He went on to criticise the grant for being too small. This accusation was rebuffed by Mr Morgan, who explained that the small direct Government grant was to try and 'encourage a close working relationship between the Association and local health authorities, including a suitable financial relationship'.[63]

The one voice of contention within the Northern Ireland House of Commons came in June 1968 from Mr Harry Diamond MP (Republican Labour Party), during the discussion of the grant made to the NIFPA. He was angry that there had been no discussion of the issue in the House and pointed out that there was 'substantial division in the community on these matters'. He contended that:

> despite the term used, this is a euphemism for artificial birth control and the promotion of abortions. In my judgement there is no right to use public funds in this connection . . . in Northern Ireland, in common with other parts of the world there has been an epidemic of venereal disease, which is increasing rapidly . . . a good deal of this is ascribed to many of the new ideas which are being promoted – abortion, the use of the pill and the establishment of clinics which seem to assure uninformed people of freedom from the risk of diseases of this kind.[64]

In response, Mr Morgan explained that the policy of supporting family planning was for situations where advice was needed for medical purposes and that 'in spite of what the hon. Member for Falls [Harry Diamond] may say I think that this is a wise and good policy to adopt and one which will be used with the greatest wisdom'.[65]

The first official statement on family planning since the Health Services Act (Northern Ireland) in 1948 came in the form of a Circular on Family Planning issued by the Ministry of Health and Social Services in December 1967. It emphasised the important role of family planning and instructed health authorities to make arrangements, either directly or through a voluntary body (the NIFPA), for the free advice and treatment of women for whom a pregnancy would be detrimental.[66] To encourage financial contributions from local authorities the circular repeated the previous financial settlement whereby the ministry would match any money given by the health authorities up to a maximum of £2,500.[67]

The circular concluded by stressing that family planning provision fell clearly within the responsibility of the local authorities and that:

> an adequate family planning service apart from its obvious benefits in promoting stable family life, will help to relieve the financial and other burdens falling on other local authority services through the physical and mental health which so frequently arises from lack of knowledge and advice. The Ministry hopes, therefore, that all health authorities will co-operate in the task of promoting the welfare of their citizens in the ways outlined in the Circular.[68]

However, it is evident that not all local authorities were forthcoming with financial help. In February 1968, the NIFPA sent a sample letter to clinics which they could send to local authorities asking for a more generous financial gesture and giving examples of the grants that had been awarded in other areas.[69] Furthermore, as explained at the BWWC Executive Meeting on 2 April 1968, the circular 'suggested but did not instruct [local authorities] to help family planning clinics; at present the amount of help varied in different localities'.[70]

The issue of providing family planning purely on medical grounds was to change with Clause 16 of the 1969 Health Services Amendment Act (Northern Ireland). This allowed health authorities to provide family planning services on social as well as purely medical grounds. As the Minister for Health and Social Services explained, this change was based on provision already in place in Great Britain and did not oblige anyone with conscientious objections to make use of the service.[71]

Further change was legislated in Article 12 of the Health and Personal Social Services (Northern Ireland) Order 1972, that required the Ministry of Health (now the Department of Health and Social Services) to arrange the provision of family planning services in Northern Ireland. However, as discussed above, it was not until 1 April 1974 that a free family planning service was made available in Northern Ireland, when Mr Paddy Devlin, Minister for Health and Social Services, announced that 'free services will be available to anyone irrespective of age or marital status'.[72]

Problems and difficulties

The establishment of clinics was not always an easy process and met with resistance from both medical staff and local authorities. The most problematic situation for the NIFPA was the establishment of clinics in the predominantly Catholic city of Derry. The Co. Londonderry Health Committee had made premises available for a family planning clinic at the Belmont housing estate on the outskirts of the city in September 1966 and a second clinic opened in 1967 in Riverside House.[73] However, Derry City Health Committee refused to give any financial help to the clinics and in March 1968 the clinics appealed to the Executive of the NIFPA for financial help.[74] This help was given, but by May 1968 the staff at the Belmont clinic had to work voluntarily.[75] The County Londonderry Health Committee discussed the situation in April 1968. Councillor Mr R.A. Brown explained 'I think it [family planning] should be carried out on a voluntary basis. The county is well covered with medical officers, health visitors and nurses all knowing what sort of advice to give people and I don't see why we should incur more expenditure.'[76] He went on to argue that it appeared to him to be 'the thin end of the wedge and that if they agreed to this family planning clinics would be springing up at every crossroads'.[77] The decision was taken by the council to defer the question for six months. Joyce Neill went to Londonderry to discuss the decision of the Health Committee in July 1968, with limited success.[78] However, when the committee returned to the debate in November 1968, while there was considerable opposition from Catholic members on religious grounds as well as from Protestant members on economic grounds, the recommendation to support the clinics was passed by a majority of one.[79] The Co. Londonderry Health Committee granted £250 to the Belmont clinic for 3 years and the City of Derry Health Committee provided a similar grant.[80]

In 1965, there had also been controversy over family planning in Londonderry, when seven Catholic members of the Londonderry branch of Oxfam resigned because the organisation supported birth control.[81] It should, however, be acknowledged that the late 1960s were a period of turmoil in Derry. The city was at the centre of the emerging civil rights movement and experiencing serious violence. The city council was at the centre of gerrymandering disputes and funding for family planning was pushed down the agenda by other more pressing contemporary events.[82]

These contemporary events, or 'the Troubles' as they became known, caused operational difficulties for the clinics themselves. In the Derry City Clinic in 1970 there was a drop in attendances of approximately 100 patients, around 20 per cent. This was believed to have been due to 'riots in the area'.[83] The Annual Report of the Omagh Clinic of the same year demonstrated similar concerns, explaining that the IUD would have been very popular 'but with the Troubles and the inconvenience of travelling to Belfast, the patients have to use other means'.[84] The Newtownards Road Clinic in Belfast reported a similar situation, with the disturbances causing a decline in attendances. However, the Troubles also provided this clinic with a surprising extra number of patients on 7 December 1970 when a bomb scare in the nearby Rupert Stanley Beauty School 'resulted in students making use of their unexpected free afternoon to visit us for supplies'.[85]

The establishment of a family planning clinic in Suffolk in West Belfast was directly related to the Troubles, the aim being to provide a 'bridging' service for patients in Suffolk and Andersonstown who might find it difficult to get to other clinics because of the present security situation.[86] However, the situation in the local area became so tense in July and early August that on four successive weeks clinics could not be held.'[87]

The impact of the security situation was also seen when six of the NIFPA clinics were to be inspected by Dr Libby Wilson from Glasgow, Chairman of the FPA Clinic Doctors' National Council.[88] Her visit coincided with a two-day general strike in May 1974 called by the Protestant Ulster Vanguard in protest at the introduction of Direct Rule from London. Over 190,000 people participated and power cuts closed down much of the Province. Vanguard supporters also barricaded and controlled Portadown, which was one of the clinics to be inspected. Dr Wilson details the complicated journey they took to get to the Portadown clinic, where of course there were hardly any patients, but all the staff were present and the inspection went ahead.[89] Their visit to the Newtownards Road Clinic the following day coincided with a march on Stormont by over 100,000 people, which passed outside the clinic premises. The result of the inspection was positive and the 'visitors were full of praise for the clinics' determination to provide as normal a service as possible at all times'.[90]

The NIFPA also had to deal with the issue of patients travelling across the border from the Republic of Ireland, where in 1929 the propaganda and advertisement of birth control had been outlawed under the Censorship of Publications Act. The 1935 Criminal Law Amendment Act went on to ban the sale and importation of contraceptives.[91] These restrictions on gaining access to contraceptives led some women to write to the FPA in London asking for contacts in Ireland, North or South. However, Olive Anderson explained the difficulties in a letter to the FPA in London in 1950: 'the position is quite difficult in the South of Ireland, it is not always possible for the women to come up here and it is almost impossible to send anything from here into the Irish Free State, so that I really cannot help these people as much as I would like to'.[92] In response, Mrs Howard explained how they 'get a constant stream of letters from people living in Southern Ireland asking for advice and we find it heart-breaking being able to do so little for them'.[93] She went on to explain the tactics used by the FPA when sending supplies to the Republic of Ireland:

> we send out parcels in plain packing. GP ointment and gels come in plain packs and volpar gels and paste have the words National Birth Control Association on them. It all rather depends on how many parcels customs open. I should think a number would get through quite easily, especially if we address them by hand.[94]

Throughout the 1950s and into the 1960s, women were continuing to travel from the Republic to Belfast for family planning. The minutes of the BWWC for 1962 record a debate concerning whether to charge a fee from women from the Republic. The decision was later taken that as the clinic was on hospital premises it was not in a position to charge these women.[95] This travel north continued into the 1970s, as did the issue over payments. It was decided in September 1971 that IUD patients from the South would not be charged differently from other patients and that 'the Dublin FP Clinics were very soon to start fitting IUDs and that IUD patients could now be checked there'.[96]

On 22 May 1971 members of the Irish Women's Liberation Movement travelled on the train from Dublin to Belfast to buy contraceptives and then returned to Dublin, challenging the customs officials to arrest them – which they didn't. Through the 1970s there were campaigns in Dublin against the contraceptive legislation in the Irish Republic.[97] In Britain in the 1920s a wide variety of women's organisations such as the Women's Institute (WI), the National Council of Women and the Women's Co-Operative Guild supported the extension and development of family planning clinics.[98] However, throughout the period from the 1920s to the 1970s, such campaigning by women's groups did not exist in Northern Ireland. In the first half of the twentieth century, as discussed above, the religious conservatism of society as a whole prevented discussion of issues such as family planning and the women's organisations, which were often associated with churches, followed this line. This religious conservatism combined with the advent of the Troubles in the late 1960s also contributed to the lack of discussion of issues such as family planning by women's groups in the 1960s and 1970s. Women were more often involved in organisations associated with peace and social reform or were politically active. As Myrtle Hill argues, it is not until 1971 that the emergence of a feminist movement in Northern Ireland, unrelated to the civil rights struggle, can be traced, and the Northern Ireland Women's Rights Movement (NIWRM) was not established until 1975.[99] However, divisions over politics split the NIWRM and concerns with more immediate issues of violence in society led to a lack of attention being focused on issues of health and reproduction. Similarly, for organisations such as the WI, that were non-denominational, open support for any potentially religious or politically contentious issue was avoided at all costs.

Patients and attendances

The attendances at Olive Anderson's Family Planning Clinic at the Royal Victoria Maternity Hospital remained relatively low at an annual rate of between 30 and 40 until the early 1960s.[100] The number of total attendances at the clinic then began to rise gradually: from 52 in 1960 to 168 in 1964, before a rapid increase to 377 in 1965, 844 in 1966 and over 2,000 in 1967.[101] Joyce Neill attributes some of this rise to the fact that oral contraceptives began to be prescribed in 1963, and partly to the fact that the clinic was held weekly rather than fortnightly from 1965, which caused an immediate increase in attendances. Added to these factors was the increased awareness among medical staff about the work of the clinic and also the group talks about family planning that were given to post-natal patients.[102] From 1965 medical students at Queen's University in Belfast and trainee midwives had been given a lecture on family planning as part of their lectures in gynaecology.[103]

Similarly, the BWWC saw an increase in patients in the 1960s, with total attendances increasing from just over 2,000 in 1960 to nearly 3,000 in 1964 and over 4,000 in 1971.[104] The figures for all the clinics of the Northern Ireland Family Planning Association indicate total attendances of 12,600 in 1968, 17,900 in 1969 and 23,250 in 1971. In particular the clinic in Ballymena saw total attendances increase from 400 in 1968 to 884 in 1971 and in Enniskillen numbers rose from 26 in 1968 to 640 by 1973.[105]

There are a number of factors which may have contributed to the rise in attendances at the clinics. Greta Jones has contended that demographic issues played an important role, with a fall in the female average age of marriage from 26.4 in 1937 to 22.6 by 1971.[106] This led to women having a longer reproductive life and increased the need for many to control their fertility. Another factor identified by Jones is the correlation between the increase in female employment and the increase in those attending family planning clinics.[107] There was a rise in the percentage of married women as a proportion of female employees in Northern Ireland from just under 21 per cent in 1951 to around 36 per cent in 1966, 47.1 per cent in 1971 and nearly 60 per cent by 1981.[108] This, it is argued, illustrates a move from 'crisis' visits for family planning towards a more positive decision by married couples to delay starting a family.[109] The importance of female employment led to changes in clinic hours, with evening clinics being established for those women who worked and could not attend during the day.[110]

However, there are other factors which come into play, particularly during the second half of the 1960s. As referred to above there was increased inclusion and discussion of family planning within medical training of both doctors and nurses. The NIFPA was very involved in

providing training and information about its services to medical personnel, which led to a greater awareness among the medical profession about
the methods of birth control available. The introduction of the pill as a
form of contraception in the early 1960s is also extremely important as
this went some way towards medicalising family planning.[111] Similarly
the publicity surrounding the pill, which existed throughout the 1960s,
ensured a growing awareness of issues surrounding family planning.
NIFPA publicity also increased over this period, with the organisation
being represented at a conference held in 1965 about family planning
in Northern Ireland and a programme on the BBC in 1966. The debates
concerning the papers encyclical on birth control, *Humanae Vitae*, in
1968 also put family planning in the public domain and while for some
Catholic women this may have discouraged attendance at family planning clinics, for others it may have drawn to their attention the possibilities and availability of family planning.

It is also important not to underestimate the importance of female
networks of friends and family in increasing awareness about family
planning clinics. While Kate Fisher has contended that men were actively
involved in the decision-making process about family planning,[112] it is
also clear that it was women who physically attended the family planning
clinics and that their decision to attend was most probably influenced by
the experiences of friends and family. Adams and Fulton in their survey
of patients attending the Belfast Women's Welfare clinic in 1960 found
that half of the patients sampled had been referred to the clinic by female
friends or relatives with the remainder referred by GPs or other medical
or social services.[113]

In addition to the increase in numbers attending clinics across
Northern Ireland there was also a change in the social class breakdown
of the women who were attending. A number of the NIFPA clinics
undertook a survey of the occupations of the husbands of women
attending clinics over a three-month period in late 1968/early 1969.[114]
There are recorded results for five clinics: Ormeau Road and Lincoln
Avenue in Belfast, Rathcoole on the outskirts of Belfast, Larne in Co.
Antrim and Coleraine in Co. Londonderry. A number of other clinics
recorded occupations but over a longer time period, which makes
comparison more problematic. The social classes are broken down
into: I – professional; II – intermediate occupations; III – skilled; IV –
semi-skilled; V- unskilled. Considering the five clinics, the percentage
of each class was: Class I, 5 per cent; Class II, 34 per cent; Class III,
27 per cent, Class IV, 10 per cent; and Class V, 24 per cent.[115] These

figures, with the largest percentage of patients' husbands' occupations coming from Class II, are markedly different from a survey made in 1960 over six months at the BWWC. This survey found that the majority of patients' husbands' occupations, 65.4 per cent, were from Class III – those of skilled occupations – with only 8.5 per cent from Class I and II and 26.1 per cent from Class IV and V.[116] There thus appears to have been a clear change in the social breakdown of those using the clinics over the 1960s. Considering the clinics individually, in the NIFPA survey, Coleraine had the highest percentage of Class I and II at 50 per cent and Larne the lowest at 29 per cent. Lincoln Avenue Clinic had the highest percentage of Class IV and V at 47 per cent and Larne the lowest at 12 per cent. For Class III, Larne had the highest proportion at 59 per cent, while the other clinics had similar percentages between 20 and 28.[117] While the figures are for a relatively short period of time it can be concluded that the percentage of women from higher social classes using the clinics across Northern Ireland had risen, as had the number from the lower social classes.

A third survey was carried out by the FPA for clinics in England and Wales in 1972. The results show a class breakdown of: Class I, 12.04 per cent; Class II, 12.16 per cent; Class III, 45.51 per cent, Class IV, 14.91 per cent; and Class V, 10.3 per cent (including unemployed).[118] Although it must be recognised that the FPA survey was over a longer period of time and covered many more clinics, there does appear to be a striking difference in the number of patients' from both the higher social classes and also the lower social classes attending clinics in Northern Ireland in comparison with England and Wales.

One of the conclusions offered by Leathard for the low numbers of working-class women attending clinics was the location of clinics and the inconvenience for these women in attending clinics and travelling long distances.[119] However, this is a factor that was clearly recognised by the NIFPA and they deliberately set up clinics in working-class areas such as Suffolk in West Belfast. Similarly, of the clinics from the 1968 survey both Lincoln Avenue and Ormeau Road in Belfast and Rathcoole on the outskirts of the city are either in working-class areas or are easily accessible by women from working-class areas. For women from Class I and II, the increased percentages in Northern Ireland may reflect changes in female employment as discussed above, with the rate of married women in employment rising in Northern Ireland from 1951, encouraging women to postpone starting families and limit the number of children they had.

Abortion

Abortion in Northern Ireland has always been in the 'twilight zone'.[120] The debate has remained relatively muted even in recent decades, in comparison, for example, with the situation in the Republic of Ireland.[121] The 1967 Abortion Act was not extended to Northern Ireland and the legal situation regarding abortion is still based on the 1861 Offences Against the Person Act which made it an offence 'to seek or procure a miscarriage . . . unlawfully'. This was further clarified in the 1929 Infant Life Preservation Act which prohibited abortion over twenty-eight weeks unless it was necessary to perform an abortion to save a woman's life. This was extended to Northern Ireland in 1945. Further definition came with the Bourne Case in 1938, where Aleck Bourne, a London gynaecologist, challenged the law after performing an abortion on a fourteen-year-old girl who had been raped. He was acquitted and the Bourne judgement allowed for doctors to perform abortions if they were for the safety of the woman's physical and mental health. The law in Northern Ireland is therefore ambiguous and open to interpretation. Whether abortions are performed is often at the discretion of the medical professionals involved and there have been legal challenges by the NIFPA to have the legislation clarified in recent years. The Department of Health, Social Services and Public Safety were due to issue guidance on the legality of abortions in Northern Ireland in October 2008, however this was not issued until March 2009. There were further attempts to extend the 1967 Abortion Act to Northern Ireland as an amendment within the Human Fertilisation and Embryology Bill as it passed through parliament in the summer and autumn of 2008. However, the debate on the amendments due on 22 October never took place and the legal situation remains unchanged.[122]

There is no doubt that through the twentieth century women in Northern Ireland, as elsewhere have been attempting to procure abortions by a variety of means, whether ingesting abortificants or attempting physical procedures either by themselves or seeking help from an abortionist.[123] Abortion is mentioned in a number of the case sheets of the Marie Stopes Clinic in Belfast and in letters written to Stopes from the clinic nurse.[124] Similarly, the clinic nurse in 1940 told Stopes how they regularly had women coming to the clinic under the impression that it offered an abortion service.[125] The court records of those prosecuted for procuring abortions in Belfast make reference to both the taking of poisons and the use of instruments.[126] Oral history evidence from women in Belfast indicates the use of a variety of substances including gin or drugs to attempt to induce abortion as well as the presence of 'handy-women' who were known abortionists.[127] Max Goldstrom, one of the founders of the Ulster Pregnancy Advisory Service which assisted and advised women travelling to England for an abortion, claimed that in the 1960s in Northern Ireland there were several backstreet abortionists at work.[128] The most skilful, he went on to suggest, was a doctor who was 'well known throughout the Province for his activities and his skills were widely called upon. It is said that the police themselves advised women who became pregnant through rape to go to him for an abortion.'[129] Even though several of his patients died he was apparently never prosecuted. Between 1967 and 1981 five women died in Northern Ireland from complications following illegal abortions, whereas no women died from similar complications elsewhere in the United Kingdom.[130] Furthermore, a 1994 survey of GPs revealed that over 10 per cent had seen evidence of illegal abortion attempts. However these numbers had declined in the years before the survey, due, it was felt, to increasing numbers of women travelling to England for abortions.[131] The number of women travelling to England from Northern Ireland for an abortion is thought to be around 2,000 per year.[132]

It is impossible to gain any accurate picture of the level of illegal abortions which took place in Northern Ireland in the twentieth century. As with a number of other issues, such as venereal disease and birth control, there was little discussion of the issue in either the medical or popular press. It was only when deaths resulted from backstreet abortions that limited discussion took place. Belfast Recorder's Court records over sixty individuals accused of attempting to procure an abortion or assisting in the attempt between 1917 and 1968 and nine deaths following attempted abortions.[133] In the majority of cases where a prosecution for abortion took place it was due to the woman becoming ill and being admitted to hospital where the doctor called the police, either following a 'confession' from the woman or due to their own suspicions.[134] In a few cases the police had been watching particular houses, obviously acting on information received, though it is not clear from whom. While much more work on the issue of abortion in early twentieth-century Northern Ireland needs to take place, it is evident from the available court records that there was a female network that supplied information and assisted in the procuring of abortions.[135] Through friends and relatives, women found someone willing to carry out the procedure, using a variety of implements, from crochet needles to syringes; they also advised which chemists supplied tablets or which combination of substances to take.

Barbara Brookes' work on England has identified similar female networks which often came to light in court records following a fatality.[136] Cliona Rattigan's work on single women seeking abortion in both the North and South of Ireland between 1900 and 1950, interestingly contends that while female networks to assist with procuring an abortion existed in Belfast, the trial records for abortion cases in Southern Ireland do not reveal a similar picture of female assistance.[137] As Brooke further argued, and the Belfast Court Records support, for many women having an abortion or carrying out an abortion was not necessarily considered to be a criminal act, but was rather more a fact of life, a regulation of menstruation or a necessary prevention of pregnancy, because of the limited family planning alternatives.[138]

It is also difficult to identify the number of legal abortions which took place in Northern Ireland. Estimates range between 250 and 500 in the 1970s and 1980s,[139] although with increased concerns about the legality of carrying out abortions the official number of abortions carried out on the NHS has been reduced to around 70–80 in recent years.[140]

Organised opposition to abortion and an extension of abortion legislation to Northern Ireland emerged in the 1990s with organisations such as Precious Life whose activities were responsible for the closure of the Ulster Pregnancy Advisory Service in 1999 and who continue to picket the premises of the Brook Clinic, a provider of free and confidential sexual health advice for young people. There is also cross-party political support on the issue of opposition to abortion.[141] This is one of the clearest issues over which both Protestant and Catholic communities are in unity.[142] Both politicians and activists frequently claim that Northern Ireland has a unique pro-life tradition and comparisons are often made with England and its more secular and by implication less moral culture.[143] This is arguably an extension of the perception held throughout the twentieth century of a higher moral and Christian identity in Northern Ireland than the rest of the UK. This extends beyond political and religious boundaries and is therefore something more complicated than simply a nationalist or post-colonial perspective. As Lisa Smyth has argued in connection with the issue of reproduction and sexuality in contemporary Northern Ireland, while these issues are often the focus for gendered national identity politics in Northern Ireland, they are characterised by cross-community agreement and disagreement.[144] This, as has been argued throughout this book, is a clear example of how, around issues of female sexuality and its regulation, there is more that draws the Protestant and Catholic communities together than separates them.

Notes

1 For example, see Katherine Side, 'Contract, Charity and Honourable Entitlement: Social Citizenship and the 1967 Abortion Act in Northern Ireland after the Good Friday Agreement', *Social Politics: International Studies in Gender, State and Society*, 13 (2006), 89–116.
2 Deborah Cohen, 'Private Lives in Public Spaces: Marie Stopes, the Mothers' Clinics and the Practice of Contraception', *History Workshop Journal*, 35 (1993), 95.
3 Jones, 'Marie Stopes in Ireland', 264–265.
4 Fisher, '"Clearing up the Misconceptions"', 118; Margaret Douglas, 'Women, God and Birth Control: The First Hospital Birth Control Clinic, Abertillery 1925', *Llafur*, 6 (1995), 113–120.
5 Jones, 'Marie Stopes in Ireland', 261.
6 Ibid., 267–268.
7 Ibid.
8 Ibid., 263.
9 Extract of letter from Dr Mary Grove White, 20 June 1953, contained in letter from Vera Houghton, International Planned Parenthood Federation to Margaret Howard, Family Planning Association London (hereafter FPA), 22 June 1953, Records of Belfast Mothers' Welfare Clinic/NIFPA, SA/FPA/A13/2, Contemporary Medical Archives Centre at Wellcome Trust for History of Medicine (hereafter CMAC).
10 Jones, 'Marie Stopes in Ireland', 265; Alan Parkes and Dee King 'The Mothers' Clinic', *Journal of BioSocial Science*, 6 (1974), 180–181; Cohen, 'Private Lives in Public Spaces', p. 108.
11 Jones, 'Marie Stopes in Ireland', 276.
12 Interview with Dr Arnold, 31 May 1950, Records of Belfast Mothers' Welfare Clinic/NIFPA, SA/FPA/A13/2, CMAC.
13 FPA to Northern Ireland Hospitals Authority, 21 June 1950, Records of Belfast Mothers' Welfare Clinic/NIFPA, SA/FPA/A13/2, CMAC.
14 Northern Ireland Hospitals Authority to Organising Secretary, FPA, 2 August 1950, Records of Belfast Mothers' Welfare Clinic/NIFPA, SA/FPA/A13/2, CMAC.
15 Mrs Howard to Dr Anderson, 4 August 1950, Records of Belfast Mothers' Welfare Clinic/NIFPA, SA/FPA/A13/2, CMAC.
16 Dr Anderson to Mrs Howard, 21 October 1950, Records of Belfast Mothers' Welfare Clinic/NIFPA, SA/FPA/A13/2, CMAC.
17 See chapter 5.
18 Fisher, '"Clearing up the Misconceptions"', 116.
19 Dr Arnold to Dr Stopes, 30 November 1950, Stopes Papers, Correspondence with Dr Arnold, Belfast 1950, SA/EUG/K.19, CMAC.
20 Constance Boyd to Mrs Howard, 5 March 1951, Records of Belfast Mothers' Welfare Clinic/NIFPA, SA/FPA/A13/2, CMAC.

21 Gayle Davis "'Every Baby a Wanted Baby?'": Family Planning Policy in later Twentieth-Century Scotland', (unpublished conference paper, International Federation for Research in Women's History Conference, Queen's University, Belfast, 2003), p. 1. My thanks to the author for providing a copy of this paper.

22 Interview with Mrs Constance Boyd, FPA HQ London, 30 August 1950, Records of Belfast Mothers' Welfare Clinic/NIFPA, SA/FPA/A13/2, CMAC.

23 Constance Boyd to Organising Secretary FPA, 20 June 1951, Records of Belfast Mothers' Welfare Clinic/NIFPA, SA/FPA/A13/2, CMAC.

24 Fisher, "'Clearing up the Misconceptions'", 108.

25 Claire Rush 'Women Who Made a Difference: The Members of the Belfast Ladies' Institute, 1867–1897', (unpublished conference paper, 'Did Women Make a Difference? Women in Higher Education, 1908–2008', Queen's University, Belfast, 2007).

26 For example Mrs Gray, who was a physiotherapist and moved to Belfast when her husband's job relocated. Put in touch with Olive Anderson by contacts from Bristol FPA, she subsequently became a secretary of BWWC.

27 Leathard, *The Fight for Family Planning*, p. 82.

28 Constance Boyd to Margaret Howard, 20 June 1951, Records of Belfast Mothers' Welfare Clinic/NIFPA, SA/FPA/A13/2, CMAC.

29 Ibid.

30 Margaret Howard to Constance Boyd, 20 June 1951, Records of Belfast Mothers' Welfare Clinic/NIFPA, SA/FPA/A13/2, CMAC.

31 Ibid.

32 Olive Anderson to Margaret Howard, 1 July 1951, Records of Belfast Mothers' Welfare Clinic/NIFPA, SA/FPA/A13/2, CMAC.

33 Constance Boyd to Margaret Howard, 23 August 1953, Records of Belfast Mothers' Welfare Clinic/NIFPA, SA/FPA/A13/2, CMAC.

34 Report of visit of Dr Joyce Neill to FPA in London, 24 March 1961, Belfast Family Planning Clinic 1960–1964, SA/FPA/A13/2A, CMAC.

35 Using the safe period as a method of contraception was acceptable to the Catholic Church as it was seen as being 'natural' as opposed to 'artificial' or barrier forms of contraception.

36 *Belfast Telegraph*, 22 March 1965, p. 5.

37 Dr Joyce Neill to Dr McKeown, 11 September 1965, NIFPA Correspondence with the Western Area Health Board, D/3543/3/2A, PRONI.

38 Dr Joyce Neill to BBC, 23 November 1965, NIFPA Correspondence, D/3543/3/1, PRONI.

39 Script of BBC 'Inquiry' programme, 14 January 1966, NIFPA Correspondence, D/3543/3/1, PRONI.

40 Ibid.

41 Ibid.

42 Dr Joyce Neill to London FPA, 4 February 1966, NIFPA Correspondence, D/3543/3/1, PRONI.

43 Annual Report of the Presbyterian Committee on International and National Problems, 1959.
44 Opposition to the provision of contraception to the unmarried and also to abortion is still present in Northern Ireland today from, in particular, the Roman Catholic and Free Presbyterian Churches. For more on current issues, see Side, 'Contract, Charity and Honourable Entitlement'; Lisa Smyth, 'The Cultural Politics of Sexuality and Reproduction in Northern Ireland', *Sociology*, 40 (2006), 663–680.
45 Dr Fulton to Dr Patterson, 24 April 1974, NIFPA Correspondence with the Western Area Health Board, D/3543/3/2A, PRONI.
46 Ibid.
47 Mary Adams and Denise Fulton, 'Family Planning: A Survey of Clinic Patients', *Ulster Medical Journal*, 32 (1963), 50.
48 Belfast Women's Welfare Clinic (BWWC) Executive Committee Meeting, 24 September 1962, Records of the BWWC, D/3691/1, PRONI.
49 Executive Committee Meeting, 2 May 1962, Records of the BWWC, D/3691/1, PRONI.
50 *Belfast Telegraph*, 28 May 1962, p. 5.
51 Ibid.
52 Ibid.
53 Executive Committee Meeting, 18 February 1964, Records of the BWWC, D/3691/1, PRONI.
54 Executive Committee Meeting, 4 November 1965, Records of the BWWC, D/3691/1, PRONI.
55 Executive Committee Meeting, 2 February 1967, Records of the BWWC, D/3691/3, PRONI.
56 NIFPA Executive Committee Meeting, 27 January 1970, Records of the BWWC, D/3691/3, PRONI.
57 NIFPA Executive Committee Meeting, 12 March 1970, Records of the BWWC, D/3691/2, PRONI.
58 Constance Boyd to Margaret Howard, 28 August 1953, Records of Belfast Mothers' Welfare Clinic/NIFPA, SA/FPA/A13/2, CMAC.
59 Adams and Fulton, 'Family Planning', 51.
60 NIFPA Annual Report 1972, Records of NIFPA, D/3543/2/3, PRONI.
61 NIFPA Annual General Meeting, 9 May 1974, Records of NIFPA, D/3543/2/3, PRONI.
62 Northern Ireland House of Commons Debates, 19 April 1967.
63 Ibid.
64 Ibid., 6 June 1968.
65 Ibid.
66 Ministry of Health and Social Services, PH Circular No. 56/1967, 4 December 1967, Records of NIFPA, D/3543/3/1, PRONI.
67 Ibid.

68 Ibid.
69 NIFPA Sample Letter to Clinics, 21 February 1968, Records of NIFPA, D/3543/3/1, PRONI.
70 NIFPA Executive Committee Meeting, 2 April 1968, Records of the BWWC, D/3691/2, PRONI.
71 Northern Ireland House of Commons Debates, 5 November 1969.
72 Statement by Mr P Devlin, 1 April 1974, Records of NIFPA, D/3543/3/2C, PRONI.
73 Executive Committee Meeting, 6 September 1966, Records of NIFPA, D/3543/ 52/3, PRONI.
74 Executive Committee Meeting, 26 March 1968, Records of NIFPA, D/3543/2/2, PRONI.
75 Executive Committee Meeting, 7 May 1968, Records of NIFPA, D/3543/2/2, PRONI.
76 *Mid-Ulster Mail*, 20 April 1968, p. 1.
77 Ibid.
78 Note added to R. Wilkins, Londonderry Health Committee, to Dr Neill, 6 June 1968, Records of NIFPA, D/3543/3/2A, PRONI.
79 *Mid-Ulster Mail*, 23 November 1968, p. 15.
80 Annual Report for Derry FPC, n.d. (c. 1969), Records of NIFPA, D/3543/3/2A, PRONI.
81 *Belfast Telegraph*, 17 March 1965, p. 1.
82 Bardon, A *History of Ulster*, pp. 647–650. There also appears to be a tradition of conservatism in the Londonderry/Derry Health Committees concerning possible contentious issues. This was also seen in previous decades concerning VD treatment provision. For more see, chapter 4.
83 Annual Report for Derry FPC, 1971, Records of NIFPA, D/3543/3/2A, PRONI.
84 Annual Report Omagh Family Planning Clinic, 1971, Records of NIFPA, D/3542/4/3, PRONI.
85 Annual Report of Newtownards Road Family Planning Clinic 1970, Records of NIFPA, D/3542/4/3, PRONI.
86 Annual Report for Suffolk Family Planning Clinic, Records of NIFPA, D/3542/4/3, PRONI.
87 Ibid.
88 Libby Wilson, *Sex on the Rates: Memoirs of a Family Planning Doctor* (Argyll, 2004), p. 162.
89 Ibid., pp. 162–164.
90 NIFPA Annual General Meeting, 4 May 1972, Records of NIFPA, D/3543/2/3, PRONI.
91 It was not until 1979 that contraception became legal in the Republic of Ireland. For more on this legislation and the situation in the Republic of Ireland, see Mary Daly 'Marriage, Fertility and Women's Lives in

Twentieth-Century Ireland *c.* 1900–1970', *Women's History Review*, 13 (2006), 371–385.

92 Olive Anderson to Margaret Howard, 31 March 1950, Records of Belfast Mothers' Welfare Clinic/NIFPA, SA/FPA/A13/2, CMAC.

93 Margaret Howard to Olive Anderson, 14 April 1950, Records of Belfast Mothers' Welfare Clinic/NIFPA, SA/FPA/A13/2, CMAC.

94 Ibid.

95 BWWC Annual General Meeting, 22 October 1962, Records of the BWWC, D/3691/1, PRONI.

96 Executive Meeting NIFPA, 23 September 1971, Records of NIFPA, D/3543/2/2, PRONI.

97 Yvonne Galligan, *Women and Politics in Contemporary Ireland: From the Margins to the Mainstream* (London, 1998), pp. 142–161.

98 See for example Fisher, '"Clearing up the Misconceptions"', 123 and Grier, 'Eugenics and Birth Control', 447.

99 Hill, *Women in Ireland*, pp. 177–179.

100 Joyce Neill, 'A Family Planning Service in a Teaching Maternity Hospital', *Ulster Medical Journal*, 38 (1969), 88.

101 Ibid.

102 Ibid.

103 Ibid., p. 90.

104 Adams and Fulton, 'Family Planning', 50.

105 Correspondence with Family Planning Clinics, 1968–1975, Records of NIFPA, D/3542/4/3, PRONI.

106 Jones, 'Marie Stopes in Ireland', 274.

107 Ibid., pp. 275–76.

108 Ibid.

109 Ibid., 275–276.

110 Mrs Boyd to Miss Cripps, FPA, 21 October 1951, Records of Belfast Mothers' Welfare Clinic/NIFPA, SA/FPA/A13/2, CMAC.

111 Lara Marks, *Sexual Chemistry: A History of the Contraceptive Pill* (New Haven, 2001), p. 117.

112 Kate Fisher, '"She Was Quite Satisfied With the Arrangements I Made": Gender and Birth Control in Britain, 1925–1950', *Past and Present*, 169 (2000), 164–165.

113 Adams and Fulton, 'Family Planning', 55.

114 Correspondence with Family Planning Clinics, 1968–1975, Records of NIFPA, D/3542/4/3, PRONI.

115 Ibid.

116 Adams and Fulton, 'Family Planning', 54–55.

117 Correspondence with Family Planning Clinics, 1968–1975, Records of NIFPA, D/3542/4/3, PRONI.

118 Leathard, *The Fight for Family Planning*, p. 171.

119 Ibid., p. 172.
120 Simon Lee, 'Abortion in Northern Ireland: The Twilight Zone', in Ann Furedi (ed.), *The Abortion Law in Northern Ireland: Human Rights and Reproductive Choice* (Belfast, 1995), pp. 16–26.
121 For more on the debates concerning abortion in the Republic of Ireland, see for example Ailbhe Smyth, *The Abortion Papers* (Dublin, 1992); Lisa Smyth, *Abortion and Nation: The Politics of Reproduction in Contemporary Ireland* (Hampshire, 2005).
122 See www.fpa.org.uk/news/policy/parliamentary-activity/detail.cfm? contentid=997#1 (accessed 19 January 2009).
123 See for example Tania McIntosh, '"An Abortionist City": Maternal Mortality, Abortion, and Birth Control in Sheffield, 1920–1940', *Medical History*, 44:1 (2000), 75–96.
124 Jones, 'Marie Stopes in Ireland', 260.
125 Ibid.
126 Crown Files at Belfast Recorder's Court, 1916–1968, BELF/1/1/2, PRONI.
127 M. Ferris *et al.* (eds), *Women's Voices: An Oral History of Women's Health in Northern Ireland, 1900–1990* (Dublin, 1992), p. 5.
128 Max Goldstrom, 'Abortion and the Law in Northern Ireland' (unpublished paper, 1981) UPAS archive.
129 Ibid.
130 Side, 'Contract, Charity and Honourable Entitlement', 98.
131 Colin Francome, 'Attitudes of General Practitioners in Northern Ireland Toward Abortion and Family Planning', *Family Planning Perspectives*, 29:5 (1997), 236.
132 'Fact sheet: Abortion in Northern Ireland', NIFPA and Health Promotion Agency, Northern Ireland (2007).
133 Crown Files at Belfast Recorder's Court, 1916–1968, BELF/1/1/2, PRONI.
134 Ibid
135 Ibid.
136 Barbara Brookes, *Abortion in England, 1900–1967* (London, 1988) pp. 34–35.
137 Cliona Rattigan, '"Dark Spots" in Irish Society: Single Motherhood, Crime and Prosecution in Ireland, 1900–1950' (unpublished doctoral thesis, Trinity College Dublin, 2007) pp. 287–288.
138 Brookes, *Abortion in England*, p. 8; Crown Files at Belfast Recorder's Court, 1916–1968, BELF/1/1/2, PRONI.
139 Goldstrom, 'Abortion and the Law in Northern Ireland'.
140 'Fact sheet: Abortion in Northern Ireland'.
141 For more on the attitude of political parties in Northern Ireland towards abortion see Farhat Manzoor, 'A Political History: Abortion in Ireland' (unpublished doctoral thesis, University of Ulster, 2000).
142 Smyth, 'The Cultural Politics', 668–671.
143 Ibid., 669.
144 Ibid., 672.

Conclusion

Female sexuality in Northern Ireland during the twentieth century was regulated in a variety of formal and informal ways. The techniques employed and the attitudes towards female sexuality were not only driven by gender and class, but influenced by the wider political, social and religious situation in Northern Ireland. All sections of the community in Northern Ireland based much of their identity upon the maintenance of high moral standards, particularly with regard to female behaviour. While Northern Ireland had a majority Protestant government intent on retaining links with Britain and appeared to have little in common with its Catholic southern counterpart, on issues pertaining to sexuality and, in particular female sexuality, they displayed more similarities than differences. Both governments saw their state as being morally superior to the British mainland. Maintaining high moral standards, or at least maintaining the image of high moral standards, was important to both the Churches and the government in Northern Ireland. Policing female sexuality played a crucial role. Women were seen as representing the communities, so their moral purity and good behaviour was essential to promote the image that was required.

The importance of women in nation-building has been illustrated with reference to the Irish Free State after partition.[1] The image of the ideal Irishwoman, a morally pure homemaker and mother, was used to help develop the image of what the Irish nation should be: pure and morally upright, particularly in comparison to its secular and immoral English neighbour. Louise Ryan has described the strong emphasis that was placed on a 'purity, virtue, integrity and honour of the nation' and that women embodied these virtues.[2] She goes on to describe women as the 'conveniently flawed boundary guards' who were susceptible to foreign influences and therefore in need of constant monitoring and policing by men.[3] The purity of Irish women and their traditions and heritage are positioned against outside impurity and modernity.[4]

The image of this ideal woman was not limited to the Irish Free State. The same rhetoric was also expressed in Northern Ireland. Both communities, across the religious and political divide, were united in the belief that women were both the moral guardians of the nation, as well as embodying the greatest threat to moral standards. The behaviour of women was linked to the identity of both unionist and nationalist communities in Northern Ireland. As Brozyna has suggested with regard to the representation of women in religious literature in Ulster, when both communities felt threatened, not only from each other but also from perceived irreligion and modernity, it was increasingly necessary to maintain and strengthen the female ideal and role.[5] As Jan Pettiman has further suggested, within nationalism the use of women as boundary markers explains the attempts to control female sexuality, as women represented the maintenance of the identity and difference between communities.[6]

In Northern Ireland, therefore, both communities tried to regulate female sexuality as a means to provide internal stability and as an attempt to maintain their identity. These identities were under continual threat: the Catholic community felt threatened by the Protestant government and the Protestant community threatened by the existence of a Catholic government in the South. In the years that followed partition, both Protestant and Catholic Church leaders were vocal in their exhortations that young women should dress modestly, not frequent dance halls or cinemas and behave in a morally upright manner. Maintaining the image of a morally pure society was extremely important.

It is however, apparent that Northern Irish society was not as morally upstanding as the rhetoric suggested. As chapter 1 demonstrated, although Belfast may have had a high proportion of women in the workforce and a wider variety of jobs available than simply domestic work, women were still entering prostitution. Whether this was as a way of supplementing income or due to limited other employment options is difficult to identify given the restricted available source material. A consideration of women who were identified as prostitutes entering Belfast workhouse reveals that the use of the term 'prostitute' to describe them appears to be a pejorative label based on physical appearance, associates, address or past behaviour rather than an involvement in prostitution at that time. For many of these women it is arguable that while the workhouse was not a pleasant option, their use of it was part of a survival system which demonstrated a 'capacity for agency' in that they were not simply victims but had a measure of control and choice.[7] These women did make choices, and while these were undoubtedly limited, they were still able to exert some control over their lives.[8]

Similarly, the investigation of the rescue homes in Belfast has illustrated that a number of women also used rescue homes as a similar
survival strategy. They entered rescue homes when it suited them, for
example when they were in financial difficulties, had no job or were ill,
and left when they no longer required assistance. Some women simply
moved from home to home.

The role of rescue homes has been discussed within the context of
social control and feminist theories.[9] Similarly, it has been viewed as
part of attempts by the middle class to reform and 'save' working-class
women.[10] It is clear that the work of rescue homes was a gendered
process. It was female sexuality that was policed. There were no corre-
sponding institutions for men who transgressed sexually. The 'crimes' of
pre-marital sex, illegitimate pregnancy, and sexual precociousness were
female 'crimes'. It is also evident that those who established and ran rescue
homes were largely from the middle class. However, the issue of class is
not as straightforward as the working class being 'saved' or 'policed' by
the middle class. A more nuanced view of the working class has been suggested in this book and the important role 'respectability' has to play has
been stressed. There was a clear division between the 'respectable' working
class and a lower working class or 'residuum', and this division was recognised by the middle class and more importantly from within the working
class itself.[11] The 'respectable' working-class shared the moral standards
and outlook of the middle class. While the girls resident in rescue homes
were largely drawn from the working class, this does not mean that alien
views were being imposed. From the beginning of the twentieth century
rescue homes were increasingly used as homes for unmarried mothers
or girls whose sexual behaviour was cause for concern, rather than for
prostitutes. Parents placed their daughters in homes when they felt they
could no longer control them or when they became pregnant outside of
marriage. A similar situation existed to that identified by Mary Odem in
the United Sates; working-class parents actively used the institutions for
their own needs and purposes and because their daughters' behaviour
clashed with their own moral codes.[12]

The contemporary portrayal of Magdalen homes and asylums has
been one of condemnation, focusing on the brutalities and horrors
experienced by some women within Catholic-run homes. It must not
be forgotten that there were a number of Protestant homes as well and
that as suggested above, they existed within a society which both actively
and tacitly ensured their continued existence. The blame for their existence cannot be placed solely with those who ran the homes, and it must

be recognised that society did not provide for these most vulnerable women.

While accepting the fact that a division existed within the working class, it is nonetheless evident that it was the perceived sexual behaviour of women from the lower working-class that caused the authorities most concern. It was the presence of these women on the streets at night during the world wars that caused greatest consternation. They were the class who were believed to be 'amateur' prostitutes and responsible for much of the spread of VD. The situation in Northern Ireland was similar to that elsewhere in that VD controls targeted women, and in particular young, lower working-class women.[13] Girls' organisations also saw lower-class women as being most in need of protection. Consequently they provided accommodation and leisure activities designed to keep them off the streets and away from bad influences. As the twentieth century progressed, the need to protect girls who were living independently from the bad influences of modernity and city life grew. In response, greater attempts were made to provide care and protection for girls considered vulnerable. However, while a variety of both religious and lay organisations sought to protect young women and maintain the perceived high moral standards, there was also a reluctance to discuss any possibly contentious issues relating to sex. This affected not only sex education in schools but also publicity and propaganda relating to both VD and family planning.

The situation in Northern Ireland concerning VD is notable for its lack of publicity about the diseases and lack of discussion about them by the medical authorities. This may have been a result of the general assumption that VD was not a serious problem in Northern Ireland. From the initial attempts to establish clinics in 1918, there was resistance from local authorities and the medical establishment and a persistence in viewing VD as a moral rather than a medical issue. The belief that women were responsible for the spread of VD also persisted into the Second World War, when concerns about the health of troops, and in particular the large numbers of US troops based in Northern Ireland, encouraged greater publicity about the diseases.

These concerns about VD were part of wider fears surrounding female sexuality during the Second World War that were intensified with the arrival of US troops. While this fear of a decline in female standards of morality, as well as the existence of a double standard which held women responsible and excused male behaviour, had a long cultural tradition in Northern Ireland, wider social and political events intensified concerns and provoked attempts to regulate and control.

The already complicated political situation in Northern Ireland was exacerbated during the Second World War with a large minority who were opposed to participation in the war, and the presence of neutral Éire. This 'incredible complexity' has led historians to exclude Northern Ireland from discussion of wartime national identity.[14] Nonetheless it is evident that regardless of political and religious divisions, young women believed to be sexually promiscuous were regarded as a threat to societal stability and identity. These fears were undoubtedly heightened by the conditions of war and the arrival of large numbers of foreign troops, which made the issue of female sexuality more pertinent and visible.

Several decades after the end of the war and similar concerns about the controlling of female sexuality were still being expounded in relation to family planning. As with issues such as VD and sex education the authorities were at pains not to offend the churches and this undoubtedly led to the slower development of family planning services in Northern Ireland than elsewhere in the UK. However, there was an absence of any large-scale religious opposition to family planning within marriage, though concerns and opposition from both religious communities were galvanised over abortion and the providing of contraception to the unmarried.

As the debates over extending the 1967 Abortion Act to Northern Ireland continue into the twenty-first century, the view of a country with higher moral standards and a more conservative, Christian tradition is still being presented. The discourse surrounding issues such as contraception, teenage pregnancy, sex education, sexually transmitted diseases and homosexuality in Northern Ireland is still overwhelmingly dominated by religious and moral rhetoric, as it was a century ago. While political and religious divisions may still run deep, there is agreement on the supposed unique moral traditions of Northern Ireland, and the need to try and control and regulate sexuality.

Notes

1 See for example Breda Gray and Louise Ryan, 'The Politics of Irish Identity and the Interconnections Between Feminism, Nationhood and Colonialism', in Ruth Roach Peirson and Nupur Chaundhuri (eds), *Nation, Empire, Colony: Historicizing Gender and Race* (Bloomington, 1998), pp. 120–138; Ryan, *Gender, Identity*; Geraldine Meaney, *Sex and Nation: Women in Irish Culture and Politics* (Dublin, 1991); Maryann Valiulis, 'Power, Gender and Identity in the Irish Free State', in Joan Hoff and Moureen Coulter (eds), *Irish Women's Voices: Past and Present* (Bloomington, 1995), pp. 117–136.

2 Ryan, *Gender, Identity*, p. 42.

3 Ibid.

4 Ibid., p. 49.

5 Brozyna, *Labour, Love and Prayer*, p. 27.

6 Jan Jindy Pettman, 'Boundary Politics: Women, Nationalism and Danger', in Mary Maynard and June Purvis (eds), *New Frontiers in Women's Studies: Knowledge, Identity and Nationalism* (London, 1996), p. 195.

7 Mahood, *The Magdalenes*, p. 165.

8 See for example Luddy, 'Prostitution and Rescue Work', p. 51; Walkowitz, *Prostitution and Victorian Society*, p. 9.

9 See for example Mahood, *The Magdalenes*, p. 163.

10 Bartley, *Prostitution*, p. 25.

11 Giles, '"Playing Hard to Get"', 243.

12 Odem, *Delinquent Daughters*, pp. 4 and 44.

13 See for example Davidson, *Dangerous Liaisons*; Lundberg, 'Passing on the "Black Judgement"'; Mooij, *Out of Otherness*.

14 Sonya O. Rose, *Which People's War? National Identity and Citizenship in Britain 1939–1945* (Oxford, 2003), p. 28n.

Bibliography

Primary sources

Cardinal O'Fiaich Library and Archives Armagh
Cardinal Logue Archive, 1887–1924
Cardinal MacRory Archive, 1928–1945
Cardinal O'Donnell Archive, 1924–1928

Church of Ireland House, Belfast
Church of Ireland Rescue League Annual Reports
Minutes Church of Ireland Moral Rescue League

Contemporary Medical Archives Centre at the Wellcome Trust for History of Medicine (CMAC)
Marie Stopes Papers
Records of Belfast Mothers' Welfare Clinic/NIFPA

Linenhall Library
Annual Report of the Ulster Magdalene Asylum, 1887
Revd Dr O'Loughlin, *Sermon in Aid of the Magdalene Asylum*, 27th March 1900, Exhibition Hall Belfast

National Archives of Ireland (NAI)
Census of Ireland, 1901, 1911
Records of Department of Health
Records of Department of Justice
Records of Department of Taoiseach

The National Archives, London (TNL)
Foreign Office, Political Department, General Correspondence: FO 371
Home Office Registered Papers: HO45
Ministry of Health, War Diaries of Second World War, 1938–1946: MH 101
Ministry of Information, Files of Correspondence: INF/1

Presbyterian Historical Society (PHS)
Annual Reports of Edgar Home, 1900–1926
Minutes of Committee of Edgar Home, 1900–1926
Minutes of General Assembly of Presbyterian Church, 1900–1970
Minutes and Records of Girls' Auxiliary, 1911–1945

Public Record Office of Northern Ireland (PRONI)
Crown Files at Belfast Recorder's Court: BELF
Dr Florence Stewart, Reminiscences of a GP in Northern Ireland, 1914–1970,
    D/3612: PRONI
Records of Alpha Club: D/1505/4
Records of Belfast Board of Guardians: BG7
Records of Belfast Midnight Mission: D/2072
Records of Belfast Women's Welfare Clinic: D/3691
Records of Cabinet Secretariat: CAB
Records of Church of Ireland Rescue League, 1924–1925: D/1362
Records of Department of Education: ED
Records of Fisherwick Women's Working Association, 1909–1915: D/1812
Records of Girl Guides, 1920–1945: D/3875
Records of Girls' Friendly Society, Diocese of Down, Connor and Dromore,
    1918–1945: D/3271
Records of Ministry of Health and Local Government: HLG
Records of Ministry of Home Affairs: HA
Records of Northern Ireland Family Planning Association: D/3542; D/3543
Records of Victoria House and Shamrock Lodge, 1925–1945: D/3606
Local Authority Records: LA

Representative Church Body Library (RCB)
Records of Girls' Friendly Society, 1871–1945: MS 578
Records of the Magdalen Asylum, Dublin, 1767–1986: MS 551

Royal Victoria Hospital (RVH) Archives
Annual Reports Royal Victoria Hospital, 1900–1945
Staff Minutes Royal Victoria Hospital, 1900–1945

Police Service of Northern Ireland (PSNI) Museum
Correspondence City Belfast RUC Commissioner's Office
Records of City Belfast RUC Commissioner's Office

Salvation Army, Belfast
Entrance Registers, Salvation Army Homes, Belfast, 1905–1945

United States National Archives Building, Maryland (MD NAB)
Belfast Consulate General Records, 1936–1945: RG 84
Records of American Red Cross, 1935–1946: RG 200
Records of European Theater of Operations, Historical Division, 1942–1946: RG 338
Records of Londonderry Naval Base, 1942–1945: RG 181
Records of Social Protection Division, 1939–1945: RG 215
Records of War Department, 1939–1945: RG 165

Women's Library (WL)
Records of National Vigilance Association, 1900–1945: 4/NVA

Parliamentary Papers
Census of Ireland 1901, PP 1902, Cd 1123, vol. CXXVI
Census of Ireland 1911, PP 1912–13, Cd 6051, vol. CXVI
Royal Commission on Venereal Diseases, Reports and Minutes of Evidence, PP. 1914, Cd 7475, vol. XLIX; PP 1916, Cd 8189, vol. XVI; PP 1916, Cd 8190, vol. XVI
Vice Regal Commission on Poor Law Reform in Ireland, PP 1906, vol. LI: Cd 3203, Minutes of Evidence, PP 1906 Cd 3204, vol. LII.

Official Publications
Criminal and Judicial Statistics for Ireland 1900–1919
Government of Northern Ireland Report on the Administration of Home Office Services, 1937–1946
Health of Belfast, Annual Reports, 1919–1945
History of the Second World War: United Kingdom Medical Series: The Civilian Health and Medical Services: Vol. 2: The Colonies, The Medical Services of the Ministry of Pensions, Public Health in Scotland, Public Health in Northern Ireland, ed. Macnalty, A.S., (London: HMSO, 1955)
Northern Ireland House of Commons debates, 1921–1970
Northern Ireland Senate Debates, 1921–1970
Ulster Year Book, 1926, 1929, 1932, 1935, 1938, 1947
Venereal Diseases, Provision for Diagnosis, Treatment and Prevention, Circulars, etc., issued by the Local Government Board of Ireland (Dublin, 1918)

Newspapers, Journals And Magazines
Armagh Gazette
Banbridge Chronicle
Belfast Newsletter
Belfast Telegraph
Catholic Bulletin
Derry Journal
Dublin Journal of Medical Science

Irish Catholic Directory and Almanac
Irish Churchman
Irish Citizen
Irish Ecclesiastical Record
Irish Journal of Medical Science
Irish Leaflet
Irish Monthly
Irish News
Irish Presbyterian
Irish Theological Quarterly
Londonderry Sentinel
Lurgan Mail
Mid-Ulster Mail
Newry Telegraph
Nomads Weekly
Northern Whig
Presbyterian Herald
Prevention: A Quarterly Journal Devoted to Public Morals
Seeking and Saving
Transactions Ulster Medical Society
Tyrone Courier
Ulster Medical Journal
Witness

Published sources

Anon., *Address to Women on Prevention of VD: By a Woman* (Southsea, 1921)

Anon., *The Belfast Book, 1929* (Belfast, 1929)

Armstrong, D.L., 'Social and Economic Conditions in the Belfast Linen Industry, 1850–1900', *Irish Historical Studies*, 7 (1950–51), 235–269

Armstrong, George A., 'After the War – What?', *Irish Presbyterian*, 23 (April 1917), 3–4

Baden–Powell, Agnes, *The Handbook for Girl Guides or How Girls Can Help Build the Empire* (London, N.D.)

Baden–Powell, Robert, *Girl Guides: A Suggestion for Character Training for Girls* (London, 1909)

Blake, John, *Northern Ireland in the Second World War* (London, 1956)

Booth, General William, *In Darkest England And the Way Out* (London, 1890)

Cherry, J.C., 'The Control of VD in Ireland', *Irish Journal of Medical Science*, 6 (1943), 161–170

Coote, William Alexander, *A Romance of Philanthropy, Being a Record of Some of the Principal Incidents Connected With the Exceptionally Successful Thirty Years' Work of the National Vigilance Association* (London, 1916)

Devane, SJ, Revd R.S., 'The Dance Hall', *Irish Ecclesiastical Record*, 37 (1931) 170–86

Donald, H.C., 'The Diagnosis and Treatment of Syphilis', *Dublin Journal of Medical Science*, 142 (1919), 70–78

Flexner, Alexander, *Prostitution in Europe* (New York, 1917)

Freeman, Flora L., *Our Working Girls and How to Help Them* (London and Oxford, 1908)

—— *On the Right Trail. Friendly Counsel for Catholic Girl Guides*, (London, 1921)

Friedrichs, Hulda, *The Romance of the Salvation Army* (London, 1907)

Giollamhuire, 'Do Irish Girls Know?', *The Catholic Bulletin*, 12 (1922), 38–39

Hayes, Richard and Kathleen Lynn, *Public Health Circular no. 1*, Sinn Fein Public Health Leaflet (Dublin, 1918)

Kumm, Lucy Guinness, *In Perils in the City* (London, 1909)

Kidd, Cecil B., 'Changing Trends in General Paresis', *Ulster Medical Journal*, 28 (1959), 197–200

Kirkpatrick, T. Percy C., 'Syphilis and the State', *Dublin Journal of Medical Science*, 145 (1918), 339–357

Leathem, W.S., *A Short History of the Church of Ireland in St Mary Magdalene Parish Belfast* (Belfast, 1939)

Maddison, Arthur, J.S., *Hints on Rescue Work: A Handbook for Missionaries, Superintendents of Homes, Committees, Clergy and Others* (London, 1898)

McCarthy, M.J.F, *Priests and People in Ireland* (Dublin, 1926)

McClure, H.I., 'Diagnosis and Treatment of Gonorrhoea in the Female', *Ulster Medical Journal*, 5 (1936), 36–40

McGlinchey, Revd James, 'Maxims and Counsels for the Christian Family', *The Catholic Bulletin*, 24 (1934), 999–1004

Mogey, John M., *Rural Life in Northern Ireland* (London, 1947)

Pailthorpe, G.W., *What We Put in Prison and Preventative and Rescue Homes* (London, 1932)

Rankin, J.C., 'Syphilis', *Transactions of Ulster Medical Society* (1921–22), 33–36

Scharlieb, Mary, *The Hidden Scourge* (London, 1916)

Sinclair, Betty, *Ulster Women and the War* (Belfast, 1942)

Spiers, M.D., *An Almoner's Work in a Women's Venereal Disease Clinic* (London, 1926)

Secondary sources

Books

Abbott, Pamela and Claire Wallace (eds), *An Introduction to Sociology: Feminist Perspectives* (London, 1990)

Akenson, David, *Small Differences: Irish Catholics and Irish Protestants, 1875–1922: An International Perspective* (Kingston and Montreal, 1988)

Akenson, Donald H., *The Irish Diaspora: A Primer* (Belfast, 1993)

Aldrich, Richard (ed.), *Public or Private Education? Lessons from History* (London, 2004)

Alexander, Ruth M., *The 'Girl Problem': Female Sexual Delinquency in New York, 1900–1930* (Ithaca and London, 1995)

Alexander, Sally, *Becoming a Woman: and Other Essays in 19th and 20th Century Feminist History* (London, 1994)

Anderson, Benedict, *Imagined Communities: Reflections on the Origins and Spread of Nationalism* (London, 1983)

Anderson, Karen, *Wartime Women: Sex Roles, Family Relations, and the Status of Women During World War II* (Connecticut, 1981)

Andrews, Jonathan and Anne Digby, (eds), *Sex and Seclusion, Class and Custody: Perspectives on Gender and Class in the History of British and Irish Psychiatry* (Amsterdam, 2004)

Anon., *The Girls' Brigade, 1893–1983* (1984)

Anon., *The War Years: Derry 1939–45* (Derry, n.d.)

Armstrong, David, *Political Anatomy of the Body: Medical Knowledge in Britain in the Twentieth Century* (Cambridge, 1983)

Baldwin, Peter, *Contagion and the State in Europe, 1830–1930* (Cambridge, 1999)

Bardon, Jonathan, *Belfast: An Illustrated History* (Belfast, 1982)

—— *A History of Ulster* (Belfast, 1992)

Barker, Philip, *Michael Foucault: An Introduction* (Edinburgh, 1998)

Bartley, Paula, *Prostitution, Prevention and Reform in England 1860–1914* (London, 2000)

Barton, Brian, *The Government of Northern Ireland, 1920–1923* (Belfast, 1980)

—— *Northern Ireland in the Second World War* (Belfast, 1995)

Beckett, J.C. (ed.), *Belfast: The Making of the City, 1800–1914* (Belfast, 1983)

Beckett, J.C. and R.E. Glasscock (eds), *Belfast: Origin and Growth of an Industrial City* (London, 1967)

Benhabib, Seyla and Drucilla Cornell (eds), *Feminism as Critique: Essays on the Politics of Gender in Late Capitalist Society* (Cambridge, 1987)

Berger, John, *Ways of Seeing* (London, 1972)

Betterton, Rosemary (ed.), *Looking at Images of Femininity in the Visual Arts and Media* (London, 1987)

Bew, Paul, *Ireland: the Politics of Enmity, 1789–2006* (Oxford, 2007)

—— Peter Gibbon and Henry Patterson, *Northern Ireland 1921–1996: Political Forces and Social Classes,* revised and updated edn (London, 1996)

Birrell, Derek and Alan Murue, *Policy and Government in Northern Ireland: Lessons of Devolution* (Dublin, 1980)

Bland, Lucy, *Banishing the Beast: English Feminism and Sexual Morality, 1885–1914* (London, 1995)

Blaney, Roger, *Belfast – 100 Years of Public Health* (Belfast, 1988)

Bond Brian and Ian Roy (eds), *War and Society: A Yearbook of Military History*, Vol. 2 (London, 1977)

Bourke, Joanna, *Working-Class Cultures in Britain, 1890–1960: Gender, Class and Ethnicity* (London, 1994)

Bowen, Desmond, *History and the Shaping of Irish Protestantism* (New York, 1995)

Boyd, Gary, *Dublin, 1745–1920: Hospitals, Spectacle and Vice* (Dublin, 2005)

Brandt, Alan M., *No Magic Bullet: A Social History of Venereal Disease in the United States Since 1880* (Oxford, 1987)

Brewer, John D., with Gareth I. Higgins, *Anti-Catholicism in Northern Ireland, 1600–1998: The Mote and the Beam* (Basingstoke, 1998)

Brewster, Scott, *et al.* (eds), *Ireland in Proximity: History, Gender, Space,* (London, 1999)

Bristow, Edward, *Vice and Vigilance: Purity Movements in Britain Since 1700* (Dublin, 1977)

Brooke, Peter, *Ulster Presbyterianism: The Historical Perspective, 1610–1970* (Dublin, 1987)

Brookes, Barbara, *Abortion in England, 1900–1967* (London, 1988)

Brophy, Julia and Carol Smart (eds), *Women in Law: Explorations in Law, Family and Sexuality* (London, 1985)

Brozyna, Andrea Ebel, *Labour, Love and Prayer: Female Piety in Ulster Religious Literature, 1850–1914* (Belfast, 1999)

Buckland, Patrick, *A History of Ireland* (Dublin, 1981)

Buckley, Anthony D. and Mary Catherine Kennedy, *Negotiating Identity: Rhetoric, Metaphor and Social Drama in Northern Ireland* (Washington and London, 1995)

Byrne, Anne and Madeline Leonard (eds), *Women and Irish Society: A Sociological Reader* (Belfast, 1997)

Calder, Angus, *The Myth of the Blitz* (London, 1991)

Campbell, D'Ann, *Women at War With America: Private Lives in a Patriotic Era* (Cambridge, MA, 1984)

Campbell, Rosemary, *Heroes and Lovers: A Question of National Identity* (Sydney, 1989)

Carroll, Joseph T., *Ireland in the War Years* (Newton Abbot, 1975)

Catterall, Peter and Sean McDougall (eds), *The Northern Ireland Question in British Politics* (London, 1996)

Clarke, Richard, *The Royal Victoria Hospital Belfast: A History, 1797–1997* (Belfast, 1997)

Clear, Caitriona, *Social Change and Everyday Life in Ireland, 1850–1922* (Manchester, 2008)

Cohen, Stanley, *Folk Devils and Moral Panics: The Creation of the Mods and Rockers* (Oxford, 1980)

—— and Andrew Scull (eds), *Social Control and the State: Historical and Comparative Essays* (Oxford, 1983)

Collins, Marcus, *Modern Love: An Intimate History of Men and Women in Twentieth-Century Britain* (London, 2003)

Conn, Johnny, *Fall In: A History of the Church Lads' and Church Girls' Brigade* (Belfast, 1991)

Cook, Hera, *The Long Sexual Revolution: English Women, Sex, and Contraception* (Oxford, 2004)

Cooter, Roger, Mark Harrison and Steve Sturdy (eds), *War, Medicine and Modernity* (Stroud, 1998)

—— *Medicine and Modern Warfare* (Amsterdam, 1999)

Costello, John, *Virtue Under Fire: How World War II Changed Our Social and Sexual Attitudes* (Boston and Toronto, 1986)

Coward, Rosalind, *Female Desire: Women's Sexuality Today* (London, 1984)

Cox, Pamela, *Gender, Justice and Welfare: Bad Girls in Britain, 1900–1950* (Basingstoke, 2003)

Cullen, Mary and Maria Luddy (eds), *Women, Power and Consciousness in Nineteenth Century Ireland* (Dublin, 1995)

Culleton, Claire, *Working-Class Culture, Women, and Britain, 1914–1921* (Basingstoke, 2000)

Curtin, Chris, Pauline Jackson and Barbara O'Connor (eds), *Gender in Irish Society* (Galway, 1987)

Daly, Mary, *A Social and Economic History of Ireland Since 1800* (Dublin, 1981)

—— (ed.), *County and Town: One Hundred Years of Local Government in Ireland* (Dublin, 2001)

Darby, John (ed.), *Northern Ireland: The Background to the Conflict* (Syracuse, 1983)

Davenport-Hines, Richard, *Sex, Death and Punishment: Attitudes to Sex and Sexuality in Britain Since the Renaissance* (Glasgow, 1991)

Davidson, Roger, *Dangerous Liaisons: A Social History of Venereal Disease in Twentieth-Century Scotland* (Amsterdam and Atlanta, 2000)

—— and Lesley A. Hall (eds), *Sex, Sin and Suffering: Venereal Disease and European Society Since 1870* (London, 2001)

Davin, Anna, *Growing Up Poor: Home, School and Street in London 1870–1914* (London, 1996)

Delaney, Enda, *Demography, State and Society: Irish Migration to Britain, 1921–1971* (Liverpool, 2000)

Derry Heritage Library, Oral History Department, *The War Years in Derry, 1939–45* (Derry, 1992)

Doherty, James, *Post 381: The Memoirs of a Belfast Air Raid Warden* (Belfast, 1989)

Douglas, Mary, *Purity and Danger: An Analysis of the Concepts of Pollution and Taboo* (London, 1965)

Dunlop, John, *A Precarious Belonging: Presbyterians and the Conflict in Ireland,* (Belfast, 1995)

Dyhouse, Carol, *Girls Growing Up in Late Victorian and Edwardian England* (London, 1981)

Earner-Byrne, Lindsey, *Mother and Child: Maternity and Child Welfare in Dublin, 1922–60* (Manchester, 2007)

Elshtain, Jean Bethke, *Women and War* (Brighton, 1987)

Fee, Elizabeth and David M. Fox, *AIDS: The Burdens of History* (London, 1988)

Ferris, M. *et al.* (eds), *Women's Voices: An Oral History of Women's Health in Northern Ireland, 1900–1990* (Dublin, 1992)

Ferris, Paul, *Sex and the British: A Twentieth Century History* (London, 1993)

Ferriter, Diarmaid, *The Transformation of Ireland, 1900–2000* (London, 2004)

Finnegan, Frances, *Poverty and Prostitution: A Study of Prostitutes in York* (Cambridge, 1979)

—— *Do Penance or Perish: A Study of Magdalene Asylums in Ireland* (Kilkenny, 2000)

Fisher, Kate, *Birth Control, Sex and Marriage in Britain, 1918–1960* (Oxford, 2006)

Fitzpatrick, David, *The Two Irelands, 1912–39* (Oxford, 1998)

Fraser, T.G., *Ireland in Conflict, 1922–1998* (London and New York, 2000)

Freedman, Estelle B., *Their Sisters' Keepers: Women's Prison Reform in America, 1830–1930* (Michigan, 1981)

Freeman, Jo (ed.), *Women: A Feminist Perspective* 2nd edn (California, 1979)

Fryer, Peter, *The Birth Controllers* (London, 1965)

Fulton, John, *The Tragedy of Belief: Division, Politics and Religion in Ireland* (Oxford, 1991)

Furedi, Ann (ed.), *The Abortion Law in Northern Ireland: Human Rights and Reproductive Choice* (Belfast, 1995)

Galligan, Yvonne, *Women and Politics in Contemporary Ireland: From the Margins to the Mainstream* (London, 1998)

Gardiner, Juliet, *'Over Here': The GI's in Wartime Britain* (London, 1992)

Gibson-Harries, Derrick, *Life-Line to Freedom: Ulster in the Second World War* (Lurgan, 1990)

Giles, Judy, *Women, Identity and Private Life in Britain, 1900–1950* (Basingstoke, 1995)

Gilman, Sander, L., *Sexuality, An Illustrated History: Representing the Sexual in Medicine and Culture From the Middle Ages to the Age of AIDS* (New York, 1989)

Grayzel, Susan, *Women's Identities at War: Gender, Motherhood, and Politics in Britain and France during the First World War* (Chapel Hill and London, 2000)

Green, Anna and Kathleen Troup (eds), *The Houses of History: A Critical Reader in Twentieth-Century History and Theory* (Manchester, 1999)

Green, Arthur, *Devolution and Public Finance: Stormont 1921–1972* (Glasgow, 1979)

Gribbon, Sybil, *Edwardian Belfast: A Social Profile* (Belfast, 1982)

Hale, Edwin R.W. and John Frayn Turner (eds), *The Yanks Are Coming* (Tunbridge, 1983)

Hall, Lesley, *Hidden Anxieties: - Male Sexuality 1900–1956* (Cambridge, 1991)
—— *Gender and Social Change In Britain Since 1880* (London, 2000)
Hall, M. Penelope and Ismene, Howes, *The Church and Social Work: A Study of Moral Welfare Work Undertaken by the Church of England* (London, 1965)
Hanna, Ronnie, *'Pardon Me Boy': Americans in Ulster, 1942–45: A Pictorial Record* (Lurgan, 1991)
Harkness, David and Mary O'Dowd (eds), *The Town in Ireland* (Belfast, 1981)
Harris, Mary, *The Catholic Church and the Formation of the Northern Irish State* (Cork, 1993)
Hayes, Alan and Diane Urquart (eds), *The Irish Women's History Reader* (London and New York, 2001)
Heatley, Fred, *The Story of St Patrick's Belfast, 1815–1977* (Portglenone, n.d.)
Hennessey, Thomas, *A History of Northern Ireland, 1920–1996* (Dublin, 1997)
Hepburn, A.C. (ed.), *Minorities in History* (London, 1978)
—— *A Past Apart: Studies in the History of Catholic Belfast, 1850–1950* (Belfast, 1996)
Hershetter, Gail, *Dangerous Pleasures: Prostitution and Modernity in Twentieth Century Shanghai* (Berkley and London, 1997)
Higonnet, Margaret Randolph *et al.* (eds), *Behind the Lines: Gender in the Two World Wars* (New Haven and London, 1987)
Hill, Myrtle, *Women in Ireland: A Century of Change* (Belfast, 2003)
Hirst, Catherine, *Religion, Politics and Violence in Nineteenth-Century Belfast: The Pound and Sandy Row* (Dublin, 2002)
Hoff, Joan and Moureen Coulter (eds), *Irish Women's Voices: Past and Present* (Bloomington, 1995)
Holloway, Pippa, *Sexuality, Politics and Social Control, in Virginia, 1920–1945* (Chapel Hill, 2006)
Holmes, Janice and Diane Urquhart (eds), *Coming into the Light: The Work, Politics and Religion of Women in Ulster, 1840–1940* (Belfast, 1994)
Holmes, R.F.G. and R. Buick Knox (eds), *The General Assembly of the Presbyterian Church in Ireland, 1840–1990: A Celebration of Irish Presbyterian Witness During a Century and a Half* (Belfast, 1990)
Hug, Chrystel, *The Politics of Sexual Morality in Ireland, 1922–95* (Basingstoke, 1999)
Hughes, John, *Toome's Wartime Airfield* (Draperstown, 1995)
Hutton, Sean and Paul Stewart (eds), *Ireland's Histories: Aspects of State, Society and Ideology* (London, 1991)
Inglis, T. *Moral Monopoly: The Catholic Church in Modern Irish Society* (Dublin, 1987)
Jackson, Alvin, *Ireland, 1798–1998* (Oxford, 1999)
Jackson, Louise, *Women Police: Gender, Welfare and Surveillance in the Twentieth Century* (Manchester, 2006)
Jeffreys, Shelia, *The Spinster and her Enemies: Feminism and Sexuality, 1880–1930* (London and New York, 1985)

Jones, Emrys, *A Social Geography of Belfast* (London, 1960)

Jones, Greta, *Social Hygiene in Twentieth Century Britain* (London, 1986)

—— 'Captain of All These Men of Death': *The History of Tuberculosis in Nineteenth and Twentieth Century Ireland* (Amsterdam and New York, 2001)

—— and Elizabeth Malcolm (eds), *Medicine, Disease and the State in Ireland, 1650–1940* (Cork, 1999)

Jordan, Alison, *Who Cared? Charity in Victorian and Edwardian Belfast* (Belfast, 1993)

—— *Margaret Byers: Pioneer of Women's Education and Founder of Victoria College Belfast* (Belfast, 1999)

Kearney, Richard (ed.), *Migrations: The Irish at Home and Abroad* (Dublin, 1990)

Kelleher, Margaret and James Murphy (eds), *Gender Perspectives in Nineteenth Century Ireland: Public and Private Spheres* (Dublin, 1997)

Kelly, Mary Pat, *Home Away from Home: The Yanks in Ireland* (Belfast, 1994)

Kennedy, Liam, *Colonialism, Religion and Nationalism in Ireland* (Belfast, 1996)

—— and Philip Ollerenshaw (eds), *An Economic History of Ulster* (Manchester, 1985)

Keogh, Dermot, *The Vatican, The Bishops and Irish Politics, 1919–1939* (Cambridge, 1986)

Kerr, Rose (ed. Alex Liddell), *The Story of the Girl Guides, 1908–1938* (London, 1976)

Kirkham, Pat and David Thoms (eds), *War Culture: Social Change and Changing Experience in World War Two Britain* (London, 1995)

Kunzel, Regina G., *Fallen Women, Problem Girls, Unmarried Mothers and the Professionalization of Social Work 1890–1945* (New Haven and London, 1993)

Lacy, Brian, *Siege City: The Story of Derry and Londonderry* (Belfast, 1990)

Langan, Mary and Bill Schwartz (eds), *Crises in the British State, 1880–1930* (London, 1985)

Leathard, Audrey, *The Fight for Family Planning* (London, 1980)

Lee, Janet, *War Girls: the First Aid Nursing Yeomanry in the First World War* (Manchester, 2005)

Lee, J.J., *Ireland, 1912–85: Politics and Society* (Cambridge, 1989)

Levine, Philippa, *Prostitution, Race and Politics, Policing Venereal Diseases in the British Empire,* (New York and London, 2003)

Lewis, Jane (ed.), *Labour and Love: Women's Experience of Home and Family, 1850–1940* (Oxford, 1986)

Liddell, Alex, *The Girl Guides, 1910–1970* (London, 1970)

Llewellyn-Jones, Derek, *Herpes, AIDS and Other Sexually Transmitted Diseases* (London, 1985)

Longmate, Norman, *The G.I.'s: The Americans in Britain 1942–1945* (London, 1976)

Luddy, Maria, *Women and Philanthropy in Nineteenth Century Ireland* (Cambridge, 1995)

—— *Women in Ireland, A Documentary History* (Cork, 1995)

—— *Prostitution and Irish Society, 1800–1940* (Cambridge, 2007)

—— and Cliona Murphy (eds), *Women Surviving: Studies in Irish Women's History in the Nineteenth and Twentieth Centuries* (Dublin, 1989)

Lynch, John P., *A Tale of Three Cities: Comparative Studies in Working-Class Life* (London, 1998)

Lyons, F.S.L., *Ireland Since the Famine* (London, 1985)

Mackenzie, John A. (ed.), *Imperialism and Popular Culture* (Manchester, 1986)

Maguire, W.A., *Belfast* (Keele, 1998)

Mahood, Linda, *The Magdalenes: Prostitution in the Nineteenth Century* (London and New York, 1990

—— *Policing Gender: Class and Family: Britain 1850–1940* (London, 1995)

Mangan, J.A. (ed.), *Making Imperial Mentalities: Socialisation and British Imperialism* (Manchester, 1990)

Mangan, J.A. and James Walvin (eds), *Manliness and Morality: Middle-Class Masculinity in Britain and America, 1800–1940* (Manchester, 1987)

Marks, Lara, *Sexual Chemistry: A History of the Contraceptive Pill* (New Haven, 2001)

Martin, Peter, *Censorship in the Two Irelands, 1922–1939* (Dublin, 2006)

Marwick, Arthur, *War and Social Change in the Twentieth Century: A Comparative Study of Britain, France, Germany, Russia and the United States* (London, 1974)

—— *Women at War 1914–18* (London, 1977)

—— (ed.), *Total War and Social Change* (London, 1988)

Maynard, Mary and Jane Purvis (eds), Researching Women's Lives from a Feminist Perspective (London, 1994)

—— New Frontiers in Women's Studies: Knowledge, Identity and Nationalism (London, 1996)

Maynes, Mary Jo, Brigitte Søland, and Christina Bennighaus (eds), *Secret Gardens, Satanic Mills, Placing Girls in European History, 1750–1960* (Indiana, 2005)

McCall, Cathal, *Identity in Northern Ireland: Communities, Politics and Change* (Basingstoke, 1999)

McHugh, Paul, *Prostitution and Victorian Social Reform* (London, 1980)

McLaren, Angus, *A History of Contraception from Antiquity to the Present Day* (Oxford, 1990)

McNay, Lois, *Foucault and Feminism: Power, Gender and the Self* (Cambridge, 1992)

Meaney, Geraldine, *Sex and Nation: Women in Irish Culture and Politics* (Dublin, 1991)

Messenger, Betty, *Picking up the Linen Threads: A Study in Industrial Folklore* (Austin and London, 1978)

Mooij, Annet, *Out of Otherness: Characters and Narrators in the Dutch Venereal Disease Debates, 1850–1990* (Amsterdam, 1998)

Morgan, Austen, *Labour and Partition: The Belfast Working Class, 1905–23* (London, 1991)

Mort, Frank, *Dangerous Sexualities - Medico-Moral Politics in England Since 1830* (London and New York, 1987)

Morton, Marian, *And Sin No More: Social Policy and Unwed Mothers in Cleveland, 1855–1990* (Columbus, 1993)

Muldowney, Mary, *The Second World War and Irish Women: An Oral History* (Dublin, 2007)

Mumm, Susan, *Stolen Daughters, Virgin Mothers: Anglican Sisterhoods in Victorian Britain* (London and New York, 1999)

Murolo, Priscilla, *The Common Ground of Womanhood: Class, Gender, and Working Girls' Clubs, 1884–1928* (Chicago, 1997)

Murphy, Cliona, *The Women's Suffrage Movement and Irish Society in the Early Twentieth Century* (Hertfordshire, 1989)

Nathanson, Constance, *'Dangerous Passage': The Social Control of Sexuality in Women's Adolescence* (Philadelphia, 1991)

Nead, Lynda, *Myths of Sexuality: Representations of Women in Victorian Britain* (Oxford, 1988)

Newton, Judith L., Mary P. Ryan and Judith R. Walkowitz (eds), *Sex and Class in Women's History* (London, 1983)

Novick, Ben, *Conceiving Revolution: Irish Nationalist Propaganda During the First World War* (Dublin, 2001)

O'Connor, Emmet and Trevor Parkhill, (eds), *A Life in Linenopolis: The Memoirs of William Topping, Belfast Damask Weaver, 1903–1956* (Belfast, 1992)

O'Connor, J., *The Workhouses of Ireland* (Dublin, 1995)

Odem, Mary, E., *Delinquent Daughters: Protecting and Policing Adolescent Female Sexuality in the United States, 1885–1920* (Chapel Hill and London, 1995)

O'Dowd, Mary and Sabine Wichert (eds), *Chattel, Servant or Citizen: Women's Status in Church, State and Society* (Belfast, 1995)

Offen, Karen, Ruth Roach Pierson and Jane Rendall (eds), *Writing Women's History: International Perspectives* (London, 1991)

O'Flannagan, Patrick, Paul Ferguson and Kevin Whelan (eds), *Rural Ireland 1600–1900: Modernisation and Change* (Cork, 1987)

Ó hÓgartaigh, Margaret, *Kathleen Lynn, Irishwoman, Patriot, Doctor* (Dublin, 2006)

O'Sullivan, Patrick (ed.), *Irish Women and Migration* (London and Washington, 1995)

Owens, Rosemary Cullens, *Smashing Times: A History of the Irish Women's Suffrage Movement, 1889–1922* (Dublin, 1984)

Pascoe, Peggy, *Relations of Rescue: The Search for Female Moral Authority in the American West, 1874–1939* (Oxford, 1990)

Patton, Marcus, *Central Belfast: An Historical Gazetteer* (Belfast, 1993)

Pelan, Renee, *Malone Place Hospital: A Short History* (Belfast, 1981)

Pivar, David, *Purity Crusade: Sexual Morality and Social Control, 1868–1900* (Westport, 1973)

Porter, Dorothy (ed.), *The History of Public Health and the Modern State* (Amsterdam and Atlanta, 1994)

Porter, Roy and Lesley Hall (eds), *The Facts of Life: The Creation of Sexual Knowledge in Britain, 1650–1950* (New Haven and London, 1995)

Porter, Roy and Mikulas Teich (eds), *Sexual Knowledge and Sexual Science: The History of Attitudes to Sexuality* (Cambridge, 1994)

Preston, Margaret, *Charitable Words: Women, Philanthropy, And The Language Of Charity In Nineteenth-Century Dublin* (Connecticut, 2004)

Prochaska, Frank, *Women and Philanthropy in Nineteenth Century England* (Oxford, 1980)

Proctor, Tammy, *On My Honor: Guides and Scouts in Interwar Britain* (Philadelphia, 2002)

Purvis, Jane (ed.), *Women's History: Britain, 1850–1945* (London, 1995)

Quetel, Claude, *History of Syphilis*, translated by Judith Braddock and Brian Pike (Cambridge, 1990)

Ramblado-Minero, Maria C., and Perez-Vides, Auxiliadora (eds), *Single Motherhood in 20th Century Ireland: Cultural, Historical and Social Essays* (Lampeter, 2006)

Reynolds, David, *'Rich Relations': The American Occupation of Britain, 1942–1945* (London, 1996)

Roach Pierson, Ruth and Napur Chaudhuri (eds), *Nation, Empire, Colony: Historicizing Gender and Race* (Bloomington, 1998)

Roebuck, Peter (ed.), *Plantation to Partition: Essays in Honour of J.L. McCracken* (Belfast, 1981)

Rose, Sonya, O., *Which People's War? National Identity and Citizenship in Britain 1939–1945* (Oxford, 2003)

Rosen, Ruth, *The Lost Sisterhood: Prostitution in America, 1900–1918* (Baltimore and London, 1982)

Ryan, James, *Picturing Empire: Photography and the Visualization of the British Empire* (London, 1997)

Ryan, Louise, *Irish Feminism and the Vote: An Anthology of the Irish Citizen Newspaper, 1912–20* (Dublin, 1996)

—— *Gender, Identity and the Irish Press 1922–37: Embodying the Nation* (New York, 2002)

Sales, Rosemary, *Women Divided: Gender, Religion and Politics in Northern Ireland* (London and New York, 1997)

Samuel, Raphael, *Theatres of Memory, Volume I: Past and Present in Contemporary Culture* (London, 1994)

Sawyer, Roger, *'We Are But Women': Women in Ireland's History* (London and New York, 1993)

Scott, Joan Wallach (ed.), *Feminism and History* (Oxford and New York, 1997)

Scull, Andrew (ed.), *Madhouses, Mad Doctors and Madmen: The Social History of Psychiatry in the Victorian Era* (London, 1987)

Sheridan, Dorothy (ed.), *Wartime Women: An Anthology of Women's Wartime Writing for Mass-Observation 1937–45* (London, 1990)

Shukert, Elfreda Berthianne and Barbara Smith Scibetta, *War Brides of World War Two* (Novota, CA, 1988)

Smart, Barry, *Michael Foucault* (Sussex, 1985)

Smart, Carol (ed.), *Regulating Womanhood: Historical Essays on Marriage, Motherhood and Sexuality* (London, 1992)

Smith, James M., *Ireland's Magdalen Laundries and the Nation's Architecture of Containment* (Notre Dame, 2007)

Smith, Harold L. (ed.), *War and Social Change: British Society in the Second World War* (Manchester, 1986)

Smith, Sarah J., *Children, Cinema and Censorship: From Dracula to the Dead End Kids* (London, 2005)

Smyth, Ailbhe, *The Abortion Papers* (Dublin, 1992)

—— (ed.), *Irish Women's Studies Reader* (Dublin, 1993)

Smyth, Lisa, *Abortion and Nation: The Politics of Reproduction in Contemporary Ireland* (Hampshire, 2005)

Snitow, Ann, Christine Stansell and Sharon Thompson (eds), *Desire: The Politics of Sexuality* (London, 1994)

Sontag, Susan, *On Photography* (London, 1978)

Sponberg, Mary, *Feminizing Venereal Disease: The Body of The Prostitute in Nineteenth-Century Medical Discourse* (New York, 1997)

Springhall, John, *Youth, Popular Culture and Moral Panics: Penny Gaffs to Gangsta Rap, 1830–1996* (Basingstoke, 1998)

Stern-Gillet, Suzanne *et al.* (eds), *Culture and Identity: Selected Aspects and Approaches* (Katowice, 1996)

Summerfield, Penny, *Women Workers in the Second World War* (London, 1989)

Szreter, Simon R.S., *Fertility, Class and Gender in Britain, 1860–1940* (Cambridge, 1996)

Thom, Deborah, *Nice Girls and Rude Girls: Women Workers in World War I* (London, 1998)

Thomson, Matthew, *The Problem of Mental Deficiency: Eugenics, Democracy and Social Policy in Britain c.1870–1959* (Oxford, 1998)

Tosh, John (ed.), *Historians on History* (Harlow, 2000)

Ungerson, Clare (ed.), *Women and Social Policy: A Reader* (London, 1985)

Urquhart, Diane, *Women in Ulster Politics 1890–1940: A History Not Yet Told* (Dublin, 2000)

Vaughan, W.E., and J. A. Fitzpatrick, *Irish Historical Statistics: Population, 1821–1971* (Dublin, 1978)

Vicinus, Martha, *Independent Women: Work and Community for Single Women, 1850–1920* (London, 1985)

—— (ed.), *Suffer and be Still: Women in the Victorian Age* (Bloomington, 1977)

Walker, Harlan (ed.), *Public Eating: Proceedings of the Oxford Symposium on Food and Cookery* (Oxford, 1991)

Walkowitz, Judith, *Prostitution and Victorian Society: Women, Class and the State* (Cambridge, 1980)

—— *City of Dreadful Delight: Narratives of Sexual Danger in late-Victorian London* (London, 1992)

Walsh, Oonagh, *Anglican Women in Dublin: Philanthropy, Politics and Education in the Early Twentieth Century* (Dublin, 2005)

Warner, Marina, *Monuments and Maidens: The Allegory of the Female Form* (London, 1996)

Weeks, Jeffery, *Sex, Politics and Society: The Regulation of Sexuality Since 1800* (London, 1989)

Whelan, Christopher (ed.), *Values and Social Change in Ireland* (Dublin, 1994)

Whelan, Imelda, *Modern Feminist Thought: From the Second Wave to 'Post-Feminism'* (Edinburgh, 1995)

White, Luise, *The Comforts of Homes: Prostitution in Colonial Nairobi* (Chicago and London, 1990)

Whitelegg, E. *et al.* (eds), *The Changing Experience of Women in Early Twentieth-Century Britain* (Oxford, 1982)

Whyte, J.H., *Church and State in Modern Ireland, 1923–1979* (Dublin, 1980)

Williamson, Judith, *Decoding Advertisements: Ideology and Meaning in Advertising* (London, 1978)

Wilson, Libby, *Sex on the Rates: Memoirs of a Family Planning Doctor* (Argyll, 2004)

Wilson, Thomas (ed.), *Ulster Under Home Rule: A Study of the Political and Economic Problems of Northern Ireland* (London, 1955)

Wilson, Tom, *Ulster: Conflict and Consent* (Oxford, 1990)

Wilson, Trevor, *The Myriad Faces of War: Britain and the Great War, 1914–1918* (Cambridge, 1986)

Winfield, Pamela in collaboration with Brenda Wilson Hasty, *Sentimental Journey: The Story of the GI Brides* (London, 1984)

Wright, David and Anne Digby (eds), *From Idiocy to Mental Deficiency: Historical Perspectives of People With Learning Disabilities* (London, 1996)

Young, Iris Marion, *Justice and the Politics of Difference* (Princeton, 1990)

Zedner, Lucia, *Women Crime and Custody in Victorian England* (Oxford, 1991)

Book chapters

Barton, Brian, 'The Impact of World War Two on Northern Ireland and on Belfast–London Relations', in Peter Catterall and Sean McDougall (eds), *The Northern Ireland Question in British Politics* (London, 1996), pp. 47–51

Beaumont, Caitriona, 'Gender, Citizenship and the State in Ireland, 1922–1990', in Scott Brewster *et al.* (eds), *Ireland in Proximity: History, Gender, Space* (London, 1999), pp. 94–109

Blair, Grainne, "'Equal sinners": Irish Women Utilising the Salvation Army Rescue Network', in Margaret Kelleher and James Murphy (eds), *Gender Perspectives in Nineteenth Century Ireland: Public and Private Spheres* (Dublin, 1997), pp. 181–192

Bland, Lucy, "'Guardians of the Race" or "Vampires Upon the Nation's Health"?: Female Sexuality and Regulation in Early Twentieth-Century Britain', in Elizabeth Whitelegg *et al.* (eds), *The Changing Experience of Women in Early Twentieth-Century Britain* (Oxford, 1982), pp. 375–388

—— 'In the Name of Protection: The Policing of Women in the First World War', in Julia Brophy and Carol Smart (eds), *Women in Law: Explorations in Law, Family and Sexuality* (London, 1985), pp. 23–49

—— "'Cleansing the Portals of Life": The Venereal Disease Campaign in the Early Twentieth Century', in M. Langan and B. Schwarz (eds), *Crises in the British State, 1880–1930* (London, 1985), pp. 192–208

—— 'Feminist Vigilantes of Late-Victorian England', in Carol Smart (ed.), *Regulating Womanhood: Historical Essays on Marriage, Motherhood and Sexuality* (London, 1992), pp. 33–53

Boyle, Emily, "'Linenopolis": The Rise of the Textile Industry', in J. C. Beckett (ed.), *Belfast: The Making of the City, 1800 – 1914* (Belfast, 1983), pp. 41–57

Brandt, Allan M., 'AIDS: From Social History to Social Policy', in Elizabeth Fee and David M. Fox (eds), *AIDS: The Burdens of History* (London, 1988), pp. 147–171

Buckley, Suzanne, 'The Failure to Resolve the Problem of Venereal Disease Among the Troops in Britain During WW1', in Brian Bond and Ian Roy (eds), *War and Society a Yearbook of Military History*, Vol. 2 (London, 1977), pp. 65–85

Burns, Robert, 'Old Ironsides', in Edwin R.W. Hale and John Frayn Turner (eds), *The Yanks Are Coming* (Tunbridge Wells, 1983), pp. 16–19

Clarkson, Leslie A., 'Population Change and Urbanisation, 1821–1911', in Liam Kennedy and Philip Ollerenshaw (eds), *An Economic History of Ulster, 1820–1940* (Manchester, 1985), pp. 137–157

Collins, Brenda, 'The Edwardian City', in J.C. Beckett (ed.), *Belfast: The Making of the City, 1800–1914* (Belfast, 1983), pp. 167–183

Cox, Pamela, 'Girls in Trouble: Defining Female Delinquency in Britain, 1900–1950', in M. Maynes, B. Søland and C. Benninghaus (eds), *Secret Gardens, Satanic Mills: Placing Girls in European History, 1750–1960* (Indiana, 2005), pp. 192–208

Cullen, Mary, 'Women's History in Ireland', in Karen Offen, Ruth Roach Pierson and Jane Rendall (eds), *Writing Women's History: International Perspectives* (London, 1991), pp. 429–443

Gray, Breda and Louise Ryan, 'Gendered Constructions on Irishness: Stagnation or Change in Irish Society Since Independence', in Suzanne Stern-Gillet *et al.* (eds), *Culture and Identity: Selected Aspects and Approaches* (Katowice, 1996), pp. 174–191

—— 'The Politics of Irish Identity and the Interconnections Between Feminism, Nationhood and Colonialism', in Ruth Roach Pierson and Napur Chaudhuri (eds), *Nation, Empire, Colony: Historicizing Gender and Race* (Bloomington, 1998), pp. 121–139

Gribbon, Sylvia, 'An Irish City: Belfast 1911', in David Harkness and Mary O'Dowd (eds), *The Town in Ireland* (Belfast, 1981), pp. 203–221

Hahn Rafter, Nicole, 'Chastizing the Unchaste: Social Control Functions of a Women's Reformatory, 1894–1931', in Stanley Cohen and Andrew Scull (eds), *Social Control and the State: Historical and Comparative Essays* (Oxford, 1983), pp. 288–312

Hall, Lesley, '"War Always Brings It On": War, STDs, the Military and the Civilian Population in Britain, 1850–1950', in Roger Cooter, Mark Harrison and Steve Sturdy (eds), *Medicine and Modern Warfare* (Amsterdam, 1999), pp. 205–223

—— 'Venereal Diseases and Society in Britain from the Contagious Diseases Acts to the National Health Service', in Roger Davidson and Lesley A. Hall (eds), *Sex, Sin and Suffering: Venereal Disease and European Society Since 1870* (London, 2001), pp. 120–137

—— 'Birds, Bees and General Embarrassment: Sex Education in Britain, from Social Policy to Section 28', in R. Aldrich (ed.) *Public or Private Education? Lessons from History* (London, 2004), pp. 98–115

Harrison, Mark, 'Sex and the Citizen Soldier: Health, Morals and Discipline in the British Army During the Second World War', in Roger Cooter, Mark Harrison and Steve Sturdy (eds), *Medicine and Modern Warfare* (Amsterdam, 1999), pp. 224–239

Hepburn, A.C., 'Catholics in the North of Ireland, 1850–1921: The Urbanization of a Minority', in A.C. Hepburn (ed.), *Minorities in History* (London, 1978), pp. 84–102

—— and Brenda Collins, 'Industrial Society: The Structure of Belfast, 1901', in Peter Roebuck (ed.), *Plantation to Partition: Essays in Honour of J.L. McCracken* (Belfast, 1981), pp. 210–228

Higonnet, Margaret and Patrice Higonnet, 'The Double Helix', in M. Higonnet *et al.* (eds), *Behind the Lines: Gender and the Two World Wars* (New Haven and London, 1987), pp. 33–36.

Jackson, Alvin, 'Local Government in Northern Ireland, 1920–1973', in Mary Daly (ed.), *County and Town: One Hundred Years of Local Government in Ireland* (Dublin, 2001), pp. 56–66

Jackson, Mark. '"A Menace to the Good of Society": Class, Fertility, and the Feeble-Minded in Edwardian England' in Jonathan Andrews and Anne Digby (eds), *Sex and Seclusion, Class and Custody: Perspectives on Gender and Class in the History of British and Irish Psychiatry* (Amsterdam, 2004), pp. 271–294

Johnson, D.S., 'The Northern Ireland Economy, 1914–1918', in Liam Kennedy and Philip Ollerenshaw (eds), *An Economic History of Ulster, 1820–1940* (Manchester, 1985), pp. 184–223

Langhamer, Claire, 'Leisure, Pleasure, and Courtship: Young Women in England, 1920–1960', in M. Maynes, B. Søland and C. Benninghaus (eds), *Secret Gardens and Satanic Mills: Placing Girls in European History, 1750–1960* (Indiana, 2005), pp. 269–284

Lee, Simon, 'Abortion in Northern Ireland: The Twilight Zone', in Ann Furedi (ed.), *The Abortion Law in Northern Ireland: Human Rights and Reproductive Choice* (Belfast, 1995), pp. 16–26.

Luddy, Maria, 'Prostitution and Rescue Work in Nineteenth Century Ireland', in Maria Luddy and Cliona Murphy (eds), *Women Surviving: Studies in Irish Women's History in the Nineteenth and Twentieth Centuries,* (Dublin, 1989), pp. 51–78

Lundberg, Anna, 'Passing on the "Black Judgement": Swedish Social Policy On Venereal Disease in the Early Twentieth Century', in Roger Davidson and Lesley A. Hall (eds), *Sex, Sin and Suffering: Venereal Disease and European Society Since 1870* (London, 2001), pp. 29–43

McAvoy, Sandra L., 'The Regulation of Sexuality in the Irish Free State, 1929–1935', in Greta Jones and Elizabeth Malcolm (eds), *Medicine, Disease and the State in Ireland, 1650–1940* (Cork, 1999), pp. 253–266

McCarthy, Aine, 'Hearths, Bodies and Minds: Gender Ideology and Women's Committal to Eniscorthy Lunatic Asylum, 1916–1925', in Alan Hayes and Diane Urquart (eds), *The Irish Women's History Reader* (London and New York, 2001), pp. 102–109

McCaughan, Alison, '"Cherchez la Femme": Women in the Presbyterian Church in Ireland and in Society, 1840–1990', in R.F.G. Holmes, and R. Buick Knox (eds), *The General Assembly of the Presbyterian Church in Ireland, 1840–1990: A Celebration of Irish Presbyterian Witness During a Century and a Half* (Belfast, 1990), pp. 112–132

McCracken, L., 'Northern Ireland, 1921–66', in T.W. Moody and F.X. Martin (eds), *The Course of Irish History* (Dublin, 1994), pp. 313–324

McKee, Francis, 'Ice Cream and Immorality', in Harlan Walker (ed.), *Public Eating: Proceedings of the Oxford Symposium on Food and Cookery* (Oxford, 1991), pp. 199–205

Meaney, Geraldine, 'Sex and Nation: Women in Irish Culture and Politics', in Ailbhe Smyth (ed.), *Irish Women's Studies Reader* (Dublin, 1993), pp. 230–244

Mort, Frank, 'Purity, Feminism and the State: Sexuality and Moral Politics, 1886–1914', in Mary Langan and Bill Schwartz (eds), *Crises in the British State, 1880–1914* (London, 1985), pp. 209–230

Nead, Lynn, 'The Magdalen in Modern Times: The Mythology of the Fallen Woman in Pre-Raphaelite Painting', in R. Betterton (ed.), *Looking at Images of Femininity in the Visual Arts and Media* (London, 1987), pp. 74–92

O'Dowd, Liam, 'Church, State and Women: The Aftermath of Partition', in Chris Curtin, Pauline Jackson and Barbara O'Connor (eds), *Gender in Irish Society* (Galway, 1987), pp. 3–37

Ollerenshaw, Philip, 'Industry 1820-1914', in Liam Kennedy and Philip Ollerenshaw (eds), *An Economic History of Ulster, 1820-1940* (Manchester, 1985), pp. 62-108

Pettman, Jan Jindy, 'Boundary Politics: Women, Nationalism and Danger', in Mary Maynard and June Purvis (eds), *New Frontiers in Women's Studies: Knowledge, Identity and Nationalism* (London, 1996), pp. 187-203

Purvis, Jane, 'Doing Feminist Women's History: Researching the Lives of Women in the Suffragette Movement in Edwardian England', in Mary Maynard and Jane Purvis (eds), *Researching Women's Lives from a Feminist Perspective* (London, 1994), pp. 166-190

Rendall, Jane, 'Uneven Developments: Women's History, Feminist History, and Gender History in Great Britain', in Karen Offen, Ruth Roach Pierson and Jane Rendall (eds), *Writing Women's History: International Perspectives* (London, 1991), pp. 45-59

Sauerteig, Luitz D.H., '"The Fatherland is in Danger, Save the Fatherland!": Venereal Disease, Sexuality and Gender in Imperialist and Weimar Germany', in Roger Davidson and Lesley A. Hall (eds), *Sex, Sin and Suffering: Venereal Disease and European Society Since 1870* (London, 2001), pp. 76-93

Simpson, John, 'Economic Development: Cause or Effect in the Northern Ireland Conflict', in John Darby (ed.), *Northern Ireland: The Background to the Conflict* (Syracuse, 1983) pp. 79-109

Smith, Harold L., 'The Effect of the War on the Status of Women', in Harold L. Smith (ed.), *War and Social Change: British Society in the Second World War* (Manchester, 1986), pp. 208-229

Summerfield, Penny, 'Women and War in the Twentieth Century', in Jane Purvis (ed.), *Women's History in Britain 1850-1945* (London, 1995), pp. 307-333

Valiulis, Maryann Gialanella, 'Neither Feminist nor Flapper: The Ecclesiastical Construction of the Ideal Irish Woman', in Mary O'Dowd and Sabine Wichart (eds), *Chattel, Servant or Citizen? Women's Status in Church, State and Society* (Belfast, 1995), pp. 168-178

—— 'Power, Gender and Identity in the Irish Free State', in Joan Hoff and Moureen Coulter (eds), *Irish Women's Voices* (Bloomington, 1995), pp. 117-136

Warren, Allen, 'Citizens of the Empire: Baden-Powell, Scouts and Guides, an Imperial Ideal', in J. Mackenzie (ed.), *Imperialism and Popular Culture* (Manchester, 1986), pp. 232-257

—— '"Mothers for the Empire"?: The Girl Guide Association in Britain 1909-1939', in J.A. Mangan (ed.), *Making Imperial Mentalities: Socialisation and British Imperialism* (Manchester, 1990), pp. 96-110

Young, Iris Marion, 'Impartiality and Civic Public: Some Implications of Feminist Critiques of Moral and Political Theory', in Seyla Benhabib and Drucilla Cornell (eds), *Feminism as Critique: Essays on the Politics of Gender in Late Capitalist Society* (Cambridge, 1987), pp. 56-77

Articles

Adams, Mary and Denise Fulton, 'Family Planning: A Survey of Clinic Patients', *Ulster Medical Journal*, 32 (1963), 49–60

Adler, M.W., 'The Terrible Peril: An Historical Perspective on Venereal Diseases', *British Medical Journal*, 19 (1980), 206–211

Allen, Ann Taylor, 'Feminism, Venereal Diseases, and the State in Germany, 1890–1918', *Journal of the History of Sexuality*, 4 (1993), 27–50

Bartley, Paula, 'Preventing Prostitution: The Ladies' Association for the Care and Protection of Young Girls in Birmingham, 1887–1914', *Women's History Review*, 7 (1998), 37–60

Beaumont, Caitriona, 'Women, Citizenship and Catholicism in the Irish Free State, 1922–1948', *Women's History Review*, 6:4 (1997), 563–585

Best, E.J., 'Health and Wealth in the Borough of Lisburn', *Lisburn Historical Journal*, 2 (1972)

Bland, Lucy, 'Purifying the Public World: Feminist Vigilantes in Late Victorian England', *Women's History Review*, 1 (1992), 397–412

Blom, Ida, 'Fighting Venereal Diseases: Scandinavian Legislation c.1800 to c.1950', *Medical History*, 50 (2006), 209–234

Brenzel, Barbara, 'Domestication as Reform: A Study of the Socialization of Wayward Girls, 1856–1905', *Harvard Educational Review*, 50 (1980), 196–213

Brozyna, Andrea Ebel, '"The Right to Labour, Love and Pray": The Creation of the Ideal Christian Woman in Ulster Roman Catholic and Protestant Religious Literature, 1850–1914', *Women's History Review*, 6 (1997), 505–528

Brumberg, Joan, '"Ruined Girls": Changing Community Responses to Illegitimacy in Upstate New York, 1890–1920', *Journal of Social History*, 18 (1984), 247–272

Bush, Julia, 'Edwardian Ladies and the Race Dimensions of British Imperialism', *Women's Studies International Forum*, 21 (1998), 277–289

Cale, Michelle, 'Girls and the Perception of Sexual Danger in the Victorian Reformatory System', *History*, 78 (1993), 201- 217

Carroll, Francis, 'United States Armed Forces in Northern Ireland During World War Two', *New Hibernia Review*, 12:2 (2008), 15–36

Carter, Julian B., 'Birds, Bees, and Venereal Disease: Towards an Intellectual History of Sex Education', *Journal of the History of Sexuality*, 10 (2001), 213–249

Ciani, Kyle Emily, '"Problem Girls": Gendering Criminal Acts and Delinquent Behaviour', *Journal of Women's History*, 9 (1997), 203–214

Cohen, Deborah, 'Private Lives in Public Spaces: Marie Stopes, the Mothers' Clinics and the Practice of Contraception', *History Workshop Journal*, 35 (1993), 95–116

Cox, Pamela, 'Compulsion, Voluntarism, and Venereal Disease: Governing Sexual Health in England after the Contagious Diseases Acts', *Journal of British Studies*, 46:1 (2007), 91–115

Daly, Mary, 'Marriage, Fertility and Women's Lives in Twentieth-Century Ireland c. 1900–1970', *Women's History Review*, 13 (2006), 371–385

Davey, Clare, 'Birth Control in Britain During the Interwar Years: Evidence from the Stopes Correspondence', *Journal of Family History*, 13 (1988) 329–345

Davidson, Roger, "'A Scourge to be Firmly Gripped": The Campaign for VD Controls in Interwar Scotland', *Social History of Medicine*, 6 (1993), 213–235

—— 'Measuring "The Social Evil": The Incidence of Venereal Disease in Interwar Scotland', *Medical History*, 37 (1993), 167–186

—— 'Venereal Disease, Sexual Morality and Public Health in Interwar Scotland', *Journal of the History of Sexuality*, 5 (1994), 267–293

—— "'Searching for Mary, Glasgow": Contract Tracing for Sexually Transmitted Diseases in Twentieth Century Scotland', *Social History of Medicine*, 9 (1996), 195–215

—— 'Fighting "The Deadly Scourge": The Impact of World War II on Civilian VD Policy in Scotland', *The Scottish Historical Review*, 75 (1996), 72–97

—— 'Venereal Disease, Public Health and Social Control: The Scottish Experience in a Comparative Perspective', *Dynamis*, 17 (1997), 341–368

—— and Gayle Davis, "'This Thorniest of Problems": School Sex Education Policy in Scotland 1939–1980', *Scottish Historical Review*, 84:2 (2005), 221–246

Douglas, M., 'Women, God and Birth Control: The First Hospital Birth Control clinic, Abertillery 1925', *Llafur*, 6 (1995) 110–122

Dunphy, Richard, 'Gender and Sexuality in Ireland', *Irish Historical Studies*, 31 (1991), 549–557

Earner-Byrne, Lindsey, 'The Boat to England: An Analysis of the Official Reactions to the Emigration of Single Expectant Irishwomen to Britain, 1922–1972', *Irish Economic and Social History*, 30 (2003), 52–71

Evans, David 'Tackling the "Hideous Scourge": The Creation of Venereal Disease Treatment Centres in Early Twentieth Century Britain', *Social History of Medicine*, 5 (1992), 413–435

Field, Geoffrey, 'Perspectives on the Working-Class Family in Wartime Britain, 1939–1945', *International Labor and Working-Class History*, 38 (1990), 3–28

—— 'Social Patriotism and the British Working Class: Appearance and Disappearance of a Tradition', *International Labor and Working-Class History*, 42 (1992), 20–39

Finnane, Mark, 'The Carrigan Committee of 1930–31 and the Moral Condition of the *Saorstat*', *Irish Historical Studies*, 32 (2001), 519–536

Fisher, Kate, "'Clearing up the Misconceptions": The Campaign to Set Up Birth Control Clinics in South Wales Between the Wars', *Welsh History Review*, 19 (1998), 103–129

—— "'She Was Quite Satisfied With the Arrangements I Made": Gender and Birth Control in Britain, 1925–1950', *Past and Present*, 169 (2000), 161–193

—— 'Uncertain Aims and Tacit Negotiations: Birth Control Practices in Britain, 1925–50', *Population and Development Review*, 26 (2000), 295–317

—— and Simon Szreter, "'They Prefer Withdrawal'': The Choice of Birth Control in Britain, 1918–1950', *Journal of Interdisciplinary History*, 34:2 (2003), 263–291

Fleming, Philip, 'Fighting the "Red Plague": Observations on the Response to Venereal Disease in New Zealand 1910–1945', *New Zealand Journal of History*, 2 (1988), 56–64

Francome, Colin, 'Attitudes of General Practitioners in Northern Ireland Toward Abortion and Family Planning', *Family Planning Perspectives*, 29:5 (1997), 234–236

Garrett, Paul, "'The Abnormal Flight": The Migration and Repatriation of Irish Unmarried Mothers', *Social History*, 25 (2001), 330–343

Gibson, K. Craig, 'Sex and Soldiering in France and Flanders: The British Expeditionary Force Along the Western Front, 1914–1919', *The International History Review*, 23 (2001), 535–579

Giles, Judy, "'Playing Hard to Get": Working-Class Women, Sexuality and Respectability in Britain, 1918–40', *Women's History Review*, 1 (1992), 239–255

Gilfoyle, Timothy J., 'Prostitutes in the Archives: Problems and Possibilities in Documenting the History of Sexuality', *American Archivist*, 57 (1999), 514–527

—— 'Prostitutes in History: From Parables of Pornography to Metaphors of Modernity', *American History Review*, 104 (1999), 117–141

Goodman, Joyce, 'Sex and the City: Educational Initiatives for "Dangerous" and "Endangered" Girls in Late Victorian and Early Edwardian Manchester', *Paedagogica Historica*, 39 (2003), 75–86

Gorman, Deborah, 'The "Maiden Tribute of Modern Babylon" Re-examined: Child Prostitution and the Idea of Childhood in Late-Victorian England', *Victorian Studies*, 21 (1978), 353–379

Grier, Julie, 'Eugenics and Birth Control: Contraceptive Provision in North Wales, 1918–1939', *Social History of Medicine*, 11 (1998), 443–458

Grobb, George, 'The Way of All Flesh: Degeneration, Eugenics, and the Gospel of Free Love', *Journal of the History of Sexuality*, 6 (1996), 589–603

Gurney, P, "'Intersex" and "Dirty Girls": Mass Observation and Working-Class Sexuality in England in the 1930's', *Journal of the History of Sexuality*, 8 (1997), 256–290

Guy, Donna, 'Stigma, Pleasures and Dutiful Daughters', *Journal of Women's History*, 10 (1998), 181–191

Hall, Lesley, "'The Cinderella of Medicine": Sexually Transmitted Diseases in Britain in the Nineteenth and Twentieth Centuries', *Genitourinary Medicine*, 69 (1993), 314–319

—— 'Impotent Ghosts from No-Mans-Land, Flappers, Boyfriends or Cryptopatriarchs: Men, Sex and Social Change in 1920's Britain', *Social History*, 21 (1996), 54–70

Hampshire, James, 'The Politics of School Sex Education Policy in England and

Wales from the 1940s to the 1960s', *Social History of Medicine*, 18:1 (2005), 87–105

Harrison, Brian, '"For Church, Queen and Family": The Girls' Friendly Society 1874–1920', *Past and Present*, 61 (1973), 105–138

Harvey, A.D., 'Prostitution in Cardiff', *Archives*, 25 (2000), 117–123

Hegarty, Marilyn, 'Patriot or Prostitute? Sexual Discourses, Print Media and American Women During World War Two', *Journal of Women's History*, 10 (1998), 112–136

Henderson, Ian, 'The GI's in Northern Ireland', *After the Battle*, 34 (1981), 1–41

Hepburn, A.C., 'Work, Class and Religion in Belfast, 1871–1911', *Irish Economic and Social History*, 10 (1983), 33–50

Hershatter, Gail, 'Courtesans and Streetwalkers: The Changing Discourses on Shanghai Prostitution, 1890–1949', *Journal of the History of Sexuality*, 3 (1992), 245–269

Horwood, Catherine, '"Girls Who Arouse Dangerous Passions": Women and Bathing 1900–39', *Women's History Review*, 9 (2000), 653–672

Howell, Philip, 'Venereal Disease and Prostitution in the Irish Free State', *Irish Historical Studies*, 33 (2003), 338–340

Jackson, Louise, '"Singing Birds as well as Soap Suds": The Salvation Army's Work with Sexually Abused Girls in Edwardian England', *Gender and History*, 12 (2000), 107–126

Jones, Greta, 'Marie Stopes in Ireland - The Mothers' Clinic in Belfast 1936–47', *Social History of Medicine*, 5 (1992), 255–277

—— 'Eugenics in Ireland: The Belfast Eugenics Society, 1911–1915', *Irish Historical Studies*, 28 (1992), 81–95

—— 'Women and Eugenics in Britain: The Case of Mary Scharleb, Elizabeth Sloan Chesser and Stella Browne', *Annals of Science*, 51 (1995), 481–502

Kingsley Kent, Susan, 'The Politics of Sexual Difference: World War I and the Demise of British Feminism', *Journal of British Studies*, 27 (1988), 232–253

Knupfer, Anne, Meis, '"To Become Good, Self-Supporting Women": The State Industrial School for Delinquent Girls at Geneva, Illinois, 1900–1935', *Journal of the History of Sexuality*, 9 (2000), 420–446

Kunzel, Regina, G. 'The Professionalization of Benevolence: Evangelicals and Social Workers in the Florence Crittenton Homes, 1915–1945', *Journal of Social History*, 22 (1988), 21–45

Lake, Marylin, 'Female Desires: The Meaning of World War II', *Australian Historical Studies*, 24 (1990), 267–284

—— 'The Desire for a Yank: Sexual Relations Between Australian Women and American Servicemen During World War II', *Journal of the History of Sexuality*, 2 (1992), 621–633

Lemar, Susan, '"The Liberty to Spread Disaster": Campaigning for Compulsion in the Control of Venereal Diseases in Edinburgh in the 1920s', *Social History of Medicine*, 19:1 (2006), 83–85

Levine, Phillippa, 'Venereal Disease, Prostitution, and the Politics of Empire: The Case of British India', *Journal of the History of Sexuality*, 4 (1994), 579–602

—— '"Walking the Streets in a Way No Decent Woman Should": Women Police in World War I', *The Journal of Modern History*, 66 (1994), 34–78

Littlewood, Barbara and Linda Mahood, 'Prostitutes, Magdalenes and Wayward Girls: Dangerous Sexualities of Working Class Women in Victorian Scotland', *Gender and History*, 3 (1991), 160–175

Luddy, Maria, 'An Agenda for Women's History, 1800–1900', *Irish Historical Studies*, 28 (1992–93), 19–37

—— 'Women and the Contagious Diseases Acts, 1864–1886', *History Ireland*, Spring (1993), 32–34

—— '"Abandoned Women and Bad Characters": Prostitution in Nineteenth Century Ireland', *Women's History Review*, 6 (1997), 485–503

—— 'Women and Charitable Organisations in Nineteenth Century Ireland', *Women's International Studies Forum*, 11 (1998), 301–305

—— 'Moral Rescue and Unmarried Mothers in Ireland in the 1920's', *Women's Studies*, 30 (2001), 797–819

Mahood, Linda, 'The Magdalene's Friend: Prostitution and Social Control in Glasgow, 1869–1890', *Women's International Studies Forum*, 13 (1990), 49–61

—— and Barbara Littlewood, 'The "Vicious" Girl and the "Street-Corner" Boy: Sexuality and the Gendered Delinquent in the Scottish Child Saving Movement, 1850–1940', *Journal of the History of Sexuality*, 4 (1994), 549–578

Malcolm, Elizabeth, '"Troops of Largely Diseased Women": VD, The Contagious Diseases Acts and Moral Policing in Late Nineteenth Century Ireland', *Irish Economic and Social History*, 26 (1999), 1–14

McCormick, Leanne, 'Sinister Sisters?: The Portrayal of Magdalene Asylums in Ireland in Popular Culture', *Cultural and Social History*, 2 (2005), 373–381

—— '"One Yank and They're Off": Interaction between U.S. Troops and Northern Irish Women, 1942–1945', *Journal of the History of Sexuality*, 15:2 (2006), 228–257

—— '"The Scarlet Woman in Person"': The Establishment of a Family Planning Service in Northern Ireland, 1950–1974', *Social History of Medicine*, 21 (2008) 345–360

McCray Brier, Lucinda, '"We Were Green as Grass": Learning about Sex and Reproduction in Three Working-Class Lancashire Communities, 1900–1970', *Social History of Medicine*, 16 (2003), 461–480

McIntosh, Tania, '"An Abortionist City": Maternal Mortality, Abortion, and Birth Control in Sheffield, 1920–1940', *Medical History*, 44:1 (2000), 75–96

McLaughlin, Dympna, 'Women and Sexuality in Nineteenth Century Ireland', *The Irish Journal of Psychology*, 15 (1994), 266–275

Morgan, Sue, 'Faith, Sex and Purity: The Religio-Feminist Theory of Ellice Hopkins', *Women's History Review*, 9 (2000), 13–34

Mort, Frank, 'Mapping Sexual London: The Wolfden Committee on Homosexual Offences and Prostitution 1954–57', *New Formations*, 37 (1999), 92–113

Morton, Marian, 'Seduced and Abandoned in an American City: Cleveland and its Fallen Women, 1869–1936', *Journal of Urban History*, 11 (1985), 443–466

Mullen, James and Frances, Dermot, '"Base One Londonderry": Derry, the Yanks and World War II', *Ulster Folklife*, 41 (1995), 12–18

Mumm, Susan, '"Not Worse Than Any Other Girls": The Convent Based Rehabilitation of Fallen Women in Victorian Britain', *Journal of Social History*, 29 (1996), 527–564

Murphy, Cliona, 'The Religions Context of the Women's Suffrage Campaign in Ireland', *Women's History Review*, 6 (1997), 549–565

Neill, Joyce, 'A Family Planning Service in a Teaching Maternity Hospital', *Ulster Medical Journal*, 38 (1969), 88–90

Nic Suibhne, Fionnuala, '"On the Straw" and Other Aspects of Pregnancy and Childbirth from the Oral Tradition of Women in Ulster', *Ulster Folklife*, 38 (1992), 12–24

Parkes, Alan and King, Dee, 'The Mothers' Clinic', *Journal of BioSocial Science*, 6 (1974), 163–182

Pierson, Ruth Roach, 'The Double Bind of the Double Standard: VD Control and the CWAC in World War II', *Canadian Historical Review*, 62 (1987), 31–58

Pilcher, Jane, 'School Sex Education: Policy and Practice in England 1870 to 2000', *Sex Education*, 5 (2005), 153–170

Pooley, Colin, 'From Londonderry to London: Identity and Sense of Place for a Protestant Northern Irish Woman in the 1930's', *Immigrants and Minorities*, 18 (1999), 189–213

Prior, Pauline, 'Mad, not Bad: Crime, Mental Disorder and Gender in Nineteenth-Century Ireland', *History of Psychiatry*, 8 (1997), 501–516

Pryke, Sam, 'The Control of Sexuality in the Early British Boy Scouts movement', *Sex Education*, 5:1 (2005), 15–28

Redmond, Jennifer, '"Sinful Singleness"? Exploring the Discourses on Irish Single Women's Emigration to England, 1922–48', *Women's History Review*, 17:3 (2008), 455–476

Riordan, Susannah, 'Venereal Disease in the Irish Free State: The Politics of Public Health', *Irish Historical Studies*, 34 (2007), 345–364

Robb, G., 'The Way of All Flesh: Degeneration, Eugenics and the Gospel of Free Love', *Journal of the History of Sexuality*, 4 (1996), 589–603

Rolston, Bill, Dirk Schubotz and Audrey Simpson, 'Sex Education in Northern Ireland Schools: A Critical Evaluation', *Sex Education*, 5 (2005), 217–234

Rose, Sonya O., 'Girls and GIs: Race, Sex and Diplomacy in Second World War Britain', *The International History Review*, 19 (1997), 142–160

—— 'Sex, Citizenship, and the Nation in World War II Britain', *American History Review*, 103 (1998), 1147–1176

—— 'The "Sex Question" in Anglo-American Relations in the Second World War', *The International History Review*, 20 (1998), 791–1072

Ruggles, S, '"Fallen Women": The Inmates of the Magdalen Society Asylum of Philadelphia, 1836–1908', *Journal of Social History*, 16 (1982), 65–82

Ryan, Louise, 'Traditions and Double Moral Standards: The Irish Suffragist' Critique of Nationalism', *Women's History Review*, 4 (1995), 487–503

—— 'Constructing "Irishwoman": Modern Girls and Comely Maidens', *Irish Studies Review*, 6 (1998), 263–272

—— 'Negotiating Modernity and Tradition: Newspaper Debates on the "Modern Girl" in the Irish Free State', *Journal of Gender Studies*, 7 (1998), 181–197

—— 'Sexualising Emigration: Discourses of Irish Female Emigration in the 1930's', *Women's Studies International Forum*, 1 (2002), 51–65

Sangster, Joan, 'Incarcerating "Bad Girls": The Regulation of Sexuality Through the Female Refuges Act in Ontario, 1920–1945', *Journal of the History of Sexuality*, 7 (1996), 239–275

Saunders, Kay and Helen Taylor, '"To Combat the Plague": The Construction of Moral Alarm and State Intervention in Queensland During World War II', *Hecate*, 14 (1988), 5–30

Schlossman, Steven, and Wallach, Stephanie, 'The Crime of Precocious Sexuality: Female Juvenile Delinquency in the Progressive Era', *Harvard Educational Review*, 48 (1978), 65–94

Seccombe, Walter, 'Starting to Stop: Working-Class Fertility Decline in Britain', *Past and Present*, 126 (1990), 151–188

Side, Katherine, 'Contract, Charity and Honourable Entitlement: Social Citizenship and the 1967 Abortion Act in Northern Ireland After the Good Friday Agreement', *Social Politics: International Studies in Gender, State and Society*, 13 (2006), 89–116

Smart, J., 'Sex, the State and the Scarlet Scourge', *Women's History Review*, 7 (1998), 5–36

Smith, Jim, 'Dancing, Depravity and All That Jazz: The Public Dance Halls Act of 1935, *History Ireland*, Summer (1993), 51–54

Smyth, Lisa, 'The Cultural Politics of Sexuality and Reproduction in Northern Ireland', *Sociology*, 40 (2006), 663–680

Springhall, John, 'The Boy Scouts, Class, and Militarism in Relation to British Youth Movements, 1908–1930', *International Review of Social History*, 16 (1971), 125–158

—— and Anne Summers and Allen Warren, Debate: 'Baden-Powell and the Scout Movement Before 1920: Citizen Training or Soldiers for the Future?', *English Historical Review*, 102 (1987), 934–950

Stanley, Liz, 'Women Have Servants and Men Never Eat: Issues in Reading Gender, Using the Case Study of Mass-Observation's 1937 Day-Diaries', *Women's History Review*, 4 (1995), 85–102

Stearns, Carol and Peter Stearns, 'Victorian Sexuality: Can Historians Do It Better?' *Journal of Social History*, 18 (1985), 309–317

Sturma, Michael, 'Loving the Alien: The Underside of Relations Between

American Servicemen and Australian Women in Queensland, 1942–1945', *Journal of Australian Studies*, 41 (1989), 3–17

Summerfield, Penny and Crockett, Nicole, "'You Weren't Taught That With the Welding": Lessons in Sexuality in the Second World War', *Women's History Review*, 1 (1992), 435–454

Taithe, Bernard, 'Morality is not a Curable Disease: Probing the History of Venereal Diseases, Morality and Prostitution', *Social History of Medicine*, 14 (2001), 337–350

Taylor, Becky and Ben Rogaly, "'Mrs Fairly is a Dirty, Lazy Type": Unsatisfactory Households and the Problem of Problem Families in Norwich, 1942–1963', *Twentieth Century British History*, 18:4 (2007), 429–452

Thane, Pat, 'Women and Poor Law Guardians in Victorian and Edwardian England', *History Workshop Journal*, 6 (1978), 28–51

Tinkler, Penny, 'Cause for concern: Young Women and Leisure, 1930–50', *Women's History Review*, 12:2 (2003), 233–60.

Todd, Selina, 'Young Women, Work, and Leisure in Interwar England', *Historical Journal*, 48:3 (2005), 789–809

Tomkins, S.M., 'Palmitate or Permanganate: The Venereal Prophylaxis Debate in Britain, 1916–1926', *Medical History*, 37 (1993), 382–398

Towers, Bridget, 'Health Education Policy 1916–1926: Venereal Disease and the Prophylaxis Dilemma', *Medical History*, 24 (1980), 70–87

Urquhart, Diane, "'An Articulate and Definite Cry for Political Freedom": The Ulster Suffrage Movement', *Women's History Review*, 11 (2002), 273–292

Vining, Margaret and Barton C. Hacker, 'From Camp Follower to Lady in Uniform: Women, Social Class and Military Institutions Before 1920', *Contemporary European History*, 10 (2001), 353–373

Voeltz, Richard A., 'Adam's Rib: The Girl Guides and an Imperial Race', *San Jose Studies*, 45 (1988), 91–99

—— 'The Antidote to "Khaki Fever"? The Expansion of the British Girl Guides During the First World War', *Journal of Contemporary History*, 27 (1992), 627–638

—— 'Reflections on Baden-Powell, the British Boy Scouts and Girl Guides, Racism, Militarism, and Feminism', *Weber Studies*, 14.2 (1997), 2011–2016

Walkowitz, Judith, 'Vice and Feminist Virtue: Feminism and the Politics of Prostitution in Nineteenth-Century Britain', *History Workshop Journal*, 13 (1982), 79–93

Walsh, Oonagh, 'Protestant Female Philanthropy in Dublin in the Early Twentieth Century', *History Ireland*, 5 (1997), 27–31

Warren, Allen, 'Sir Robert Baden-Powell, the Scout Movement and Citizen Training in Great Britain', *English Historical Review*, 101 (1986), 376–398

White, Luise, 'Prostitutes, Reformers and Historians', *Criminal Justice History*, 6 (1985), 201–227

Williamson, Noeline, 'Laundry Maids or Ladies? Life in the Industrial and

Reformatory School for Girls in New South Wales. Part II: 1887–1910', *Journal of the Royal Australian Historical Society*, 68 (1983), 312–324

Wimshurst, Kerry, 'Control and Resistance: Reformatory School Girls in Late Nineteenth Century South Australia', *Journal of Social History*, 18 (1984), 196–214

Woollacott, Angela, '"Khaki Fever" and its Control: Gender, Class, Age and Sexual Morality on the British Homefront in the First World War', *Journal of Contemporary History*, 29 (1994), 325–347

Unpublished papers and theses

Austoker, Joan, 'Biological Education and Social Reform: The British Social Hygiene Council 1925–42' (unpublished master's thesis, University of London, 1981)

Ball, Gillian Tyler, 'Practical Religion: A Study of the Salvation Army's Social Services for Women, 1884–1914' (unpublished doctoral thesis, University of Leicester, 1987)

Blom, Ida, 'Sexuality and Public Policy: Prevention of VD in Scandinavia, c.1900–1950' (unpublished paper, presented at IFRWH Conference, Belfast, August 2003)

Boyle, Michael, 'Women and Crime in Belfast 1900–1913' (unpublished doctoral thesis, Queen's University, Belfast, 1997)

Davidson, Roger, 'The Great Scourge: Approaches to the History of VD in Modern Europe' (unpublished paper, February 2003)

Davis, Gayle, '"Every Baby a Wanted Baby?": Family Planning Policy in later Twentieth-Century Scotland' (unpublished paper, presented at the International Federation for Research in Women's History Conference, Queen's University, Belfast, August 2003)

Goldstrom, Max, 'Abortion and the Law in Northern Ireland' (unpublished paper, 1981)

Gray, William Paul, 'Patterns of Illegitimacy in Twentieth Century Northern Ireland' (unpublished master's thesis, Queen's University Belfast, 1989)

—— 'A Social History of Illegitimacy in Ireland from the late Eighteenth Century to the Early Twentieth Century' (unpublished doctoral thesis, Queen's University, Belfast, 2001)

Hamill, Jonathan, 'A Study of Female Textile Operatives in the Belfast Linen Industry: 1890–1939' (unpublished doctoral thesis, Queen's University, Belfast, 1999)

Hughes, Peter, E, '"Cleanliness and Godliness": A Sociological Study of the Good Shepherd Refuges for the Social Reformation and Christian Conversion of Prostitutes and Convicted Women in Nineteenth Century Britain' (unpublished doctoral thesis, Brunel University, 1985)

Jeffery, Keith, 'Canadian Sailors in Londonderry: A Study in Civil–Military Relations, 1942–45' (unpublished paper, n.d.)

Jordan, Alison, 'Voluntary Societies in Victorian and Edwardian Belfast' (unpublished doctoral thesis, Queen's University, Belfast, 1989)

Larmour, Sandra Ruth, 'Aspects of the State and Female Sexuality in the Irish Free State, 1922–1949' (unpublished doctoral thesis, University College, Cork, 1998)

Leane, Marie, 'Female Sexuality in Ireland, 1920–1940: Control and Regulation', (unpublished doctoral thesis, University College, Cork, 1999)

Manzoor, Farhat, 'A Political History: Abortion in Ireland' (unpublished doctoral thesis, University of Ulster, 2000)

Morrow, Alison, 'Women and Work in Northern Ireland, 1920–1950' (unpublished doctoral thesis, University of Ulster, 1995)

Neil, Margaret, 'Women at Work in Ulster, 1845–1911' (unpublished doctoral thesis, Queen's University, Belfast, 1996)

Rattigan, Cliona, '"Dark Spots" in Irish Society: Single Motherhood, Crime and Prosecution in Ireland, 1900–1950' (unpublished doctoral thesis, Trinity College, Dublin, 2007)

Robinson, Peter, 'The Impact of Competing Nationalisms on Women in Northern Ireland' (unpublished master's thesis, Queen's University, Belfast, 1998)

Rush, Claire, 'Women Who Made a Difference: The Members of the Belfast Ladies' Institute, 1867–97', (unpublished paper, presented at 'Did Women Make a Difference? Women in Higher Education, 1908–2008' Queen's University, Belfast 2007)

Simpson, Audrey, 'A Sociological Analysis of the Theory and Practice of Sex Education in Post-primary Schools in Northern Ireland' (unpublished doctoral thesis, University of Ulster, 2001)

Ware, Helen, 'The Recruitment and Regulation of Prostitution in Britain from the Middle of the Nineteenth Century to the Present Day' (unpublished doctoral thesis, University of London, 1969)

Index

abortion
  back-street 188, 199
  female networks 199, 200
  legislation 180-181, 198, 200
    opposition 200, 203
  methods 198, 199
alcohol
  links with prostitution 23, 31, 32,
    51, 53-54, 59, 98, 164
  US troops and 155-156
America 155, 172
  see also United States
American 56, 139
  Consul 150, 152
American Red Cross 152, 155, 160,
  168, 171
American troops 148, 150,
  172-173
  alcohol 155-156
  prostitution 159-160
  race 162-163
  relations with locals 150-151
  relations with women 152-154,
    155-158
    controlling contact 161-162
  VD 163-169
  war brides 169-172
Anderson, Olive 182-185, 188,
  193-194
Andersonstown, Belfast 187,
  192

Antrim
  County 86, 116, 120, 157, 196
    Council 125, 142,
Armagh
  County 31, 99, 116, 119
    Council 118
  prison 28
  Armagh Guardian 153, 166, 168
Arnold, Charlotte 183
Australia 5, 81, 148, 164

Baden-Powell, Robert 83
Bailie, H.W. 116, 123-124
Ballymena 119, 124, 189, 195
Band of Hope 82
Bangor, Co. Down 89, 189
Bartley, Paula 4, 39, 63, 80
Bates, Dawson 27, 137
BBC 186, 188, 196
Belfast
  brothels 27, 28
  economy 2-3
  employment, 29-30, 44, 84, 94
  hostels 81, 86-89
  housing 20-21
  prison 29
  prostitution 17, 20-21, 29, 32,
    156
    prosecutions 13, 23, 25
  rescue homes *see* individual
    institutions

Belfast (*cont.*)
    VD rates 115, 138-140
    Women's Patrols 29, 95-96, 159
Belfast Corporation 2
    housing 17, 20
    Maternity and Child Welfare
        Committee 103
    Public Health Committee 102
        VD 116-117, 120-121, 123-127,
            134-136
Belfast Girls' Club Union 85, 89-91
Belfast Midnight Mission 37, 41, 66,
    92
    see also Malone Place
Belfast Newsletter 127, 157, 172, 188
Belfast Union Workhouse 119
    Lock Wards 114, 119
    women recorded as prostitutes 13,
        15, 17, 18-19, 31-32, 37, 47,
        208
Belfast Women's Welfare Clinic
    (BWCC) 183-185, 188, 191,
    194-195, 197
    see also NIFPA
birth control *see* contraception; family
    planning
Booth, William 52
Boyd, Constance 183-185
Boyle, Michael 17, 22-23
British Army 129-130, 152, 155, 169
Brookes, Barbara 200
Brozyna, Andrea 100, 208
Buhrman, Parker 150, 163

Canadian 126, 131, 159, 168, 174
Carrigan Committee 133
Catholic Church
    abortion 200
    cinema 98, 133
    family planning 181-183, 185-187,
        196
    female behaviour 149, 151,
        153-154, 208

female dress 98-100, 208
girls' clubs 88, 91
hostels 89
Magdalen homes 3, 37, 39, 41-42,
    46-48, 67-71, 94, 209
moral purity movements 26
relations with Stormont 2, 180,
    182-183
scandals 3, 6-7, 80
sex education 102
VD propaganda 117-118, 124, 127
Catholics
    nationalism 150
    recorded as prostitutes 18-19
censorship 193
    Second World War 154-155,
        157-158, 173
Church of Ireland
    family planning 187
    preventative work with girls 80, 89
    recorded as prostitutes 18-19
    rescue homes 47
    VD propaganda 122
Church of Ireland Moral Welfare
    Association 25, 35, 154
Church of Ireland Rescue League 53,
    96
cinema
    immorality 71, 97-98, 133, 208
    US troops 152-3
    VD propaganda 126
Coleraine, Co Londonderry 117, 189,
    197
Collins, Marcus 90
Contagious Diseases Acts 95, 114,
    122
contraception 6, 71, 180-181, 186-187,
    190, 192-193, 196, 202-204,
    211
    see also abortion; family planning
Cooke, Herbert 169
court visitors 40-41
Cox, Pamela 79

Criminal Law Amendment Act (1885)
  24, 91
  (1912) 24, 43-44
  (1923) 24, 26
  (1935) 193

dancing
  Church attitudes 98, 133, 208
  dance halls 96, 133
  US troops and 153, 155-156,
    159-163, 173
Davidson, Roger 132
De Valera, Eamon 150
Defence of the Realm Act (DORA)
  131
  Regulation 33B 134-136, 166
  Regulation 40D 131-132, 165
Derry 3, 86, 130
  Catholic Bishop 99, 100, 117, 124
  family planning 191-192
  US troops 153-154, 156, 158-159
  see also Londonderry
Devane, Richard, S., SJ 28
Devlin, Paddy 191
Diamond, Harry 190
Docks 139
  immorality 20-22, 32, 50
Dublin 3, 47, 63, 67, 70, 81, 86, 150,
  163
  family planning 194
  Monto 28
  prostitution 25, 133
  purity campaigns 28, 89, 94-95
  VD 115, 131, 138
Duff, Frank 28, 133-134
Dufferin and Ava, Hariot,
  Marchioness 86-87, 92
Dungannon, Co. Tyrone 119, 186, 189
Dyhouse, Carol 4, 80

Edgar Home 27, 31, 37, 39, 46, 71, 92
  daily life 60-61
  discipline 64-66

entering and leaving 42-44, 48-49,
    53, 63-64
  laundry work 59, 60-63
  missioner 40, 41
  religious affiliation 46-48, 60
  size of home 45-46, 66-67
Eire 124, 183
  Second World War 3, 150, 158, 171,
    211
  see also Irish Free State, Republic of
    Ireland
emigration 81
employment
  domestic service 19, 29-30, 40,
    63-64, 81, 85, 87, 89-92, 94,
    208
  factory work 17, 44, 63, 80, 85
  family planning 195, 197
  mill work 20, 30, 45, 54, 63, 85,
    87-90, 104
  prostitution 16, 23, 29, 31, 208
  World Wars 83, 94, 153
Enniskillen, Co. Fermanagh 189, 195
eugenics 51

family planning 1
  Belfast Women's Welfare Clinic
    (BWWC) 184, 188
  clinics 188-189, 194-196
  establishment of service 6, 8, 180,
    182, 191
  Family Planning Association (FPA)
    182-183, 184-185, 187
  legislation 180, 189-191
  Northern Ireland Family Planning
    Association (NIFPA) 185-189
  opposition 180, 182-183, 186-187,
    190-192
  publicity 185-186, 188, 196
  see also abortion; Belfast Women's
    Welfare Clinic; contraception;
    Marie Stopes
Farrand, Louise 155, 161

Fermanagh, County 27, 116-117, 120, 130
Finnegan, Frances 4, 48
Fisher, Kate 183, 196
First World War 1
  employment 3, 17, 44, 94
  Khaki Fever 4, 26, 80, 83-84
  preventative work 80, 83, 94
  prostitution 26, 28, 43
  Women's Patrols 29, 94-97, 154
  VD 5, 129, 131, 134, 165

Girl Guides 4, 80, 82-84
Girls' Auxiliary (GA) 80, 82-84, 100, 104
Girls' Friendly Society (GFS) 4, 27, 80-82, 84, 88-89, 99, 122
  hostels 85, 86, 87-89, 92, 104
Glasgow 4, 98, 193
Goldstrom, Max 199
Gonorrhoea 130, 167
  rates 115, 135, 139-140
  treatment 119, 135
  see also syphilis; VD
Good Shepherd Convent (GSC) 7, 31, 37, 39, 41
  daily life 50, 59-60
  entering and leaving 46, 49, 57, 64, 67
  laundry 61-2
  preventative work 67, 89, 91
  religious affiliation 47
  size 45

Harrison, Brian 4, 81
Hill, Myrtle 194
Hopedene House 82
Howard, Margaret 182, 185, 193

ice-cream parlours 98
illegitimacy 16, 23, 31-32, 46, 55, 71, 115, 172, 209
  see also unmarried mothers

infanticide 54
Ireland
  high moral standard 8, 79, 93, 115, 118, 130, 140, 149, 151, 169, 200, 207-211
Irish Citizen 85, 93-95, 107, 115, 131, 138
Irish Free State 2-3, 70, 119
  Catholic Church 70, 127
  family planning 193
  purity campaigns 28, 133
  role of women 207-208
  see also Eire; Republic of Ireland
Irish Presbyterian 97, 99
Irish Republican Army (IRA) 150, 156, 171
Irish Women's Liberation Movement 194

Jackson, Louise 95
Jeffery, Keith 169
Jones, Greta 122, 181, 195

Khaki Fever 4, 26, 83, 94-95, 97
Kilkeel, Co. Down 119, 148

Larne Co. Antrim 122, 189, 196-197
Leathard, Audrey 197
Legion of Mary 28, 69, 89, 91, 133
Levine, Philippa 96
Lisburn, Co. Antrim 38, 48, 119-120, 125, 158, 189
Local Government Board Ireland 114, 116-117, 119, 123-124
Local Health Authority 189
Lock hospital 22, 50, 114, 120
lodging houses 20-23, 32
Londonderry 2
  family planning 189, 191-192
  US troops 148, 151, 153, 155-161, 163-164, 169-172, 174
  VD 116-117, 120-121, 124
  see also Derry

Londonderry Sentinel 160-161, 164, 170
Luddy, Maria 3-4, 21, 29, 48, 119, 131
Lurgan Co. Armagh 99, 119
Lynn, Kathleen 129

Magdalen homes *see* individual institutions
Magdalene Sisters 67-70
Mahood, Linda 4, 15, 61
Malone Place 42, 47, 66, 183
   see also Belfast Midnight Mission
Mater Hospital 117, 121, 138-139, 147
McHugh, Charles 99, 117, 124
mental illness 46, 51, 178, 190, 198
   feeblemindedness 51, 56-58, 164
Methodist 47, 89, 102
Midgley, Harry 126, 181
military authorities 8, 26, 155, 160, 165,
   British 162, 166
   United States 7, 162, 165, 169-170
Ministry of Home Affairs 2, 24, 25,
      27, 29, 117, 119, 121, 125, 128,
      130, 136, 137
Mooji, Annet 132
Morgan, William 189-190
Morton, Marian 38
Mullan, Peter 67, 69

National Council for Combating Venereal
   Diseases (NCCVD) 122-124
      Ulster branch 116, 122-123
National Health Service 2, 13, 180
National Vigilance Association 91
Nationalists 2, 182, 200
   Second World War 150, 171
   VD propaganda 129-131
Neill, Joyce 185-188, 192, 195
Neville-Rolfe, Sybil 123-124, 126
Newtownards Road, Belfast 189, 192-193

Northern Ireland Family Planning Association (NIFPA)
   clinics 189, 193 legislation 189-191, 198
   publicity 186, 188, 196
   relations with FPA 184-185
   training 195
   see also birth control; contraception; family planning
Northern Ireland House of Commons 2, 189-190
   see also Stormont
Novick, Ben 129
nuns 47, 59, 62, 68, 70
   see also Good Shepherd Convent

O'Brien, Brian 114-115
Odem, Mary 59
Omagh, Co. Tyrone 189, 192
O'Neill, Phelim 189
Ormeau Road, Belfast 37, 89, 91, 189, 196-197

partition of Ireland 2, 3, 119, 130, 207-208
Pascoe, Peggy 48, 56
philanthropy 53, 96, 184
police 38, 56
   abortion 199
   prostitution 14, 21, 23-26, 28-29, 131
   Second World War 155-159, 164, 170-171
   women 95-96, 104, 154
   see also RUC
police courts 40, 71
Poor Law Commission (1906) 31, 44
Portadown, Co. Armagh 189, 193
Precious Life Society 200
Presbyterian
   women entering rescue homes 47
   women entering workhouse 18-19

Presbyterian Church 2
  concerns female behaviour 96, 99,
    154
  family planning 187
  preventative work 27, 85–86, 88, 90,
    96
  VD 122
prostitute
  amateur 131–134, 210
  networks 22–23
  reform 4, 38, 46, 49, 51
  terminology 14–16, 37, 50, 208
  VD 113, 131–135, 167, 169
  workhouse 14, 15–19, 208
prostitution
  Belfast 20–22
  casual occupation 15, 52, 208
  impact of World Wars 28–9, 43,
    156–158, 163–164, 166
  prosecution 23–28
  poverty 29–31
prison 17, 22, 24, 28–29, 31, 40, 54,
  71, 159
  see also Armagh Prison; Belfast
  Prison
Procter, Tammy 83
Protestant 1, 3, 4, 19, 127
  Churches 2, 7, 18, 28, 98, 102, 151
  community 8, 151, 208
  concerns female behaviour 100,
    103, 153, 208
  family planning 183, 187, 192, 200
  moral superiority 130, 149
  preventative work 81, 89, 90, 99
  rescue homes 41–42, 45–49, 61, 67,
    69–71, 209

Queen's University Belfast 27, 195

Regina Coeli Home 69, 89, 108
Republic of Ireland 7, 67, 69–70
  family planning 193–194, 198
  see also Eire; Irish Free State

Rescue Homes *see* individual
  institutions
Rose, Sonya O. 149, 162–163
Rosen, Ruth 58
Rosevale Home, Lisburn 38, 48
Royal Commission on Venereal
  Disease (RCVD) 5, 114, 116,
  122, 137
Royal Ulster Constabulary (RUC) 25,
  29, 158, 171
  see also police
Ryan, Louise 207

Salvation Army 96
  rescue home 21–22, 30, 37, 40–43,
    45–53, 55–58, 61–62, 64–67, 71
Sancta Maria hostel 89, 198
Scotland 4, 86, 101, 115, 120, 125–126,
  135–166, 139–140, 180–183
scouts 4, 10, 80, 83
Second World War 150, 211
  American troops 148, 152
  concerns female behaviour 5, 8, 90,
    140, 149
  employment 3, 153
  prostitution 28
  VD 101, 113, 125, 128, 134, 137,
    139, 165, 168, 210
sex education 101–103, 129, 210–211
single women 20, 30, 44, 85, 89, 200
  see also unmarried mothers
Sinn Fein 129
Smith, James 68–69
social workers 40, 122
Sponberg, Mary 133
Stopes, Marie 181–183, 198
Stormont 2, 70, 121, 127–128, 180, 193
  see also Northern Ireland House of
  Commons
suffrage 43, 91–93, 95, 129
syphilis 54, 102, 115, 120, 125–126,
  129, 132, 135, 137–140
  see also gonorrhoea; VD

Thomson, Charles 101-102, 128, 134-137
Thomson, Matthew 58
Troubles, The 3, 192, 194
Tuberculosis (TB) 2, 122

Ulster Female Penitentiary 37, 39, 60
Ulster Hall 43, 126
Ulster Magdalen Asylum 37, 41-42, 45-48, 54, 61-62, 66-67, 87-88
Ulster Medical Journal 135
Ulster Pregnancy Advisory Service 199-200
Unionist 2,150, 172, 179, 181, 208
United States 8, 59, 81, 152, 172
    VD 134
    see also America; American
unmarried mothers 6, 21, 28, 31, 44, 50-51, 55-56, 66-72, 82, 187, 203, 209, 211
    see also illegitimacy; single women
urban life 20, 92, 115, 119-120, 137

venereal disease (VD) 71
    churches 127-129

publicity and propaganda 122-127, 167-168
rates 137-140, 168-169
RCVD 5, 114-116
soldiers 129-130
treatment 24, 50, 116-120, 135-137
US troops 163, 166
women 113, 131-135
World Wars 166
vigilance organisations 91-94, 108
Voeltz, Richard 83

Waddell, John 39, 53, 100-101
Walkowitz, Judith 23, 32
White Slave Trade 26, 43, 80, 91-94, 108,
Women's Institute (WI) 194
Women's Patrols 26, 29, 94-97, 104, 122, 159
Woollacott, Angela 95, 97
Workhouse 7, 13, 15, 44, 46, 48, 66, 69, 208
    see also Belfast Union

Young Women's Christian Association (YWCA) 7

EU authorised representative for GPSR:
Easy Access System Europe, Mustamäe tee 50,
10621 Tallinn, Estonia
gpsr.requests@easproject.com

www.ingramcontent.com/pod-product-compliance
Lightning Source LLC
Chambersburg PA
CBHW061722270326
41928CB00011B/2084